ta Clara County Free Library
San Jose, Calif.

NAVAL DUTY

in California

BY JOSEPH WARREN REVERE, *1812-1880*

LIEUTENANT, UNITED STATES NAVY

WITH MAP
AND PLATES FROM ORIGINAL DESIGNS

FOREWORD BY JOSEPH A. SULLIVAN

209975

BIOBOOKS · OAKLAND, CALIFORNIA
1947

FOREWORD

You will recall that in Peter Burnett's *An Old Pioneer* we discussed the King James Grant to the Virginia Colony, and the tenacity of this Grant as a living force in the securing of California for the Union. It is our purpose here to explore another contemporary grant that had an equal influence in the settlement and conquest of the Pacific Coast.

Facilitated through the kindness and courtesy of the Oakland Public Library we were enabled to select and utilize for Number Eleven of the California Centennials Editions the scarce, informative and valuable work of Joseph Warren Revere, using for our copy their first edition, published in 1849 at New York by C. S. Francis & Co.

Lieutenant Revere, a native of Massachusetts, was a grandson of Paul Revere, the Revolutionary patriot, "Mechanic, silversmith, engraver, church bell and cannon maker." Our author bearing as well the proud name of his grandfather's intimate friend Major General Joseph Warren, who was killed during the Battle of Bunker Hill June 17, 1775.

Also you may recall that in Ide's *The Conquest* Revere was appointed the Commandant at Sonoma for the northern district with instructions to raise the American Flag, thereby terminating the Bear flag revolt. According to Davis, under date of July 9, 1846, Revere wrote Mr. Kern at Sutter Fort that Montgomery, from the U.S.S. *Portsmouth,* on this date had unfurled the National Flag at Yerba Buena, that our Lieutenant had followed suit at Sonoma, that he was sending Kern by messenger a U. S. Standard with instructions that it be hoisted at the Fort at New Helvetia.

Somehow it seems fitting that history selected this specially named New Englander to take over Drake's New Albion. In the more or less easy task at hand Revere explored parts of his territory; it ran to the Oregon. He furnishes the earliest description of Clear Lake as well as excellent portraits of some interesting Californians, Yount, Vallejo and Murphy. This book is the accepted authority on the change-over, a perfect follow-up to those other Massachusetts Bay men, Robinson and Farnham. Like Robinson he describes well and, as with Robinson, made his own fine plates, here reproduced, supplements Farnham by knowing

Isaac Graham, fills in a gap in the history of that colorful character, who relates Revere, was exploiting the Palo Colorado in a commercial way near Big Basin as early as 1846. The map we use is from Revere's edition and may be misleading to the unwary. The New Almaden quicksilver mine is not indicated on the map; it is situated about 10 miles south of the City of San Jose or the Mission of Santa Clara.

Revere published the Governor Mason report, retained here, but without the Sherman Map. See General Sherman's *Recollections*. Quite likely Sherman as adjutant had a major part in preparing the report, it will, however, properly continue to be credited to Colonel Mason.

Someone writes that Revere was a graduate of Annapolis.* This would appear to be unlikely, for the Naval Academy was not instituted until 1845-46. From his keen interest in sport, we feel sure that our Lieutenant would have been very much interested in joining the 80,000 people who gathered in Memorial Stadium this afternoon to attend the football game between the students of the Academy and the University of California, the large crowd a tribute to the quality and growth of these fine schools. The game, the setting and the spirit shown reflecting the development of both this country and this state over the century.

Briefly, the destruction of the Spanish Armada redirected the course of history, tremendously quickened the gentlemen of London to take over their new world, readily claimed after the naval victory, and resulted as we recounted, in the Virginia Grant. Its strong man John Smith, who named New England. The second great grant was to the council for New England dated November 3rd, 1620, followed presently by Patents and Grants to Massachusetts 1629, Connecticut 1662, The Carolina Proprietors 1665 and to the Hudson Bay Co. 1670. The Letters Patent by Charles the First to the Governor and Company of the Massachusetts Bay in New England, in its original is in the Massachusetts State Archives and bears an endorsement in perpetuity.

These several grants disposing of the territory on a line from Florida to the Rio Grande, extended below the mouth of the Colorado River and to the northern limits of Canada. Although the Virginia and Massachusetts Grants overlapped each other three whole degrees of latitude, they caused no serious difficulties between the Colonies. Lieutenant Revere's

*See correspondence of Captain John B. Heffernan, U.S.N.

Flag raising at Sonoma was the official sealing of the Massachusetts as well as the Virginia and Carolina Grants.

Having travelled the United States forth and back a number of times, we this past summer, having in mind the Revere book, determined to travel the Massachusetts Patent from Boston west to see what we could see.

Boston and Salem both date from 1630 and have from that time contributed very heavily to the development and culture of this country. Visiting Boston today one is struck by its activity, its friendliness and its apparent thriving condition as well as its historic consciousness. We drove the Albany Turnpike, Cambridge, Concord, Walden Lake, Wayside Inn, the Beautiful Lenox in the Berkshires, crossing the Hudson at Albany we followed the Mohawk Trail to Niagara, not without having a wonderful warm day Strawberry Collins before dinner at the Hotel Syracuse. Somewhere on the road becoming aware of the projected Boston Culture expressing itself in the extended Colonial architecture, this culture again quite noticcable, even to the casual view, in the many small boats on the Five Finger and Great Lakes, this Boston Bay heritage carrying through to the North Mississippi River.

To a semi-arid Californian, a dabbler in Chionology and its subdivision Ecology the gripping thing is the abundance of water in natural post-glacial storage basins and flowing freely to the sea, we could envy such abundance. In the making of the Continent, the Rocky Mountain up-thrust gave the long side East making the Atlantic seaboard the terminal moraine.

The pilgrims, multiplying and ever thrusting West for more land had but to follow the natural water courses, consolidating as they went along, taking with them their non-conformist ideas (every village has a Baptist, Congregational or Lutheran church) and their outstanding mechanical adaptation, in both leaving a profound mark on the political and economic structure of the West, they, like the Virginians, were land appropriators and exploiters, the land was to be had and they owned the Grant to the farther Sea.

Before consolidation there was a chore to do and in the doing changed the course of history, they had considerable help tendered from the Southern Grants as well as from the continent. The destruction of the

Armada having determined who was to control the Western world, the American Revolution determined how it was to be controlled, the cleavage resulting in a burst of whirling energy that has not yet abated, the pulsing rippling waves from this intellectual dynamism still travelling at high speed.

The social institutions, Common, Church, School and Township following the deeply etched pattern of the Puritan Founders and while partially blended with the Virginia system of delegating power, the Democratic seeds scattered by New Englanders are still the dominant note of the middle West. They, skeptical and canny, economical and long headed, were the inventors of the mechanical wheat harvester, probably the real decider in the war between the states, almost every improved method and engine in office and field, in war and peace on land, sea and air, came from the hands of the receivers of the Massachusetts Grant.

California history cannot be written nor understood without reference to the Boston Men, their energetic bid for commerce made them the real openers of California and of the Hawaiian Islands, one of their sons won at Lake Erie, another with the same name opened Japan, again this name was first at the Pole, it was from this same locality came what many think the most useful and beautiful vehicles for the doing of the job ever wrought by man, the early American West is very closely tied in with the designers of Clipper and Concord.

We made night's lodging at Candlelight Lodge in Westfield, learning of that fruitful and profitable Coöperative Grape Juice Industry and there cinching an idea that had been of continuous interest from East of the Connecticut River, in the Garden of the Lodge was an enormous and beautiful Horse Chestnut, the tree 20 feet in circumference, and we were sure we had made a cultural discovery on the Massachusetts Oregon Trace, for all along had been directed plantings of deciduous trees, the annuals of Southern New England carried along and placed in double rows on either side of the main street in almost every settlement, now Elms, now Chestnuts, now Walnuts but always of a pleasing pattern, we came to look for them as we drove and were not disappointed in Ohio, Michigan, Illinois, Wisconsin, Minnesota. The finest planting on that magnificent Summit Drive at St. Paul. There must be many fine stands in the Oregon Country.

You will find these tree patterns even to the town of St. Peter, later we discovered one in an obscure place at Chamberlain on the Missouri Crossing and, a pleasant surprise, the pattern reproduced on a small scale opposite the railroad station at Redding, in California they did it in Palms!

Climbing the slope for 2000 miles from Plymouth Rock was an education in how the world was made. We fell in love with the alert and clean looking Twin Cities, at Minneapolis stopping at the Curtis, excellent accommodations, courteous service, reasonable prices, good food, and marvelous water. We obtained permission to stay over and used part of the time to view a movie, an exceptional theatre, the leading picture shown in natural color, the review of the Minnesota Aquacentennial, a four star, also a good second picture with to us the warming title "Welcome Stranger."

It was harvest time and with heat like the Great Valley when we crossed South Dakota (why hasn't someone the fortitude and the sense of historic values to change the name of that state to Jefferson? and for that matter West Virginia should be Lincoln), through Rushmore, Black Hills and Bad Lands to Yellowstone, shades of Sam Adams and John Hancock they charge $3.00 to enter the National Commons and in this legal no-man's land impose an additional sales tax, although the washboard roads were the least excusable we found on the continent. However at Old Faithful we were given desirable seats for the Thor-Mars rebroadcast of the battles of the Argonne and Okinawa, with sound effects! At 7000 feet it was spectacular.

Intrigued by the progress and development in the Snake River Valley, where we saw the first echelon of south flying ducks on a Poplar lined horizon, we travelled through Boise to sturdy Alturas, quaint Weaverville and the Coast Redwoods home, due to lack of time missing the great Western Oregon country and the Sunset end of the Massachusetts Grant. The Yankees however were there, Ledyard's report was known to the great capitals of the world and in Boston something was done about it, its commercial men were emerging from the War and sent Captain Gray to the West Coast with instructions, he found the Columbia and naming it for his Boston Ship, thereby, in a magnificent historic gesture registering the surname of the stalwart explorer and sailor on the West's greatest river, further completing by right of discovery the title to the Oregon and assuring the eventual acquisition and occupation of the Virginia and Carolina Grants.

Says Lieutenant Revere, "Perhaps a hundred years hence, some curious book-worm, while exploring a musty library, may alight on this forgotten volume, and will be tempted." Roger, Lieutenant, we hope you like it, we have not edited your fine account, our emphasis has rather been to make the printing worthy of the great state you foresaw and foretold.

We take liberty to dedicate your book to Dr. Robert Semple, native of Kentucky, who came to California overland with the Hastings Party, by trade a printer and dentist, prominent in the revolt at Sonoma, "A pronounced filibuster and conspirator," with Colton published the first newspaper at Monterey, was president of the Constitutional Convention, founder of the town of Benicia, owner of the ferry across the Strait during the Gold Rush, organizer of the earliest public school in California, selector and early settler of the town of Colusa, 6 feet 8 inches tall, a good natured, popular, honorable man.

Our dedication plate is through the coöperation of Librarian Leslie E. Bliss and the Huntington Library and Art Gallery.

JOSEPH A. SULLIVAN

September 27, 1947
at Oakland 10, California.

Yerba Buena Jan. 7th 1847.

I hereby certify that Henry Smith joined a party which was sent out by Col. Fremont at Yerba Buena under my charge on the first of July 1846, as a on the volunteer; that he continued in the service faithfully during my command, and that he was transferred to Lieut. Hensley as a volunteer, who was sent to the San Joaquin by water, and so far as I know of Smith he received no compensation.

R. Semple.

NAVY DEPARTMENT
OFFICE OF
NAVAL RECORDS AND LIBRARY

WASHINGTON, D. C.

October 7, 1947.

Dear Sir:

In response to your recent request, I am pleased to furnish the desired data concerning Lt. Joseph Warren Revere and a brief history of the U.S.S. PORTSMOUTH.

Joseph Warren Revere was born in Boston, Mass. May 17, 1812; a citizen of and appointed from the state of New York.

He was appointed an Acting Midshipman in the U.S. Navy April 1, 1828. At that time Midshipmen received most of their training on ship board where they performed regular duties. The larger ships, which employed most of them, had a schoolmaster or a chaplain who instructed them in mathematics and navigation and sometimes gave attention to other subjects including the classics. There were so-called naval schools at the navy yards or stations to which young officers were sent prior to examination for promotion for periods of from six weeks to three months. Midshipman Revere was allowed to attend the naval school at New York from June to October 1828 and then was ordered to the U.S. Frigate GUERRIERE in which he made a three year cruise in the Pacific. During Nov.-Dec. 1832 he attended the naval school at Norfolk, and in 1833 he spent about ten weeks at the naval school New York. From September 1833 to February 1834 he was attached to the U.S.S. ST. LOUIS cruising in the West Indies. In May 1834 he took his examination and on June 14th was warranted a Passed Midshipman.

Lt. Revere was attached to the U.S.S. PORTSMOUTH in the Pacific from 1846 to 1848. He entered on board that vessel February 14, 1846 from the U.S.S. CYANE at Mazatlan. He was an officer of the PORTSMOUTH in San Francisco Bay in July 1846 when, under orders of Commander J. B. Montgomery, he landed at Sonoma to read the Proclamation of Commodore Sloat and hoist the U.S. Flag at that place.

Yours very truly,

John B. Heffernan,
Captain, U.S.Navy,
Director, Naval Records and Library.

Mr. Jos. A. Sullivan,
515 Weldon Avenue,
Oakland 10, Calif.

Encl.- 1

U.S.S. PORTSMOUTH

(2nd of name)

The sloop-of-war *Portsmouth* was built at Portsmouth, N. H., Navy Yard. She was built to carry 20 guns but the number composing her battery varied according to the service she was on. Her hull was of live oak, with the following dimensions: burthen, 1022; length, 153 feet; beam, 38 feet 1 inch; depth of hold, 16 feet 9 inches; draft, 16 feet 6 inches. Her crew consisted of about 200 men but this number also varied at times.

The *Portsmouth* was launched October 23, 1843, placed in commission November 10, 1844, Commander John B. Montgomery commanding, and sailed on January 25, 1845 for the Pacific to join the squadron of Commodore Sloat, which was being increased in anticipation of the outbreak of hostilities with Mexico. After touching at Rio de Janeiro and Valparaiso the *Portsmouth* arrived at Callao, Peru, April 19th where she joined the U.S.S. *Savannah*, Sloat's flagship. In May she conveyed Hon. Wm. Crump and his secretary to Valparaiso; returned to Callao June 18th and in a few days sailed for the Sandwich Islands to procure provisions; from thence she proceeded to the coast of Mexico. In December she went from Mazatlan up the Gulf of California as far as Guaymas—where there was an outbreak—to protect American citizens and property and to examine that harbor and others on the east coast of the Gulf. During the early months of 1846 the *Portsmouth* cruised along the coast of California, off Monterey, affording protection to our citizens and their interests in that country.

War with Mexico was declared April 26, 1846. During the greater part of the Mexican War the *Portsmouth* was very actively engaged on the coast of California and Mexico. On July 9, 1846 her commander took possession of Yerba Buena, now San Francisco, and a few months later she accompanied the flagship to the Gulf of California where she took up a position off the town of Guaymas. The American colors were raised over San Jose on March 30, 1847 and early in April San Lucas and La Paz were occupied, after which the *Portsmouth* returned to her former station until relieved by the *Dale* in November. After the conclusion of hostilities she returned home, arriving at Boston, Mass., on May 9, 1848.

From August 1848 to June 1851 the *Portsmouth,* as flagship of Commodores Benjamin Cooper and Francis H. Gregory, cruised off the coast of Africa where we kept a few ships which cooperated with the British for the suppression of the slave trade.

On December 16, 1851 she left Boston to join the squadron of Commodore McCauley in the Pacific, where she cruised for three years protecting American citizens and trade. Upon her return to the United States in 1855 she was placed out of commission at Norfolk on April 9th.

In the following spring the *Portsmouth,* under command of Commander Andrew H. Foote, was sent to the East Indies to join the squadron of Commodore Armstrong. She sailed from Hampton Roads May 4, 1856 and after a passage of 94 days, in which she encountered heavy gales, reached Batavia and proceeded from there to the coast of China where troubles had broken out between the natives and the English. While engaged in protecting the lives and property of American residents at Canton one of the boats of the *Portsmouth* was fired upon by the Chinese. An explanation was at once demanded, but no satisfaction being received, the *Portsmouth, San Jacinto* and *Levant* proceeded to attack the Barrier Forts on November 20. The *Portsmouth* took the most prominent part in the capture and subsequent destruction of four of the Forts, each mounting from 40 to 50 guns. She was under fire for three days and received 18 shot in her hull and rigging; two members of her landing party were killed and five wounded. In January 1857 she visited the Chinese ports opened to American commerce by treaty, and later went to Bangkok, where the ship was visited by one of the kings of Siam. She continued to cruise on the station until the end of 1857, visiting various ports, and then returned to the United States and was placed out of commission at Portsmouth, N.H. on June 21, 1858.

In 1859-60 the *Portsmouth* cruised off the coast of Africa. On the outbreak of the Civil War she was recalled from the African Station and assigned to blockading duty off the coast of Texas. In February 1862 she captured the schooner *Wave* and the sloop *Pioneer.* In April, upon being relieved by the *Montgomery,* she joined Flag Officer Farragut's squadron in the Mississippi River. During the passage of Forts Jackson and St. Philip by the fleet, on the morning of April 24, the *Portsmouth* was towed within range of the enemy works for the purpose of enfilading them. But soon after she came to anchor, the spring was shot away and the ship swung around, so that none of the guns could be brought to bear upon Fort Jackson. The *Portsmouth* soon became the target for the enemy's guns and it was found necessary to slip her cable and drop down stream out of range. After the surrender of New Orleans the *Portsmouth* was anchored off the city for the protection of the troops left to garrison it, and remained in that position until the end of the war. She left the Mississippi River in August 1865 for New York, where she was placed out of commission on September 11th.

In 1866 the *Portsmouth* was employed on ordnance duty, and used a part of the time as quarantine vessel in New York Harbor; 1867-68 she was on special service under Commander Joseph S. Skerrett; from April 1869 to August 1871 she cruised on the coast of Brazil and countries south, with a short visit to the coast of Africa during the early part of 1870; in 1872 she served for a brief time on the South Atlantic Station.

In December 1872 the *Portsmouth* sailed for the Pacific Ocean for surveying duty. In September 1874 she sailed for Alaska with a Committee of Icelanders who were interested in a colonization project. In August 1876 she was put out of commission at the Mare Island Navy Yard.

Early in 1878 the *Portsmouth* arrived at Washington, D.C. from San Francisco, and the next month sailed with articles for the Exposition at Paris, France, returning to the United States with them in December. From 1879 to 1895 she was used as a training ship for naval apprentices, following which she was loaned to the naval militia of the state of New Jersey. She was returned on March 4, 1911, to the Navy Department, which loaned her to the Marine Hospital Service. The *Portsmouth* was stricken from the Navy List on April 17, 1915.

ABOUT MIDSUMMER, in the year 1845, we sailed from the Chesapeake in the fine sloop-of-war Cyane, to join the United States Squadron cruising in the Pacific. We had a long passage of fifty-six days to Rio Janeiro, nothing of consequence occurring to break the monotony of the trip, the ship's company being chiefly occupied in the exercises customary on board a man-of-war, at the commencement of the cruise, which are necessary to render the crew efficient to contend either with "the battle or the breeze." We crossed the equator in longitude 21 deg. west, and in a few days afterwards took the S.E. trade; but, unluckily, in latitude 20 deg. south, we encountered an equinoctial storm, after which we had head winds until our arrival at Rio. Our stay there was short, as we were under orders to get on our station as soon as possible, in view both of the threatening aspect of our relations with Mexico, and of the expectation which then prevailed that England might interfere in case our forces on the Pacific should land to take possession of any portion of the Mexican territory.

After leaving port, we had more head winds, and a gale from the eastward. Arriving off Staten land on the twenty-second day out, we found ourselves near the coast, with the Straits of Le Maire lying most invitingly open before us, and a fine leading wind from the northward, which would have carried us through in a few hours. Had we taken advantage of our favorable position we should have shortened our passage by a fortnight of its worst weather; but instead of doing so, we stood to the eastward round Cape St. Juan, thereby depriving ourselves of sixty miles of westing, for which we paid dearly. During twenty-five days we had the wind dead ahead, veering from W. N. W. to W. S. W., with a head sea, and gales of wind succeeding each other in rapid succession, blowing in heavy squalls, accompanied with snow and hail.

Our gallant ship, however, proved herself a good sea-boat and weatherly enough, although very wet and uncomfortable, like all single-decked sloops-of-war. She ran no risk except once, when, at the close of a tremendous squall, a huge "comber" came curling over the lee-quarter, and stepped on board, deluging the deck, fore and aft, waist deep, and washing away some light articles. Had this ugly customer come in to windward it might have proved troublesome, for one of those mountainous seas fairly shipped would swamp a deep-waisted ship of this class. Thus, and slowly enough, wore away the tempestuous month of November off Cape Horn. In this stormy region the squalls come up in massy threatening clouds, which lurk near the horizon, while the sky above is perfectly clear; but suddenly the tempest bursts upon the devoted ship with a fury which would do credit to a legion of unchained demons, and the lurid clouds, like an assailing army, discharge volleys of sleet and hail-stones, with the velocity, and almost with the effect of small shot from muskets, rapidly retreating to leeward as they discharge their vexatious weapons. Suddenly the sun shines out again as brightly as ever, his brilliant and joyous rays contrasting strangely with the stern scene presented by the noble ship struggling with turbulent waves under close-reefed main-topsail, her slippery deck exhibiting a piteous spectacle in the persons of the drenched and shivering "watch." In these high latitudes the principal dangers to be dreaded are the floating icebergs, which sometimes encumber the ocean, and on which has been wrecked many an unfortunate vessel, painfully looked for until hope has fled from the anxious hearts of those concerned in her sad fate. The thermometer always indicates the approach of the ship to the vicinity of these dangerous floating islands of ice, but a good look-out is also invariably kept.

One cold, wet, and stormy night, having the deck in the mid-watch, and thinking of the warm beds and snug snoozes of the folks at home, or it may

be of the fine weather which existed at that very time in Lima, and the
good accommodations at the "Golden Ball" or "Morius," I was suddenly
aroused from my meditations by some of the men running aft and singing
out, as I thought, "ice! ice!" Suspecting we were close on board an iceberg,
I ordered the helm up, when I saw a volume of thick smoke pouring up
the main hatchway, and my heart actually seemed as if all at once it would
fall into my very best India rubber waterproof boots, of Horace Day's
patent, as the conviction forced itself upon me, that it was the opposite and
more dreaded element of *fire* we should have to contend with. "Up courses!
rig the pumps! beat to quarters!"—and before the little drummer had
found either his wits or his drum, the hammocks were stowed, the hatch-
ways battened down, and the crew mustering at their quarters at the windward battery, while the marines, with fixed bayonets, their officer at their
head, occupied the lee-side of the quarter-deck.

Hackneyed as I am, by long familiarity with such scenes, I cannot help
feeling that there is something very impressive in the *morale* of man-of-
war discipline on an occasion like this. Should an alarm of fire be given on
board a United States ship, "quarters" are to be beaten as soon as possible,
while the first lieutenant, carpenter, and a "fire party" promptly repair to
the scene of the conflagration. If reinforcements are necessary, they are
provided in detachments from the "divisions" who remain at their guns.
On the present occasion the fire was caused by the accident or negligence
of the hospital steward, who was making some pleasant mixture in which
spirits of turpentine was an ingredient, and being brought into contact
with his candle by a sudden lurch of the ship, instantly blazed up, and for
the short time the fire lasted, smoked and burnt most infernally. Very
luckily, the flames did not communicate with the principal vessel, containing about a gallon of spirits, and which stood near, or the whole inflam-
mable contents of the dispensary, as well as the light and dry wood work of
the shelves, &c., would soon have raised a beautiful blaze, and the whole
of us might have been sent as a burnt sacrifice to Davy Jones, in this remote
corner of his "locker." Our crew, although for the most part young and
new to the "service," behaved with remarkable steadiness, mustering at
their quarters as if for combat with a mortal foe, while the moon's pale
light, as she came forth fitfully from the ragged storm-clouds, was reflected
back from cutlass and bayonet. Thus, as if he were about to meet sternly

face to face a human enemy, the seaman prepares to grapple with his most dreadful and insidious foe, from which, surrounded as he is by the opposite element, and cut off from all the world, there can be no retreat, no hope of escape, save in coolness, discipline, and courage.

At this period of the year the days are long, and through the hours of darkness we were favored with the zodiacal light shooting from the horizon to the zenith. But although it is accounted a favorable season of the year, we gained every mile by hard carrying through a high sea, and against constant adverse winds.

I have made this passage several times, and should at any season of the year, get well to windward, say to 90 deg. west longitude, before attempting to get to the northward, north-west winds generally prevailing on the coast of Patagonia, and the current setting constantly in a south-easterly direction on that of Tierra del Fuego. I should *always* attempt to go through the Straits of Le Maire. The only risk is being becalmed there, in which case, currents *might* drift a vessel near the shore. This, however, is a rare occurrence in these high latitudes, where there is generally rather more wind than is at all times agreeable; although, in a strait fifteen miles wide, and hardly so long, between the main land and *an island,* it would scarcely be possible, without the exercise of some ingenuity, to make a lee-shore with any wind. The passage through the Straits of Magellan, from the eastward, in a square-rigged vessel, is generally admitted, by those who have made it, to be attended with as much labor and anxiety as that around Cape Horn; and, in the majority of cases, is longer. It would not, therefore, be advisable to attempt it in any other than steam-vessels, and small fore-and-afters. This was the unanimous opinion of the officers of H. B. M. Frigate *Fisgard,* which ship I met in the Pacific, after she had been nearly two months in the Straits; and this opinion agrees with that of all experienced masters of merchant-men with whom I have conversed on the subject, but who advocated going through these straits in passing from the Pacific to the Atlantic. Now that we possess extensive and accurate charts of that part of the world—(thanks to the labors and scientific accomplishments of Captain Fitzroy, of H. B. M. surveying vessel *Beagle,* and his officers)—the passage through Magellan's Straits, from the west, is made perfectly easy, and will soon be the common route. It was accomplished by the British bark, *Cape Horn,* while I was on the station, in sixty hours, twelve of which were spent at anchor. It was the first time the master had made the passage, and he stated, that, with an experience of four voyages around the Cape, he should altogether prefer the new route.

The relentless Storm Spirit, who presides over the Atlantic, pursued us even beyond the legitimate bounds of his sovereignty; for, not until we arrived in the latitude of the Archipelago of Chiloé, did the kind and beneficent fairy, who rules the pleasant breezes and smooth sea of the charming Pacific, take us under her protection. But once secure in her embraces, our weather-beaten ship was thenceforth bathed in her balmy breath, and while her favorite south-east trade was especially detailed to wait upon us—our wet pea-jackets were hung up in the rigging to dry!

We arrived at Valparaiso in fifty-three days from Rio, which was only nine days less than the entire passage of the U. S. sloop-of-war Portsmouth, in the preceding spring, from the Capes of Virginia to the same port, touching at Rio—but the Portsmouth went through the Straits of Le Maire. I presume I may hazard the remark, without being accused of originality, that this is a forcible example of the uncertain duration of voyages to distant parts of the world, in vessels propelled by the wind alone.

From Valparaiso we had a short and agreeable trip to Callao; and a visit to Lima, partly restored us from the fatigues of Cape Horn. The glories of this once famed "city of the kings," have sadly departed since I first saw it, some eighteen years since, shortly after the war of Independence. Then its beautiful architectural ornaments, its aqueducts, bridges, and fountains, bore evidence of the wealth which had been lavished upon it by the Spanish Viceroys. But now everything presented the appearance of neglect and decay. The fine paved road, raised above the level of the plain through which it runs nearly in a straight line from the Castle of Callao to the handsome gateway of the city, flanked on each side by the extensive Alameda, with its shade trees and pleasant promenades, is now in ruins. The Castle itself, which was the scene of the obstinate defence of the royalist General Rodil, and which I remember in fine order, is now dismantled and decayed. In that delicious climate these admirable public works might have been kept in good repair at little expense and trouble; but the republican system which works so admirably with us, seems to engender sloth, anarchy and desolation, among the Spanish race.

Let us pass the gateway, and observe the interesting group assembled there. Here is a dirty little fellow who represents that universal nuisance, the dreaded corps of Custom-House Officers, who infest every civilized shore, and are the especial aversion of travellers. The day must come when their valuable services will be dispensed with, and the sooner the better. The specimen before us evidently takes the world easy, as he complacently puffs his cigarito beneath his huge sombrero. But he is "not a circumstance" to the military heroes around him. The City Guards of Lima, like those of New York, are a "uniformed corps," but the resemblance is not striking, and indeed it would take a Fluellen to detect it at all. The fact is, these Peruvian soldiers were very much in the plight, so far as regarded externals, of our own brave volunteers, when they returned from Mexico. The evident attempt to ape the French was ludicrous in the extreme, and one might fancy that they had decorated themselves with rags picked up at Austerlitz or Jena. The grotesque "bonnets de police," manufactured of what was once red flannel, were particularly conspicuous, and impressed the spectator the more forcibly on account of their peculiar adaptation to a tropical sun. Such a lazy, loafing, ragged, worthless set of vagabonds, have not been seen since the days of Falstaff. One of them, literally "at ease," stood sentry, while the rest amused themselves with *hunting*, the game being found in great abundance, and with little effort, on their own persons. To complete this pleasing family group, a large assemblage of fragrant buzzards graced the scene with their presence, and indeed I could not help thinking them the most respectable part of the company.

The population of Lima has decreased since the overthrow of monarchy, and the Peruvians, like all the Spanish colonists, have proved themselves unequal to the task of ameliorating the condition of the masses, and have satisfied the world of their inability to conduct a republican government. It is melancholy to observe how heavily the hand of desolation has been laid upon the beautiful city of Lima. Here, in the heart of the new world, where everything should naturally possess the vigor of youth, we behold those vestiges of ruin and decay which mark the decline of ancient nations which have flourished for centuries, and having had their day of greatness and glory in its full length, have finally yielded to a natural process of dissolution. But Lima, like many of her sister cities, totters in a premature old age; ruinous and deserted buildings are scattered through her suburbs; great architectural works of public utility, left unfinished by the viceroys, have been wholly neglected under republican sway. The whole city presents a melancholy aspect of past magnificence; peace is not within her walls, nor plenteousness within her palaces; but anarchy and idleness, those master architects of ruin, have already more than half achieved their labors. If you would see the proximate causes of the demoralization of the people, and the consequent decline of prosperity, you have only to walk the streets. "He who runs may read, and the wayfaring man, though a fool, shall not err therein." The Church, the State, the Camp, each furnishes its hordes of canker worms to eat out the very heart of the republic. This crowd of priests of all degrees, in shovel hats and various clerical costumes, must be maintained in idleness and dissipation at the expense of the people, who in return are taught to be superstitious, bigoted, and devoted to the interests of the priesthood. I would not be understood as assailing the Catholic religion in particular, for I am not ignorant of the many good things it has accomplished, nor unacquainted with the history of many holy and philanthropic men, whose noble qualities have become developed and expanded under the influence of its teachings. But wherever priestcraft prevails, whether it be Catholic or Protestant, Hindoo or Mohammedan, there the people are enslaved, besotted, and dissolute. Where there is no established religion, the people are in little danger from the sacerdotal authority, because the competition of the various sects for proselytes leads to a minute exposure of all the weak points, errors, and dangers of the rival systems; and indeed the worthy "padres" are not slow in drawing upon their imaginations to disparage those whose theology is not cut after their favorite pattern. But where a national religion, excluding all other forms of faith, lies at the foundation of the civil government, and, as in the Spanish republics, forms the "first article" of the political constitution, the "drum ecclesiastic" beats no alarum to awaken the conscience and reason of the people, but keeps up an everlasting and monotonous tattoo, to lull suspicion, prevent inquiry, and preserve implicit faith and obedience. So much for the hierarchy. Now let us glance at the oligarchy; for the sham republic of Peru is governed by a few, as compared with the mass of the inhabitants, and yet, Heaven knows, the privileged classes are sufficiently numerous to "eat out the substance of the people." In fact, the great men of Peru are a set of rank aristocrats, and all the petty officials who depend upon their patronage and favor, ape their superiors as closely as possible. The bearing of the higher classes in Lima reminds one of the titled fools in the petty despotisms of continental Europe. Perhaps the Lima aristocrats are not so particular as those of Germany about their quarterings, and do not care to trace their genealogy beyond Adam; but they have the same contempt for the common people, and look down with the same haughty condescension and scorn upon those engaged in commerce and the mechanic arts. Their wealth is derived from corruption, oppression and extortion, and such justice as they administer is sold to the highest bidder. In that country it is settled doctrine, that "the longest pole knocks down the persimmons."

The military authority is so entwined with the civil, that both in effect form one united despotism. The army is, of course, a mere caricature of an army, but it answers all the purposes of enabling the higher officers to fleece and oppress the people. Even when the rogues fall out, honest men do not come by their rights; but whichever faction may chance to be uppermost, it is about the same thing to the people, who are most impartially and religiously plundered on all hands.

Long continued intercourse with foreigners, since the opening of commerce, has deprived the Limeños—and, alas! the fair Limeñas also—of many of their former national characteristics. Our own country is responsible, in a great measure, for this change, and the New England manufacturers have many sins to answer for to Apollo and the Graces, for their innovations here, as well as in almost every other country under the sun. Omnibuses, built in Newark, now travel the road from Callao to Lima, and infest the narrow streets of the latter, originally designed for the equestrian only. English saddlery has nearly superseded the cumbrous but picturesque and showy caparisons which formerly decorated the *monture* of a Peruvian cavalier, and which consisted of the demi-pique saddle, covered with a gay-colored fleecy pillion, the pommel and cantle richly mounted with silver-chased ornaments, elaborately carved wooden stirrups, and a profusion of silver buckles, studs, and bosses, which covered the plaited bridle, and hung jingling from all parts of the equipment. This outfit was formerly considered necessary to every one, female as well as male; and when both sexes, equipped in gay and fine *penchos,* hanging in graceful folds, were mounted on the fiery little jennets of the country, you might see as dashing, tasteful, and gallant a turn-out as any country could show. The ladies were especially attractive, with their *penchos* falling below the saddle, their long braided locks hanging over the shoulders from beneath the Panama man's hat, and their little silk stockings and delicately slippered feet thrust into *both* stirrups, the nicely turned ankles being invisible—of course. Sometimes the "mount" was a mule, or even a sleek party-colored ass; but in all cases the equestrians vied with each other in the taste and costliness of the adornments of their animals, in which an agreeable variety prevailed. At a little distance it was difficult to distinguish the sexes of the party, owing to the similarity of their costume, and also to the fact that the ladies often rode the most spirited horses. A group of these dames and their attendant squires, when prancing and curvetting on the road to Charillos and other points, to which the inhabitants of Lima repair for their favorite sea-bathing, with the glorious accessories of the towering Andes in the background, and Lima lying at their base, presented a truly national and characteristic picture, such as Leopold Robert would have delighted to paint. In the streets of Lima, gay *militaires*, reverend ecclesiastics, and *Cholos,* in the embroidered Andalusian *zamarra,* vest and breeches of velvet, with lots of little dangling filagree buttons, alternated with Sambos and Sambitos,* in flaunting colored shawls and dresses, their woolly locks plaited with bits of pure gold, and their ears decorated with huge ear-rings of the same metal; while the fair Limeños, in *saya y manta*—then of a different and closer fashion from the corresponding garment now worn—moved like shadowy spectres of fairy land amid the bustling throng.

But now, *"on a changé tout cela!"* English tailors have transmogrified the men, and French milliners have played the deuce with the women; Lowell fabrics and straight coat-tails have come in with the march of civilization; and I looked almost in vain for the national traits which were wont to delight the eye of youth in Peru's proud capital. The never-to-be-sufficiently-anathematized *marchandes des modes* have Frenchified even the captivating saya, and converted it into a mere *pelisse à la reine*—an offence which the eye of taste views with horror. There is, however, one national feature of which even milliners cannot divest the Peruvian women. They

---

*The Cholos and Cholitas are those of Indian blood; and the Sambos and Sambitos are of the duskier race of Africa.

inherit it from their Spanish ancestry; and it is an infallible sign of that ancestry in all the varied races in which Spanish blood has intermingled. Go north or south, east or west, it shows itself alike in the different shades of the Mexican and South American Indian, in the Tagolo of Manila, and even in the blue-eyed Fleming; and in no part of the world, where haughty Spain has displayed her bannered lions and castles, not even in

"Fair Cadiz rising o'er the dark blue sea,"

can this national feature be found in greater perfection than in Lima, among all classes, the dama, the cholita, and the sambita—I allude to the foot and ancle. The *chaussure,* too, although somewhat too fanciful among the lower orders to suit the taste of our northern fair, is always perfect in its way; and the little embroidered slipper of a Limeña would excite the envy of Cinderella.

The walking dress of the Limeñas, although often graphically described by tourists, has, I believe, never been deemed worthy of a leaf in the *Petit Courier des Dames.* The saya is a silk petticoat plaited so as to cling to the form without impeding the fair wearer's motions in walking, and as originally cut, displays the form in the most *faithful* manner, from the waist to the tapering and delicate ankle, graciously revealing a generous share of the latter. The manta envelops the head and face, except one eye, and is skilfully managed at the pleasure of the gypsy, whose little jeweled fingers are coquettishly employed in so arranging it as to display an exquisitely moulded arm, or a full swelling *neck,* costumed *au naturel.* The concealment of the fair incognita is perfect, and numberless are the anecdotes, comic, tragic, comico-tragic, and tragico-comic, melo-dramatic, and farcical, related in Lima, of husbands, brothers, lovers, and strangers "taken in and done for," all hinging upon this masquerading promenade dress. If universal report may be accredited, those graceful and *svelte* Limeñas are not exactly vestals, and some censorious persons insinuate that these seductive walking-dresses were invented and are still kept up for purposes of intrigue. But the world is given to lying on such subjects, and the best way is to doubt and disbelieve in the absence of actual demonstration. The cunning wearers are very eloquent in expatiating upon its convenience to slip on in haste when they go to mass, and attribute to it various other perfections; but other ladies are of the same way of thinking as a fair Chilena, who replied to my inquiry as to her opinion of the *saya y manta,* "I acknowledge it shows the shape to great advantage, but it does little honor to the character of her who wears it."

The national amusement of the bull-fight, so characteristic of the mother country, has, I believe, gone out of fashion in a great degree, but in place of it there is now established a very tolerable opera. At the date of my visit, the famous Ravel family, whom I had last seen at Niblo's, were playing an engagement at the opera-house, and it is needless to say they were great favorites. On Sunday afternoon I saw an oily "padre" with a cock under his *soutane* walking towards the suburbs, from which I conclude that one elevating amusement has not yet been abrogated, either in church or state. As to bull-fights, since my last visit to Lima, I had witnessed the feats of the famed Montes, in the "plaza de toros" at Seville; and the unscientific chicken-murder practiced here, had no charms for a *connoisseur.* The superior science displayed by our well-trimmed and gaffed birds, as compared with the clumsy work done with vile "slashers," reminds the spectator of a skilful *escrimeur* with his slender rapier, pitted against a clownish fellow with a huge broadsword,

"A ton of rusty iron in the hilt."

There are few public edifices in Lima worthy of notice save the cathedral, palace, and a few churches. The façades of these buildings are painted in sized colors, with a variety of designs, bearing at a little distance an humble resemblance to the façades of some European churches, that of the basilica of St. Paul at Rome, for instance; but there is this important difference, that the latter is executed in mosaic.

Many of the private houses are peculiar in several respects. The *patios* (court-yards) are in many instances tastefully, but somewhat fantastically pictured on their inner walls and verandahs in landscape, while the doors are guarded by grim giants, knights in armor, and ugly dwarfs. Sometimes the "heavenly host," is called in to the aid of the artist in the decoration of the ceiling. The most frequent scene, however, is the festival of the "Amancaes," a plain near the city, resorted to upon the anniversary of the blossoming of a little flower of that name, by all the inhabitants in full dress, from the highest to the lowest. This mode of decorative painting must always be peculiar to Lima, for in a different climate this ornamental feature in external architecture would be washed away by the first shower. It never rains in Lima, but the mists are sometimes as heavy as a "sixteen-dram fog" in old Virginia, where the density of a fog is *barometrized* by the number of horns it takes to cut it.

The town of Callao, the sea-port of Lima, which I remember as consisting of a few adobe* houses, and a scattered assemblage of Cholo huts, crouched between the north and south castles, has begun to present the appearance of a populous town. The castles themselves, as before remarked have been dismantled, and are now fast falling into decay; in which respects they resemble other expensive structures of the same kind erected by the Spaniards for the security of their colonies, and in pursuance of that system of exclusive and jealous monopoly of their commerce which led to the almost total prevention of intercourse with any other than the mother country; a system which established a forced trade by adventurous smugglers from the interdicted nations, among which our own was somewhat notorious. This illicit trade, connived at by the authorities, laid the foundation of many a tale of fiction, as well as some solid fortunes. Taking into consideration the expense of keeping these extensive castles in a state of repair, and how constantly they caused revolutions in the *republic* of Peru, it is doubtless a blessing to the people and country that they have been suffered to fall into decay. It is indisputable that they are master-pieces of the art of fortification. Commanding the harbor and its entrances, and situated on a low point—extending far into the sea—they moreover command the road to Lima on the land side, and the wide plain between it and Callao, as far as the guns can carry, so that the possessor of the castles can interdict communication for every warlike purpose between the city and the place of embarkation. In the frequent *emeutes,* dignified by the name of revolutions, it was always a great point to seize the castles by gaining over the garrison; and this fine fortress, which witnessed the intrepid and obstinate defence of a Rodil, continued through several years against a vastly superior besieging and blockading force, and until he had been reduced almost to starvation, has since been sometimes taken by a *coup-de-main,* by a half-starved ensign at the head of a scarecrow sergeant's guard.

---

*Sun-baked mud bricks.

Nothing more impressively demonstrates the ephemeral duration of empires, and of systems destined by their haughty authors to be perpetual, than such ruins as these. They abound in all the Spanish-American colonies, which were at once the source of the wealth and of the downfall of the mother-country. The Moro Castles of Havana and of St. Iago, the noble castle of San Juan de Ulloa, and the extensive and imposing fortifications of St. Johns of Porto Rico, are all more or less neglected and decaying. But more prominent than all, is the stupendous fortification of "Cartagena de los Indias," which is a system of castles, triple-walls, and bulwarks of every description, in which ingenuity is stretched to the utmost in devising plans for defence, fort rising above fort, castle surmounting castle, from the bosom of the ocean in which the foundations are laid to the battlemented heights in the rear. From these towering battlements once proudly flaunted the gorgeous red and yellow stripes with the crown and shield of Castile and Leon, announcing the dominion of his Most Catholic Majesty, "Rey de España y los Indias" in this his principal depôt of treasure, sent from all other parts of South America to be freighted in the galleons to Cadiz. Of these fortifications, the king of Spain remarked, that they must have been built of silver, so many millions did they cost him. But now—

> "Alack! and what shall good old York there see
> But empty lodgings and unfurnished walls,
> Unpeopled offices, untrodden stones?"

Alas for Carthagena of the Indies! What is she now? A broken and miserable sea-port of the "Costa Firme," of little commerce, and small consideration; while her mother, in old Spain, with her spacious but deserted quays, her noble but neglected royal arsenal, and the infrequent feluccas lying at her desolate wharves, presented, when I was there, a sad and startling counterpart. And it has been my fortune also to see the shapeless remains of the once mighty ancestress of the Spanish Carthagenas. I have stood on the site of that Carthage, made illustrious by the great deeds of Hamilcar, Asdrubal, and Hannibal—of that Carthage over whose ruins the bloodthirsty and fugitive Marius brooded—of that Carthage, victorious on land and sea, which was once the terror and the scourge of Rome—of that Carthage, twice subjugated in the Punic wars by the Scipios. But the Carthage of Africa—the Carthage of Queen Dido—is no more! A few wretched huts occupy the places of her citadels and temples; a miserable vagabond race are unenvied masters of the classic soil, once trodden by the most famous heroes of antiquity; and it would seem that destiny has written the sentence of Cato upon the very name, wherever found—*"Delenda est Carthago!"* The Carthagena of Murcia, founded by Asdrubal, whose mines of silver sustained Hannibal against the serried hosts of Rome is falling into decay; whilst her once opulent namesake in the new world is thus early almost forgotten. Let him who would study the romance and the philosophy of history read the story of the African, the Spanish, and the American Carthage—

> "The boast of heraldry, the pomp of power,
> And all that beauty, all that wealth ere gave,
> Await alike the inevitable hour.
> The paths of glory lead but to the grave!"

We spent New-Year's day at sea, running before a fine trade westerly. The S. E. trade-winds blow, as a general rule, on the west coast of South America, from 35 deg. of south latitude to the equator, and extend west as far as 100 deg. west longitude. North of the line, and near the coast, the N. E. trades blow, although not so steadily as the former. In the tropics, easterly winds generally prevail; and on the coast of North America, in Oregon and California, N. W. winds prevail; while on the coast of Mexico, southers, with an occasional gale, accompanied with almost constant showers, are usual in the summer season. Farther west, in the Sandwich Islands and other groups, the N. E. trade blows constantly. Gales of wind are of very rare occurrence. The climate of the whole Pacific is mild and pleasant, and the voyager in that "summer sea" is seldom or never chilled by the almost universal damps, dews, and disagreeables of the ungenial Atlantic.

WE FOUND THE COMMODORE at Mazatlan with a squadron, consisting of two first-class frigates and three sloops of war, which composed our entire force in this important sea, on the eve of a war which, at the outset, threatened to embroil us with the first naval power in the world.

On the other hand, that power had on the station the Admiral's Flag ship, the Collinwood, of 80 guns, the America razee, of 60 guns, and four sloops of war, besides two splendid war steamers, which would have proved an important adjunct, perhaps a fatal one for us, in case of a collision. We not only had no war steamers in this ocean, so well adapted to that class of vessels, but none were expected, nor did any arrive in the course of the war which ensued. This looks very much as if there had been an understanding concerning Mexican affairs between the Cabinets of St. James' and Washington, although the Mexicans were led to think very differently.

Since the royal administration of affairs in Mexico, Acapulco and San Blas have silently fallen into decay, and Mazatlan, although destitute of a good or safe harbor, has become the most important commercial town possessed by Mexico on the Pacific. This is owing to the facility of communication with the northern provinces and the mining districts, as well as to its proximity to a large population, and consequently to a market. The town has been built up and its prosperity maintained by its merchants, who are exclusively foreigners, and chiefly English, Americans, and Germans. The imports are such European productions as are required by a non-productive population like that of Mexico. The exports are logwood, and a few cheap articles exchanged for agricultural products, coast-wise, with the small ports on the Gulf of California, at the southern extremity of which Mazatlan is situated.

So many of my countrymen have lately joined in several little parties of pleasure to the Aztec capital itself, that it is unnecessary to describe the appearance of the town, which, like all fourth-rate Mexican towns, possesses a full complement of slip-shod women in ragged *rebosos,* and *léperos* swaggering about in parti-colored *sarapes,* gambling, drinking, and stabbing, *á discretion.*

After remaining here about two months and a half, during which time the Mexicans had no less than five *pronunciamentos,* and of course as many governors, the new and beautiful ship to which I had been transferred, sailed, by order of the commodore, to look after our interests in Upper California.

But before getting under way, I will add a few words touching the interesting emporium of commerce we are about to leave. To be frank, the place is a perfect nuisance, and all hands took leave of it without shedding many tears. Its revolutions are the most laughable and farcical *"coups d' état"* imaginable. In other countries, especially our own, tariffs of duties are made and unmade, altered and amended, without exciting anything more than a temporary grumbling or exultation, according to political bias; producing on one side the most solemn assurances that "the country is ruined," and on the other equally positive asseverations that "the country is safe." Perhaps now and then, if an election occurs before the change is forgotten, Mr. Jones, the champion of the opposition, is triumphantly elected to Congress, and Mr. Brown, who voted for the bill, is decidedly "rowed up salt river." It may even happen, when an unfruitful season, making provisions scarce and dear, or an over-productive one, making wheat to "rule low," can be clearly traced to and identified with, "the new tariff," that the party in opposition may obtain a "glorious victory," and cry "all hail," at the expense of that which foolishly altered the rate of duties without first consulting the almanac. But neither a "revenue tariff" nor a "protective tariff," neither "discriminating duties" nor "incidental protection," can excite popular commotions in the United States. They manage these things differently, however, in Mazatlan. In that great mart, a revolution turns upon the duties which shall be levied upon the last cargo of Nuremberg nick-nacks, or of French *liqueurs* and silk stockings, or of English every-things fresh from Brummagem, or of Yankee notions just imported from "the States." Thus a modest merchant-ship, which sails on a peaceful trading expedition, suddenly finds herself the head and front of a political revolution, and lights up the fires of patriotism as effectually as if she had poured in a broadside of hot shot. While we remained at Mazatlan there was, on an average, only one revolution every fortnight; but I take it for granted that these long spells of tranquillity were in a measure owing to the proximity of our guns.

Another delightful feature about this lovely town is its anchorage. Poor Mr. Mantalini was sorely afflicted by "one dem'd eternal grind," but his mangle was not a circumstance to the never-ending rollers of Mazatlan harbor. We did nothing but roll from morn till dewy eve, and from dewy eve till morn, insomuch that it became doubtful whether we should ever be able to adopt any other system of locomotion. But these vile rollers are not the most formidable evil of Mazatlan harbor, as the uninitiated may find out to their cost. It is a most uncomfortable fact, that no boat, the bottom of which is not coppered or sheathed, can lie a week in the water without being utterly destroyed by the *worms*. These insidious little "varmints" are provided with a head compounded in equal parts of screw-augur, saw, and piercer. They insinuate themselves into the bottom planks, through holes into which it would be quite as impracticable to insert a cambric needle as a crow-bar, and when they once get into the solid wood, presto! they riddle it in no time. They traverse it in every possible direction with labyrinthine sinuosity, reducing the inside of the board to an almost impalpable powder, whilst the two surfaces appear intact. I will mention "a case in point," which exhibits a perseverance and ingenuity on the part of these little sea-monsters, worthy of a better cause.

A British vessel of war, having collected a large amount of specie, and the captain having intelligence that the *contrabandistas* had a considerable quantity of *plata* ready at a point up the Gulf, left her largest and best boats at anchor here, with several hundred thousands of dollars in them, and equipped for rolling a fortnight at anchor. But the submarine guardians of the Mexican waters, not being bribed like their amphibious brethren in the custom-house, set diligently to work to revenge the outraged revenue laws prohibiting the exportation of the precious metals, and speedily but silently made minced meat of the preciously freighted boats, insomuch that an unlucky step in the vicinity of the "garboard streak" must inevitably have compelled the crews to swim for their lives, and committed the treasure to "the kelpies' keeping." Luckily, however, they stepped lightly, and did not discover the danger they had escaped until the return of their ship. When, however, the boats were hoisted in, the sea no longer sustaining them, their bottoms very unceremoniously dropped out and vamosed, probably supposing there was no further occasion for their services. Thanks to a kind Providence, the crews were not injured. Indeed Jack has almost every day to be grateful for escaping a premature fate, and hence, perhaps, his proverbial recklessness.

Standing to the westward across the Gulf of California, we soon fell in with the N. W. winds prevalent on the coast of North America, and which blow very fresh at this season of the year. In twenty-two days after leaving Mazatlan, we made the land, being Point Año Nuévo, (New Years), the northernmost cape of the large indenture of the coast, in whose southern corner is the town of Monterey.

I had heard so much of California since arriving on the coast, that my curiosity was highly excited. It had been represented as the El Dorado of this part of the continent; and the fact that it would probably soon be annexed to the United States, even whether war gave it to us by conquest or not, made it of additional interest to us.

The approach to these almost virgin shores, showed us a high, bold coast, totally different from the flat, same, and barren coast of our Atlantic seaboard. The magnificent and prominent mountains of the coast-range skirting the back-ground, with their wavy and picturesque play of lines; the apparently well-wooded heights stretching their sombre foliage to the brink of the ocean; the abrupt and broken precipices, whose projecting points caught the last rays of the setting sun—all these accessories reminded me strongly of the Maritime Alps, as seen while coasting the northern shores of the Mediterranean.

Sketched by J. W. Revere U. S. N.

MONTEREY - CAPITOL OF CALIFORNIA.

Lith. of Wm. Endicott & Co. N. York.

In coming into the harbor it is always best to make Point Año Nuévo first on falling in with the land, that being far to the westward of Point Pinos, which is the southern promontory of the bay. Having got well under the high lands of Santa Cruz, a S. E. course by compass takes you direct to the anchorage at Monterey. I mention this because, in falling in with the land at night, or in hazy weather, which is very prevalent here, the high lands of Santa Cruz can always be seen, when the lower land about Monterey cannot. The risk, in making Pinos, is falling to leeward and being becalmed—north-west being the prevalent wind—in which case, were a vessel to drift close inshore, she would probably be obliged to anchor in foul ground, either near that point, or in Carmel Bay.

We arrived at Monterey at a very interesting time. A Junta was in session, composed of some of the leading Californians, who had met to take into consideration what line of conduct should be adopted in the existing state of affairs. The Californians had just succeeded in getting rid of Micheltoréna, the last Mexican satrap sent to plunder them and mal-administer the affairs of the Province. They had shipped him, and as many of his fustian officers and scarecrow soldiery as they could lay hands on, back to Mexico, and had elected a native of the Province, by name José Castro, as their commander-in-chief. The civil governor was Don Pio Pico, and the views of these two worthies entirely corresponded, both being in favor of annexation to an European power. I have been favored, by an intelligent member of the Junta, with the following authentic report of the substance of Pico's speech to that illustrious body of statesmen:

"Excellent Sirs! to what a deplorable condition is our country reduced! Mexico, professing to be our mother and our protectress, has given us neither arms, nor money, nor the material of war for our defence. She is not likely to do any thing in our behalf, although she is quite willing to afflict us with her extortionate minions, who come hither in the guise of soldiers and civil officers, to harass and oppress our people. We possess a glorious country, capable of attaining a physical and moral greatness corresponding with the grandeur and beauty which an Almighty hand has stamped upon the face of our beloved California. But although nature has been prodigal, it cannot be denied that we are not in a position to avail ourselves of her bounty. Our population is not large, and it is sparsely scattered over valley and mountain, covering an immense area of virgin soil, destitute of roads, and traversed with difficulty; hence it is hardly possible to collect an army of any considerable force. Our people are poor, as well as few, and cannot well govern themselves and maintain a decent show of sovereign power. Although we live in the midst of plenty, we lay up nothing; but, tilling the earth in an imperfect manner, all our time is required to provide proper subsistence for ourselves and our families. Thus circumstanced, we find ourselves suddenly threatened by hordes of Yankee emigrants, who have already begun to flock into our country, and whose progress we cannot arrest. Already have the wagons of that perfidious people scaled the almost inaccessible summits of the Sierra Nevada, crossed the entire continent, and penetrated the fruitful valley of the Sacramento. What that astonishing people will next undertake, I cannot say; but in whatever enterprise they embark they will be sure to prove successful. Already are these adventurous land-voyagers spreading themselves far and wide over a country which seems suited to their tastes. They are cultivating farms, establishing vineyards, erecting mills, sawing up lumber, building workshops, and doing a thousand other things which seem natural to them, but which Californians neglect or despise. What then are we to do? Shall we remain supine, while these daring strangers are overrunning our fertile plains, and gradually outnumbering and displacing us? Shall these incursions go on unchecked, until we shall become strangers in our own land? We cannot successfully oppose them by our own unaided power, and the swelling tide of emigration renders the odds against us more formidable every day. We cannot stand alone against them, nor can we creditably maintain our independence even against Mexico; but there is something that we can do which will elevate our country, strengthen her at all points, and yet enable us to preserve our identity and remain masters of our own soil. Perhaps what I am about to suggest may seem to some, faint-hearted and dishonorable. But to me it does not appear so. It is the last hope of a feeble people, struggling against a tyrannical government which claims their submission at home, and threatened by bands of avaricious strangers from without, voluntarily to connect themselves with a power, able and willing to defend and preserve them. It is the right and the duty of the weak to demand support from the strong, provided the demand be made upon terms just to both parties. I see no dishonor in this last refuge of the oppressed and powerless, and I boldly avow that such is the step I would now have California take. There are two great powers in Europe, which seem destined to divide between them the unappropriated countries of the world. They have large fleets and armies not unpractised in the art of war. Is it not better to connect ourselves with one of these powerful nations, than to struggle on without hope, as we are doing now? Is it not better that one of them should be invited to send a fleet and an army, to defend and protect California, rather than we should fall an easy prey to the lawless adventurers who are overrunning our beautiful country? I pronounce for annexation to France or England, and the people of California will never regret having taken my advice. They will no longer be subjected to the trouble and grievous expense of governing themselves, and their beef, and their grain, which they produce in such abundance, would find a ready market among the new comers. But I hear some one say, "No monarchy!" But is not monarchy better than anarchy? Is not existence in some shape better than annihilation? No monarchy! and what is there so terrible in a monarchy? Have we not all lived under a monarchy far more despotic than that of France, or England, and were not our people happy under it? Have not the leading men among our agriculturists been bred beneath the royal rule of Spain, and have they been happier since the mock republic of Mexico has supplied its place? Nay, does not every man abhor the miserable abortion christened the Republic of Mexico, and look back with regret to the golden days of the Spanish monarchy? Let us restore that glorious era. Then may our people go quietly to their ranchos, and live there as of yore, leading a merry and thoughtless life, untroubled by politics or cares of State, sure of what is their own, and safe from the incursions of the Yankees, who would soon be forced to retreat into their own country."

Fortunately for California, and, as the sequel proved, for the views of the government of the United States, which already embraced the acquisition by treaty or purchase of that important territory, with its fine seaports, so essential to the interests of our growing commerce in the Pacific, a man was found at this crisis whose opinions were more honest and enlightened than those of the military and civil rulers of his country. Like a true patriot, he could not endure to see the land of his birth traded away to any European monarchy, and he rightly judged, that although foreign protection might postpone, it could not ultimately avert the "manifest destiny" of California. Possessed at the time of no political power, and having had few early advantages, still his position was so exalted, and his character so highly respected by both the foreign and native population, that he had been invited to participate in the deliberations of the Junta. This man was Don Mariano Guadalupe Vallejo. Born in California, of Mexican parents, he commenced his career in the army as an "alferes," or ensign, and in this humble grade, he volunteered, at the suggestion of the Mexican government, with a command of only fifty soldiers, to establish a colony on the north side of the bay of San Francisco, for the protection of the frontier. He effectually subdued the hostile Indians inhabiting that then remote district, and laid the foundation of a reputation for integrity, judgment, and ability, unequalled by any of his countrymen. Although quite a young man, he had already filled the highest offices in the province, and had at this time retired to private life near his estates in the vicinity of the town of Sonoma. He did not hesitate to oppose with all his strength the views advanced by Pico and Castro. He spoke nearly as follows:

"I cannot, gentlemen, coincide in opinion with the military and civil functionaries who have advocated the cession of our country to France or England. It is most true, that to rely any longer upon Mexico to govern and defend us, would be idle and absurd. To this extent I fully agree with my distinguished colleagues. It is also true that we possess a noble country, every way calculated, from position and resources, to become great and powerful. For that very reason I would not have her a mere dependency upon a foreign monarchy, naturally alien, or at least indifferent, to our interests and our welfare. It is not to be denied that feeble nations have in former times thrown themselves upon the protection of their powerful neighbors. The Britons invoked the aid of the warlike Saxons, and fell an easy prey to their protectors, who seized their lands, and treated them like slaves. Long before that time, feeble and distracted provinces had appealed for aid to the all-conquering arms of imperial Rome; and they were at the same time protected and subjugated by their grasping ally. Even could we tolerate the idea of dependence, ought we to go to distant Europe for a master? What possible sympathy could exist between us and a nation separated from us by two vast oceans? But waiving this insuperable objection, how could we endure to come under the dominion of a monarchy?—for although others speak lightly of a form of government, as a freeman, I cannot do so. We are republicans—badly governed and badly situated as we are—still we are all, in sentiment, republicans. So far as we are governed at all, we at least profess to be self-governed. Who, then, that possesses true patriotism will consent to subject himself and his children to the caprices of a foreign king and his official minions? But it is asked, If we do not throw ourselves upon the protection of France or England, what *shall* we do? I do not come here to support the existing order of things, but I come prepared to propose instant and effective action to extricate our country from her present forlorn condition. My opinion is made up that we must persevere in throwing off the galling yoke of Mexico, and proclaim our independence of her for ever. We have endured her official cormorants and her villainous soldiery until we can endure no longer. All will probably agree with me that we ought at once to rid ourselves of what may remain of Mexican domination. But some profess to doubt our ability to maintain our position. To my mind, there comes no doubt. Look at Texas, and see how long she withstood the power of united Mexico. The resources of Texas were not to be compared with ours, and she was much nearer to her enemy than we are. Our position is so remote, either by land or sea, that we are in no danger from a Mexican invasion. Why, then, should we hesitate still to assert our independence? We have indeed taken the first step, by electing our own governor, but another remains to be taken. I will mention it plainly and distinctly: it is annexation to the United States. In contemplating this consummation of our destiny, I feel nothing but pleasure, and I ask you to share it. Discard old prejudices, disregard old customs, and prepare for the glorious change which awaits our country. Why should we shrink from incorporating ourselves with the happiest and freest nation in the world, destined soon to be the most wealthy and powerful? Why should we go abroad for protection when this great nation is our adjoining neighbor? When we join our fortunes to hers, we shall not become subjects, but fellow-citizens, possessing all the rights of the people of the United States, and choosing our own federal and local rulers. We shall have a stable government and just laws. California will grow strong and flourish, and her people will be prosperous, happy, and free. Look not, therefore, with jealousy upon the hardy pioneers who scale our mountains and cultivate our unoccupied plains; but rather welcome them as brothers, who come to share with us a common destiny."

Such was the substance of Vallejo's remarks; but his auditors were far behind him in general intelligence, and what reason they possessed had not been quickened by the application, on the part of our government, of those convincing arguments which convert multitudes who do not believe that "virtue is its own reward." The arguments of Vallejo failed to carry conviction to the majority, but the stand taken by him caused a sudden *sine-die* adjournment of the Junta, without arriving at any definite conclusion upon the weighty matter concerning which they had met to deliberate.

As soon as Vallejo had retired from the Junta, he addressed a letter to Don Pio Pico, embodying the views he had expressed, and refusing ever again to assist in any project having for its end the adoption of any protection other than that of the United States. He also declared in this letter that he would never accept office under a government which advocated the surrender of California to an European power; and he then left Monterey for his home, resolved to await the issue in retirement.

Castro and Pico, and their adherents, were not alone in their jealousy of the American settlers. The Mexican government had taken the alarm, and repeated orders were issued both to the *"gefe politico"* and to the *"commandante militar"* to drive back these dangerous self-invited guests "to the deserts from which they came." A wholesome dread, however, of the formidable western rifle deterred these distinguished men from obeying the easily given orders of the *"gobierno supremo;"* and, moreover, they were well aware of the difficulty of collecting a force of their compatriots to undertake the execution of orders so directly contrary to their own interests—the enterprising strangers having ingratiated themselves with the natives. Instead, therefore, of obeying the impotent mandates of Mexico, the worthy patriots, Castro and Pico, very unceremoniously threw off their allegiance, and sought to barter themselves and their country for French or English gold, hoping to be continued in their high offices, and decked out with stars and garters and ribbons. Their party was large and powerful, consisting of subordinate military officers from Mexico, petty employées of the custom-house, and a considerable number of rancheros, who had been won over by magnificent promises. Their ablest adherent was José Antonio Carillo, who reflected the views of Pico, and officiated as his especial mouth-piece.*

---

* It is even probable that the speech I have attributed to Pico was in fact delivered by Carillo, my informant being likely to speak of the acts of the latter as those of Pico.

The Junta met about the time of our arrival at Monterey, and I had the pleasure of making the acquaintance of General Vallejo.* At that time, however, I knew nothing of the existence of the Junta, the object and deliberations of which were secret; nor did I know anything of the state of politics in the country, except the notorious facts that two parties existed, and that General Vallejo was supposed to be the leader of the American party, while Castro was at the head of the European movement. Subsequently, however, I obtained from persons concerned in the Junta, and also from documentary evidence, all the facts which I have before related, as well as sketches of the principal speeches.

It happened some weeks after our arrival that I met Don José Castro in the Pueblo de San José, and in the course of a conversation I had with him, he inquired whether the government of the United States would give him a brigadier-general's commission in case he decided to "pronounce" for the establishment of their authority? He spoke apparently in jest, but I could perceive that the promise of such an appointment would have had its effect. His excellency, when out of the filagree Mexican uniform, was dressed in the calzoneros, botas, gaiters, sarape, &c., usually worn by the Californians, and his heels were armed with spurs of formidable length. His forehead is high but not broad, indicating a fair average of brains; his hair, black as a raven's wing, is arranged in thick clustering curls; his black bushy whiskers and moustaches form an unbroken cordon of hair from ear to ear *via* the upper lip, similar to the same appendage on the face of the king of Hanover; his complexion is a dark olive; his eye a brilliant black, indicating intelligence; his lips are thick, his nose aqueline, and his figure stalwart, inclining to stoutness.

The anchorage at Monterey is in the S. E. corner of the bight which forms the harbor, anywhere inside of a line from Point Año Nuévo drawn through Point Pinos, or where the two points lap. The bottom is apt to be either rocky or too hard for good holding ground in any other part of the harbor, which, being open to the N. W., is rarely smooth anywhere else. In from four to six fathoms you have in that part of the road a stiff clay bottom.

---

* Pronounced "Val-ya-ho."

THE OFFICERS who had preceded us, gave glowing accounts of the hunting in California. According to some of their stories, the whole territory was stocked with game, as various as it was abundant. As soon, therefore, as we had secured our ship at her anchors, we got up a party to pay our respects to these interesting natives. I had done some little shooting in my day, on the north-western prairies, and was not at all loth to try my hand on the shores of the Pacific. A couple of our countrymen residing at Monterey, kindly consented to act as our henchmen, and beat up the quarters of our unsuspecting victims. Having sent forward to a place of rendezvous divers beasts of burthen loaded with a variety of creature comforts, we set out from Monterey well mounted and equipped for the excursion. After riding several miles through a dark pine forest, we emerged upon a level plain, having before us a stream of water singing its way merrily to the sea, which was spread out in "boundless continuity" upon our right. Upon a small elevation at no great distance, we saw the ruined towers of an old church, and also some walls built of adobe, which had evidently enclosed extensive and commodious buildings, now fallen into utter decay. This was the ancient mission of Carmel, which, in common with all the other missions, had been suppressed by an act of the Mexican Congress for reasons which I am unable to disclose.

This consecrated spot, so long the abode of holy men, is now the property of a private person, and has fairly "gone to grass." Whether the surrounding Indians are any the worse Christians, or more troublesome neighbors, may be easily guessed by those who know that Catholic missionaries exert a more wholesome influence over the aborigines than any others. It seems to be a peculiarity of the Roman priesthood, to accommodate themselves to circumstances, and to render their religion as attractive as it is powerful. As a general rule the reverend padres are popular men, and make friends wherever they go.

We rode along the ruins of what had once been a neat and convenient aqueduct, watering a now uncultivated vineyard. We pursued our way along a plain which bore evident traces of the taste and industry of the missionaries and their docile Indian pupils, and leaving to the left a collection of huts, whose wretched appearance and squalid inmates furnished no favorable commentary on the change which had followed the expulsion of the padres, we struck at once into the hilly country.

After surmounting several lofty hills, and winding through some lovely valleys, following all the way the devious course of a bridle-path, we stopped to rest upon a spur of the coast mountains, having travelled about fifteen miles from Monterey. We now refreshed man and beast, and starting again, in high spirits, we reached in the afternoon a beautiful and fertile valley, and camped on the bank of a "purling rivulet." Now "camping" in California, is not precisely the same thing that is implied by that term in other countries, but "on the contrary, quite the reverse." It is a sort of *lucus-a-non-lucendo* operation, the "camp" part of the performance being decidedly minus. In fact, it consists of nothing more, than stripping your saddle and depositing it on the first convenient spot of mother earth. To select a tree or a bank would be deemed rather fastidious, but to collect bushes for a hut, would be considered by a true Californian frightfully effeminate. However, the saddle used in California, is admirably contrived for the primitive system of camping which prevails there. The "muchillas" and "coraza," serve as a capital bed—the solid leather of which they are composed, keeping off the dampness of the ground, while the "fusta" furnishes a pillow, by no means to be sneezed at by the weary traveller. In addition to these comfortable equipments, the Californian always takes with him, even when he leaves home only for a day or two, the "armas de pélo," which consist of two entire goat skins tanned with the hair on, and depend from the saddle-bow on either side of the horse. In wet weather these are drawn around the waist of the horseman, covering the lower part of the person, and extending below the stirrups; and with this and his well-woven "sarape," and broad-brimmed hat covered with oil-skin, the cavalier is rendered impervious to the heaviest showers. It may be surmised that these little articles come comfortably into the account while travelling in a country where the ranchos are far apart and the wayfarer is often compelled to put up at this kind of indigenous "California Hotel," which I have described. Nor is this simple mode of lodging any hardship in the lovely climate of California during the dry season; for sleeping in the open air in that pure and balmy atmosphere, is far preferable to being smothered in the close and ill-contrived houses of the rancheros, where travellers, without respect of persons, are generally devoured by those inseparable and nimble companions of the Spanish race, which manage to elude all attempts to entrap them.

Not having been accustomed to the saddle for some time we had private reasons for going no farther that night, and accordingly made preparations for concocting coffee, and taking lodgings "au naturel." But ere we had commenced operations, our shore friends, whom we had left a short distance behind, came along, dragging the corpse of a huge grizzly bear, which they had shot within the sound of a rifle from our camp, and moreover, they gladdened our hearts with the carcass of a fat doe, which a few moments before had had no idea of taking a journey on horseback. Now, while we freely forgave them the doe, we could not help bemoaning our hard luck at not being "in at the death" of Bruin, as we had heard terrible tales concerning game of that species; but swallowing our regrets like true philosophers, we set instantly to work with our knives, and speedily stripped the ungracious rascal of his shaggy coat, exposing to view a set of nerves and muscles which indicated that the proprietor would have proved rather unpleasantly affectionate at a close hug. Our friends first saw him on the plain, and in utter contempt of the laws of chivalry took him at a disadvantage, and despatched him with repeated rifle-shots before he could get to cover. As I could not participate in his "taking off," I feel it incumbent upon me to deliver his funeral sermon, and like Anthony on a similar occasion, I beg the reader to "bear with me." But in performing this duty, I cannot follow established usages, and eulogise the great defunct. A proper regard for truth compels me to say that, like old Joey B., he was rough and tough albeit not "devilish sly." In fact his flesh was about as easily masticated, and not half so digestible as whipcord. I do not intend to dispute with those who aver in the abstract, that bear steaks are a luxury; but, so far as this particular bear was concerned, I am not to be convinced "in spite of my teeth." But if the bear was not to be borne, the doe was not in the same category, and we took a sweet revenge upon her fat ribs, which we roasted with savage delight, and discussed with ravenous appetites. Having supped full of doe, we gathered around a fire which the cool air of evening rendered extremely comfortable, and drawing our blankets over our heads to escape the effects of a thick mist which was gathering around us, we gradually talked ourselves asleep, not without misgivings that the next of kin of our tough friend might undertake to avenge the murder of their clansman.

At early dawn we were again in the saddle, and dividing into pairs, started off in different directions for the morning hunt—for after the sun is up the deer catch the scent far quicker than when the dew is upon the grass. My companion and guide was an accomplished woodsman, well skilled in the "art of venerie," like most of our compatriots, who have crossed the Rocky Mountains. We immediately ascended to the top of the highest range of hills in sight, and I found an abundant reward for my pains in a view of the most beautiful, singular and novel scenery I had ever before beheld. It was the charming month of May, and the heights on which we rode, although thousands of feet above the level of the sea, were lavishly strewed with wild flowers of a hundred hues, larger and more beautiful than any I had ever seen. On the plain below was growing a crop of oats, sowed and cultivated by nature's hand alone, and the bright green stems shot up more thickly and luxuriantly than in any cultivated field I have ever beheld, the rapidly filling ears giving promise of an abundant crop, destined to furnish food only to the wild beasts of the field and the fowls of the air, while what remained would be sown broadcast by the winds of heaven, to be reproduced a hundred fold the next season. The deep vales were filled with fine timber and thick underbrush, and while we stood upon a lofty eminence forming a portion of an amphitheatre of hills, the glorious sun rose above a distant range, producing effects which varied every moment with his increasing altitude. The space between us and those opposite distant hills was like a misty lake, bounded by them as though they were remote shores, while here and there a wooded peak shot up like an island, the seeming lake rolling its agitated and unsubstantial waves of pearl and opal to our very feet. This magnificent scene was gradually dissipated by the rising sun, and at length a few evanescent clouds clinging to the mountain's sides alone told of the splendid morning picture we had witnessed. Yet what remained after these brilliant accessories had passed away, was beautiful exceedingly—as beautiful as the real can be when divested of the ideal. Here were majestic mountains, expansive plains, rugged ravines, fragrant groves, verdure of exquisite freshness, flowers of a thousand tints, and fast-flowing rivulets dashing on to that benignant old ocean whose blue waves seemed to stretch out in one direction into boundless space. And here we were alone with nature, for the habitations of men were not to be seen, and we stood on virgin soil unstained by crime, and seldom trodden by any of Caucasian blood. And what could be more exciting amidst such primitive scenes than the bound of the deer startled at the approach of hostile strangers? Alas! that man should be so frail, so inconsistent, as to admire nature, and yet be intent upon destroying the poor harmless animals which inhabit her wildest and most secluded haunts. But so it was; and when I popped at a fat buck, dashing by us at the top of his speed, all I regretted was, that I had only a shot gun instead of a rifle. I had no sort of regard for the poor creature's life, but thirsting for innocent blood, thought only to slay and eat. Imagine then the awkwardness of a shot-gun for hunting such game! However, in a few hours, *we* killed no less than five good fat deer—that is to say my companions killed four and wounded a fifth, which I *finished* with a charge of buck-shot. We selected the choicest parts of the poor creatures, and bore them triumphantly to our camp, where we arrived at noon, and made such a breakfast as can be eaten only by sportsmen.

We staid here a few days hunting around the country, but, to my great sorrow, we saw no more bears, they having probably taken the alarm from my shot-gun. Yet some of that interesting family were undoubtedly not far from us—a fact which was shown by the appearance of a luxuriant field of wild clover growing up as high as the bellies of our horses, which the bears had evidently been demolishing. Bruin, like some other animals, loves to be "in clover," and his choicest Apician morsels consist of the ripe sweet heads of that fragrant grass, which he takes by way of dessert after venison. But he seems to hate man as cordially as Lord Byron did, loves solitude equal to Zimmerman, and, like many other prejudiced and ill-bred beasts of the wilder sort, gives the lord of creation as wide a berth as possible. Let a man come within the beat of bruin, and he will be smelt out and avoided, unless he come upon the beast unawares; and indeed, it may be remarked, that wild animals in general seem to regard man as the most ferocious and dreadful among all the beasts of prey—with what justice, let those decide who know the gentle and peaceful habits of human kind.

On our way homewards, we made a small *detour* to a wild and savage glen, shut in by perpendicular precipices and "horrid crags," very aptly called by the people "los infernos." This interesting locality is said to be a favorite resort of the bear population, who retreat to these damp and gloomy solitudes for coolness and shade. It is chiefly remarkable for a group of monstrous red-wood trees, greatly resembling the cedars of Lebanon, which taking root in the humid earth of "los infernos," (which by good rights should be dry), shoot upwards to the light, pushing their spiry tops to a level with the brink of the precipice, at least two hundred feet above. These trees were of enormous girth, and I rode into the cavities of several which would easily have held another horse and man at the same time. Vegetation, like every thing else, is on a vast scale in California, which will yet prove one of the brightest stars in the American galaxy.

A few days after our return "to town," another hunting party was formed, consisting in part of several of our officers. This time they resolved to "see the elephant," that is, the bear. Accordingly, after spending a day or two at the "camp," they selected a spot for placing the bait, which was composed of the carcasses of several deer which had yielded their tender haunches and savoury saddles to the camp fare. With guns and rifles ready for execution, the party lay *perdu* until daylight, meditating a violent death to "cuffee," should he be tempted by the "broken victuals." But having waited in vain, they returned to camp, breakfasted, and prepared for the morning hunt. The sun was already up when they started, and they were passing the remote and shady nook where the bait had been left, without supposing it had been visited by the wary bear. But sure enough, there was bruin, alias cuffee, in his own proper person, busily employed in burying the dainty morsels, which were as yet too fresh and recently killed to suit his fastidious taste. Probably feeling that he had been trifled with, and not relishing the interruption, the enraged animal, at one fierce bound, seated himself *en croupe* with Tom Cole, the guide and file-leader of the party, taking that intrepid son of Nimrod in his arms with a truly fraternal embrace. Those behind drew bridle, dismounted, prepared their pieces, but dared not shoot, so close was the identity of Tom and the bear. But if they could not succeed by force of arms, they were more fortunate in using the force of lungs, and were well supported in the rear by Tom's horse, who intimated very strongly his disgust at this novel way of carrying double. By these means Tom was liberated from his dangerous neighbor, his *gamusa* (buckskin) having been proof against the teeth and claws of the monster. But now it was Tom's turn. With perfect self-possession, he dismounted his trembling charger, and the very next instant his unerring rifle had sent its fatal messenger through the lungs of the retreating foe. No second shot was needed, although a whole broadside was poured into the brute from shot-guns, rifles and pistols. In fact, every one enjoyed the luxury of a shot at the bear, but the huge hide was awarded to the intrepid hero of the feat, whose skill, coolness and deliberate courage were fully appreciated, under circumstances so emphatically impressive. I believe our American woodsmen, especially the elder race of trappers and hunters, the Saturns and Titans of our forests, are not surpassed in *nerve* by any men in the world. With muscles of iron, and souls that know not fear, no effort discourages, no peril daunts them; but, like honest Tom Cole, their aim is as steady and deadly in a moment of imminent danger, as it would be at grouse shooting on a summer's day.

It would give me pleasure, in the course of these pages, to impart a faithful idea of California to those who choose to read them; but as it is not my design to write a treatise by rule and compass, nor to trouble the reader with exact measurements and tedious details, that "gentle" personage must learn, if at all, from general observations, and abide rather by the spirit "which maketh alive" than by the letter "which killeth." I detest the diary form of writing, and hope no sensible man cares to know exactly where a traveller slept on each particular night, the precise distance he travelled every day, and each dish of which he partook at every meal. Nor shall I strain after being particularly entertaining, or faultlessly methodical; and it may often happen that I shall write without point, and in a discursive, egotistical, desultory style. For instance, here is an account of a ride without a bear, which many will find dull and some may think instructive.

Early one fine morning I left Monterey with a companion to conduct me to Salinas, where we arrived about noon. Every thing connected with this ride was delightful. The fresh morning air was redolent of the sweetest perfume ever wafted to the celestial "daughter of the dawn." It was none of your common-place Atlantic atmospheres, but laden with fragrance; soft and voluptuous, yet not enervating, but gently bracing. In truth there was a pervading reality in the sweet gales which wooed us, seeming to impart to them intense vitality, and to establish sympathy if not familiarity with the viewless spirits who "people the sun-beam." Our way lay through delicious plains, richly enamelled with those exquisite wild-flowers varying from palest blue to brightest flame-color, which are produced spontaneously in all parts of California. Occasionally we wound through groves of oaks verdant as misseltoe, and arranged in clumps with a skill which man might vainly imitate, through the openings of which the startled deer darted with lightning speed as our cavalcade dislodged them from their leafy coverts. The balmy air, the perfume of countless flowers, combined with scenery now sweetly beautiful, now grandly bold, gave zest and life to the conscious enjoyment of the free and rapid motion of our steeds, which united to fleetness and spirit perfect obedience to the rider's will. I am not aware of any higher and truer enjoyment of mere physical existence than this kind of travelling in California, which the world can hardly match. I have travelled in all sorts of ways, in all sorts of countries; in the toiling diligences of France, and on the broad pack-saddle of a contrabandista's mule in Spain; I have been whisked across the Pontine marshes by half-wild colts, guided by shouting postillions; been jolted half to death in Syria and Egypt on the unsteady deck of a "desert ship," conducted by Arabs clamorous for "bucksheesch;" travelled "dawk" in India, with the "last new novel" in a palankeen; and once had the pleasure to back an elephant in the Island of Ceylon. But all these were vulgar joys compared with the rapturous pleasure of travelling in that part of the United States of America called California. Seated in your firm and chair-like saddle, your horse held well in hand, but not irritated by the severe and subduing

Spanish bit; going on a full gallop, which is the travelling gait of the country, the shouting *vaquero** (outrider) driving on the road far ahead a *"caballada"* of rushing steeds, and changing your horse for a fresh one at the slightest symptom of fatigue, what can be more delightful, more satisfying, surrounded as you are with such glorious accessories, breathing the fulness of life into every sense? Who cares for the artificial world across the continent, when he can thus enjoy wild and uncontrolled independence? Who cares for the wealth of Wall street, when, dashing over the painted plains and far-surveying hills, he may exclaim with Goldsmith—

"Creation's heir, the world, the world is mine!"

We arrived early in the evening at the rancho of Don Francisco Pacheco, having accomplished, since morning, with perfect ease, an equestrian journey, which, on our side of the continent, would have been considered a great performance.

---

*Vaquero means herdsman, outrider or groom.

NEAR THE HOMESTEAD of Señor Pacheco, and on his land, is the *Picacho Verde,* one of the highest mountains of the coast range, elevated many hundred feet above the level of the sea. From its summit we had a magnificent and extensive prospect. To the north-east lay the flat meadow land of the Tulare Valley, with the river San Joaquim winding through it, while the distant heights of the Sierra Nevada, or Snowy Mountains of California, bounded the view on that side. Toward the west we beheld the beautiful little Rattlesnake Vale seemingly at our feet, and presenting a miniature of the large valley on the other side. The Sierras of the mission lands of San Juan, and a distant sheet of water, which appeared like mist, completed the panorama. That sheet of water was the renowned Bay of San Francisco, the most magnificent harbor in the world. On our return to Monterey, we visited the mission of San Juan, the buildings of which are as yet in tolerable preservation, but fast falling into decay.

Crossing a high mountain we proceeded thence to Santa Cruz, a town situated near the bay, on the north side of the same indenture of the coast where stands Monterey. The population is small, and composed partly of Americans; but the inhabitants have improved their time, and the place presents a busy aspect. The people here are chiefly engaged in the lumber trade, excellent saw-mills having been erected by Mr. Graham and others, which are constantly in operation, all the lumber they can produce selling readily at high prices. The principal timber here is the *palo colorado,* or red-wood, which grows to a monstrous size, and appears somewhat like a huge cedar, to which species it belongs. The timber is soft and easily cut up, and is of a reddish color, like the cedar of the United States. The fibre is perfectly straight, and the wood will split its entire length as true as if sawed. It is slightly odoriferous, as if impregnated with an essential oil, and, when kept dry, is incorruptible, so that it is probably the best wood in the world for beams, rafters, shingles, joists, &c. Pine is also abundant, and is sawed at this place for flooring, the red-wood being too soft for that purpose. I was informed, by authority not to be doubted, that a single red-wood tree had produced the enormous quantity of 113,000 feet of lumber, sawed into clapboards. The lumber is shipped from the beach for the leeward ports of California, where the timber exists only in almost inaccessible mountains, the ravines of which are inhabited only by Indians.

In excursions of this kind, we passed the time pleasantly enough—now hunting deer, now shooting ducks and partridges, and now fishing. Game and fish are abundant, and the emigrant who is anything of a sportsman, is in no danger of starvation, even when the gold mania rages. Occasionally we had a *merienda* (pic-nic), a few miles into the country, or a *bayle* (dance) at the house of one of our polite and hospitable friends. We wound up the month of April with a grand ball, given by the officers of the ship, at which the American and Mexican flags gracefully and lovingly intertwined in a most fraternal embrace, forming one of the most conspicuous decorations of the room. Don José Castro, *commandante general,* was our principal guest. But little more than a month afterwards, the same national symbols were arrayed against each other in hostile feud, and the illustrious Don José, preferring a race to a fight, was riding express, with all his braves, towards the lower country.

CAPTAIN FREMONT, of the United States Topographical Engineers, had entered California, with his party, just before our arrival, depending upon the resources of the country for subsistence and recruits,—his little band being sorely exhausted by their wearisome journey across the most rugged part of the continent. As far as I could understand, the duty of this topographical party was to explore the route to the Pacific, on the line connecting the head-waters of the Gila with the Rio Grande del Norte. The able and accomplished leader of this expedition had already completed the reconnaisance of the route, through the immense unknown region of country lying in the vicinity of the Great Salt Lake, vaguely known under the name of the Great American Desert. Among civilized nations, scientific expeditions are always treated with courtesy and hospitality, even if they are in a country actually at war with their own. As far back as the reign of Louis XIV, that monarch imprisoned the officers who seized the builders of the Eddystone lighthouse, saying that he was at war with England, and not with mankind. But, in the present instance, our government did not rely upon custom, but obtained positive assurances from the Mexican government that the exploring party should receive good treatment. But, notwithstanding these pledges of hospitality, and the universal usage of civilized nations, General Castro in perfect consistency with the treacherous character of his government, and in a spirit of ignorant and arrogant assumption, fulminated a proclamation denouncing Fremont as an invader of the sacred soil of the republic, and characterizing his party as robbers and cut-throats. This was followed, upon Fremont's advance to Monterey, by another paper volley, in the usual vainglorious and bombastic style of such Mexican productions, calling together the people in arms to defend their glorious country, polluted by a foreign and unholy invader. This proclamation contained the usual flourishes in which these heroes indulge, in common with the Chinese, and wound up with the stereotyped but unreverenced names, *"Dios y Libertad."* The Americans residing in the country, with a zeal which did them honor, volunteered to defend their countrymen; and numbers would have poured into Fremont's camp had the gallant captain encouraged them to do so. Knowing, however, as I imagine, his own party quite competent to compete with any force that Castro could bring against him, and fearing perhaps to compromise his countrymen who would have suffered in person and property, had Castro, by any unexpected circumstance, proved successful—Fremont quietly entrenched his little band in a well-selected position, every approach to which was commanded by their rifles—and calmly awaited the terrible onset of the truculent Castro. Don José summoned to the field a force of two hundred men; and, with a six-pounder or two, advanced towards the hill from which floated the starry flag, beneath whose folds common men are transformed into heroes. And never did it wave over a more resolute band of gallant hearts than on this memorable occasion, when a few hardy trappers, adventurous young men, and Delaware Indians—ever the faithful allies of ourselves and our forefathers—stood ready, in the midst of a remote and hostile country, to meet all odds which might be brought against them. But Don José was rather in the humor of that renowned king of France, who,

—"With twenty thousand men,
    Marched up the hill, and then—marched down again."

He vapored, he curvetted, he pranced,—he made all manner of demonstrations and manœuvres, which he doubtless thought no small beer of, in the hope of "striking terror," after the manner of his Chinese prototypes. But he finally concluded to break up his forces and withdraw, without venturing to approach within rifle-range, or to commit an outrage upon that flag which he could not have assailed without diminishing his own importance, and endangering the crockery in the undefended towns under his command.

The bad faith of the Mexican authorities, and perhaps the want of a friendly feeling on the part of the people of the country, partially defeated the object of the expedition, and Captain Fremont shortly after took the road to Oregon. About the same time, (May, 1846,) Lieut. Gillespie, United States marines, was landed from the United States sloop-of-war which had brought him from the coast of Mexico, he having crossed that country with despatches for Fremont, and, finding he had left, instantly started in pursuit of him. He left Sutter's fort on the Sacramento, travelling north, and expecting to overtake Captain Fremont's party before they got clear of the valley of that river. They followed the trail, however, until they got beyond that section of country, and arrived in the country of the Klamet Lakes, inhabited by roving bands of Indians of that name, who are great thieves and very hostile to the whites. They met, however, with attention and kindness from a party of these Indians whom they encountered fishing in a river for salmon, who even assisted them to cross over with their animals, although the little party, consisting of only six persons, was completely at the mercy of these savages. This apparent forbearance, however, only shows the deep wile of the Indian character; for they acted on the principle of the spider, who allows his victim to become well entangled in his web ere he strikes the fatal blow. About a day or two after they had crossed the river, finding it almost a hopeless case to pursue the trail of Fremont, so rapidly did he travel, and their horses being almost "used up," Gillespie encamped with four men, and sent the remaining man, an in-

trepid and skilful mountaineer—Joe Neal, by name—on the best horse of
the party, to overtake Fremont, if possible. This he succeeded in doing, at
an immense risk, having been obliged to charge through a party of Indians
who obstructed his passage. With the bridle in his teeth, and firing his rifle
and pistols to "port" and "starboard" amongst them, and receiving in return a volley of arrows, which luckily did him no injury, he gallantly made
good his way, and finally reached Fremont's camp in such a state of exhaus-
tion that he fell from his horse, and had barely strength to say that Gillespie
was in danger, and to describe the situation of his camp. Taking with him
his seven brave Delawares and two Canadians, Fremont instantly started
on the back trail, leaving the rest of the camp in its bivouac. He arrived at
Gillespie's station just at dusk, and after having supped and sat until a late
hour by the camp fire, the whole party fell sound asleep. Their slumbers,
however, were not of long duration, for they were suddenly aroused by the
loud war-whoop of a party of Indians, who were charging the very centre
of their camp. If a man ever requires the "four o'clock in the morning"
courage, of which Lord Byron speaks, it is on occasions like this, when suddenly aroused from sound slumber, in the dead of night, he is called upon
to confront a dimly-seen and skulking savage foe, whose force he cannot
estimate. But courage was the last thing lacking in the gallant party led by
Fremont and Gillespie. Kit Carson and the Delawares bravely sent back
the war-whoop, and the enemy was repulsed with loss. Their chief alone
continued to fight, and he did it after the most approved rules of war
adopted by these Indians—yelling aloud, dancing from side to side to elude
the aim of the hostile rifles, and discharging his sharp arrows with the
rapidity of thought. At length he also was brought down, and proved to be
the same chief who had helped Gillespie to ford the river. The arms and
accoutrements of the little party had excited the cupidity of the Indians,
who dogged the trail, expecting an easy conquest. The almost providential
accession of force to the way-worn little band was unknown to the savages,
who found in the end that they had reckoned without their host. After
inflicting summary chastisement on the village of these marauders, Fremont returned to Sutter's Fort.

On hearing of Fremont's unexpected return, the valorous Castro became again greatly excited. Proceeding to the Pueblo San José and occupying the barracks, he called together as large a posse as he could raise, and
pompously gave out that he intended to march at once up the Sacramento

Valley, and clear it of all suspicious characters. He declared, with a great show of sincerity, that he should attack the fort which, (he said,) ever since its establishment by Captain Sutter, had been the rendezvous of seditious and revolutionary foreigners—that he would raze the fort to the ground, and thus destroy the stronghold from which the legitimate government had been threatened; and finally, that he would either exterminate or drive out all foreigners who refused to become strictly Mexican citizens. How faithfully these magnificent threats were carried into effect, is somewhat notorious, even out of California.

In order to be near the probable scene of action, and to afford "aid and comfort" to Captain Fremont's party, which they much needed, our ship sailed from Monterey on the first of June, and keeping close in with the land on our way up the coast, we entered, on the third, between the huge basaltic cliffs forming the portals of the magnificent bay of San Francisco, and anchored at Sausalito.

In approaching the entrance to *this* harbor, look out for a white rock fronting its entrance, called Alcatraz, if you are coming from the southward. When you have it in a line with the fort on the southern point of the entrance, you have the best mark for crossing the bar in six fathoms of water. If coming from the north, the same fort on a line with Yerba Buena Island leads in, in four fathoms; and the entrance should not be attempted either to the northward or southward of these lines, as there is generally more of the rolling swell, which is sometimes rather heavy. There is almost always a leading wind, and the long and narrow entrance is entirely clear of any hidden dangers while the water is bold up to the very base of the cliffs. After you get in, the only danger to be avoided is a sunken rock, called Blossom Rock, near the south-east corner of Alcatraz, or Bird Island, bearing from it E. S. E. by compass, distant eight cables length. There is great depth of water over the whole bay. The latitude of the fort on the Presidio point is 37 deg. 48 min. 30 sec. N. Longitude, 122 deg. 27 min. 23 sec. west. Outside and bearing south 60 deg. west from the fort, and distant from it twenty-five miles, is a cluster of peaked rocks, called the Farullones. The tides here are very irregular. The usual watering-place is at Sausalito, on the north side of the bay, where also all kinds of supplies of vegetables, fruits, &c., may be obtained.

YERBA BUENA, now called San Francisco, is situated on the south side of the entrance of the bay, and at the period of this visit contained about half a dozen houses, and somewhat less than one hundred inhabitants. Of course, the place must have since grown considerably, notwithstanding the migration of the population to the gold region.*

The Indians have a tradition, that at no remote period of time the Bay of San Francisco was a great inland lake or sea of fresh water, the only outlet being the Rio de los Pejanos, (Bird River), which still empties into the Bay of Monterey. General Vallejo informed me, that a very old Indian had told him that he had heard his father say, that *his* grandfather had travelled by *land* to the "Pui," or feast, at Monterey, from the north to the south side of the bay, across what is now its entrance, but which was then a mountain, and that an earthquake rent the mountain asunder, and opened the present passage into the Pacific. Of course, the level of this huge lake was much higher than the Pacific, and it must have covered the whole of the valleys leading down to it, including the vast Tularé valley and plains. All these valleys bear evidence of having once been the bed of a large body of water, which has been partially drained off. The former existence of such a wide-spreading sheet of water may still be traced, and its channel is still

---

* It is to be regretted, that the author's sketch of this town has been lost, or stolen.

noticeable in examining the Tulé lakes, all of which communicate at a high stage of water with the San Joaquim. The shells and other deposits are appropriate to fresh water, and can be accounted for on no other hypothesis than the Indian tradition. There appears also to have been an upheaval of the low lands—lands now high above the valley streams being covered with a growth of *young* timber rapidly growing larger. In the valley of the Napa, a ranchero assured me, that some low lands on his rancho, now fit for cultivation, were, when he took possession in 1834, merely a salt water tulé marsh. A geological survey will, in my opinion, show that large bodies of land about San Francisco Bay have been reclaimed by a natural drainage caused by volcanic disruptions, and our government should institute a scientific expedition to examine into this subject, in connection with the origin of the vast deposits of gold which have lately been discovered in that neighborhood.

The usual preliminaries having been gone through with on entering port, I made arrangements in company with a brother officer to visit San José, the chief town of this district of country. We landed at Yerba Buena, and sat up, or rather stood up, all night at a ball, at which we had specimens of all the fair *rancheras* from around the bay, including the "contra costa," as the south-east side of it is called. I fear some good people will be scandalized, when they are informed that these gay damsels are gathered together at a ball with great ease, and think nothing of a journey of thirty or forty miles in quest of a dance.

Although we felt more like taking a nap than anything else, my comrade and myself mounted our horses early in the morning, and, after a little time spent in getting the "caballada" ahead of us, we pursued our journey.

Passing near the mission of Dolores, along the Porto Suelo of San Bruno, which is a steep chain of lofty and precipitous hills, extending from the point of that name on the bay across the Peninsula to the sea, and converting the northern end of it into a natural fortification, we saw the sea and bay at once on either hand, and both so near that a thirty-two pounder could have carried to either beach. Hence the road lies across a level prairie with the bay to the east, and a chain of lofty hills called the Santa Clara Mountains, on the west or ocean side. This plain, which is more than sixty miles in length, and averages nearly thirty in width, is said to be the largest single body of good agricultural land in all California. With the exception, however, of the little "milpas," near the different ranchos, it is not cultivated, although it affords grazing to vast herds of cattle and sheep, and numerous "manadas" of brood mares and colts, and "caballadas" of tame horses, of which we saw great numbers on both sides of our road. This extensive plain is divided into ranchos of four and eight square leagues in extent, and the soil is a black loam many feet deep, as any one can see in passing the dry beds of what, in the wet season, are running streams, emptying into the bay. This great prairie is sprinkled here and there with points or islands of timber, and reminded me very strongly of similar land which I have seen in the State of Illinois.

Passing through the mission of Santa Clara, we arrived at San José about dark. Having rested a day, and looked around the straggling village of San José, which is hardly worth describing, we visited several ranchos and also the famous quicksilver mine in the vicinity.

The depôt is situated in a secluded and romantic glen, about three leagues from San José. The mine itself is on the top of a high mountain, and the ore is brought down on mules, the path being very precipitous. The ore is the red cinnabar, and the quality is extremely rich, yielding from thirty to forty per cent., even by the rude and inadequate process which is adopted by the miners, although all the quicksilver might be easily disengaged from the ore. The process is as follows: Large whalers' try-pots are inverted over a heap of ore laid on an iron grate, beneath which a stream of water is made to pass. The edges of the pots being luted to the hearth in which the grate is fixed, a fire is made on the outside of the pots, and the dense mercurial vapors, evolved from the ore as it bakes, finding no vent save through the interstices of the grate, is condensed, and falls, in its metallic form of quicksilver, to the bottom of the little well or stream beneath. The vein is very rich, and the whole surrounding hills appear, from their reddish color, as if they contained inexhaustible quantities of ore. The cavity in the mountain, of about twenty cubic feet, was at this time worked by two Indians, with picks, who threw out quantities of the ore as fast as it could be broken up. This place has been resorted to by the Indians from time immemorial, for vermillion, to apply to their interesting persons; but the value of the deposit was first ascertained by Señor Castillero. This gentleman was educated at the school of mines in the city of Mexico; and, having visited California, his superior knowledge enabled him to detect the value of this mine, which he at once *"denounced,"** and commenced working.

When the truculent and doughty Don José Castro, alarmed at the first gleam of the bayonets of our tars, took refuge in inglorious flight from his entrenched camp of La Mesa, at Los Angeles, he first directed his furtive steps to the neighboring province of Sonora, to demand arms and money from the governor thereof, with the avowed purpose of rescuing California from the clutches of the "injusto opresor." Old Zack's victories, however, had knocked all the calculations of the Mexican "benemeritos de la patria" into a cocked hat, and the governor of Sonora was inclined to "acknowledge the corn" and give in. But if Castro's patriotic blustering was at a discount, he had still one possession which was above par, and that was his interest in the quicksilver mine. The commercial house transacting business in Tepic, under the name and style of Barron & Forbes, is a shrewd establishment with a vigilant eye to the main chance. Little cared they who governed the country, what faction was up to-day or down to-morrow; their thoughts were intent on the quicksilver, and they commissioned a score of Mercuries to get hold of it in their behalf and at their expense. Their emissaries and correspondents in California were instructed to hunt up Castro, and in the most benevolent and disinterested manner to furnish him money and other facilities to reach with all despatch the city of Tepic, and especially that quarter thereof in which the aforesaid commercial house exhibited its shingle. This mercantile hue and cry proved more efficacious than military pursuit, and Don José was picked up one fine morning with all his suite, in the town of Mazatlan, then closely blockaded by our fleet. To say that in a financial point of view, this discomfited patriot was decidedly "short," is hardly to do justice to the abhorrent vacuum which existed in his pockets; and it may easily be imagined that in his straitened situation he looked with complacency upon the thousand hard dollars with which he was kindly and unexpectedly furnished on the simple condition of visiting the pleasant city of Tepic. He did not therefore stop to be asked twice, but pocketed the money with avidity, and spent the whole of it in one day, between champagne and monte. All great men have their faults, and if Don José had one besetting sin more inveterate than

---

*Any one who discovers a mine, although it be on land not his own, may, by the law of Mexico, *denounce* it (as it is called) to the authorities. If he works it, the produce becomes his, under certain restrictions.

any other, that sin was a devotion to the game of monte. But he was a man of nerve, and with a coolness not to be surpassed, he complained to his sympathizing friends that it would now be quite impossible to go to Tepic —that he was in fact without money, and after all, that duty called upon him to stand by "la patria," and to maintain "el honor militar Mexicano," which required that every true and valiant soldado should muster beneath his country's glorious colors and die in her defence. He therefore announced with great solemnity, that, like a true hero, he should join the army then in the field under Santa Anna, and fall in the front rank, bravely battling for the liberties of his country. Now I never heard it objected to commercial gentlemen that they are slow at taking a reasonably broad hint, and the agents of the Tepic house were constrained to arrive at the melancholy conclusion that they must risk another cool thousand to allay the martial longings of Don José. It came like drawing teeth and with much higgling—but it *came*—and the bold and for once successful soldier mounted a noble steed, and rode to the city of Tepic. Here he was appointed to command the artillery, (being a colonel of that arm,) his ordnance consisting of a few dilapidated Spanish pieces of ancient date, and his force of half a dozen ragged artillery-men. But like a genuine old Mexican campaigner, he took advantage of one of those rare moments when the Supreme Government were in funds, and drew full pay and rations for a batallion. As to the quicksilver mine, *that* was a foregone conclusion. He was induced to sell out his shares on terms by no means ruinous to the opulent and sagacious firm at Tepic, who acquired the ownership or control of the whole mine, and sent up Mr. Alexander Forbes with English miners from the unproductive silver mines, and bought up all the empty *"frascos"* (cast iron flasks) which they could lay hands on. The first vessel they sent was the brig William, under English colors; but as she was proved to be a Mexican vessel, she was condemned by our admiralty court at Monterey, sold in pursuance to the sentence of that tribunal, bought in by the owners, and sent directly back by those enterprising men under neutral colors, having been purged of her Mexican character by the little formalities exacted by the admiralty.

This mine must prove a fertile source of wealth to all concerned in it. The ease with which the metal is extracted from the ore; the facility of transporting it to the ready market afforded by the gold and silver mines of Mexico, Lower California and South America; its extensive consumption for other than mining purposes, and the present monopoly of the article by Rothschilds and a few others, all contribute to render it very valuable. The yield of the precious metals has decreased in Mexico since that country became a republic, not only in consequence of the great insecurity of property in that country, but also on account of the high price of quicksilver. The prosperity of gold and silver mines has always been in proportion to the cheapness of quicksilver. The monopoly of the Rothschilds raised the price of this article from $100 to $150 per quintal, and sometimes, of late, it is quoted at eighty-seven and a half cents per pound. In 1590, when quicksilver was worth $107 per quintal, there was little product from the mines; when, in 1750 quicksilver fell to $82, there was a great increase in the yield of precious metals; and in 1782, when quicksilver was down to $42 per quintal, an immense impulse was given to mining operations. These fluctuations are not surprising when we consider that the richest silver mines in Mexico yield only three or four ounces of silver to one hundred pounds of ore, and that in some instances the quicksilver lost amounted to more than the silver that was obtained.

The process of using the quicksilver is very simple. It is mixed with the pounded and washed ore, and the affinity of the two metals causing them to unite, the mercury is driven off by heat and the silver remains. It is said that an ingenious American, residing in Guanajuato, has invented a method of condensing the mercury thus driven off, so that it can be used again.

Quicksilver is destined to become a most important article of Californian commerce, and one of its great sources of wealth. The doctors and men of science, and the mines before mentioned, will use it extensively; and it will also be employed in the mines of Upper California. Gold, platina, silver, quicksilver, lead, copper, iron and coal, are all known to exist in our California; and to her mineral wealth there will be no end.

There is a silver mine at Santa Inez, and the same metal is found in other parts of Upper California. There are also numerous *placers* of native gold, the metal being obtained by merely washing the earth in a rude and inartificial manner. These deposits are found on and near several streams running into the Tulé lakes.*

---

*This was written several months prior to the discovery of the vast deposits of gold in California. "The streams running into the Tulé Lakes" are probably still unexplored; and it being known that gold exists in their vicinity, who can say to what extent it may be found?

We only require the means of rapid and certain inland communication between California and the Atlantic States, to make all these treasures the property of our own people, and place our country in a position of paramount power as the great regulator of the currency of the world.

It may not become me to advise the powers at Washington, but I would confidently assure the people of the United States that the whole commercial world will "put in" for a footing in California, and seek to divert her golden streams into distant countries. England will do her utmost to reap this golden harvest, and if France ever gets a bona fide government, she will reach out for a moderate share. It is not unlikely that we shall have all sorts of "reciprocities" offered us, looking to the free admission of French, English and German goods into California, and the free abstraction of her mineral treasures towards Europe. But there is little danger that our government can be entrapped into driving the trade of California into foreign hands by rendering American competition hopeless. We shall possess advantages by the free admission of American manufactures, for which a vast market will be opened; and the warehousing system, so successfully introduced by the enlightened Secretary Walker, will enable American ships to carry large amounts of foreign goods. The Atlantic States will, therefore, secure profitable returns for their merchandise and freights, in the precious metals, which, I trust, will ere long be coined at San Francisco. But California is still very distant from us, and cannot be truly and surely ours until she is made more accessible to us than to other nations. It is, therefore, incumbent upon us to use all proper means to establish, as rapidly as possible, means of rapid and safe communication with the resplendent Star of the West. Measures should be taken to insure the immediate construction of a railroad across the Isthmus of Panama—but that is merely a step, and is to be first taken because it is the shortest step. Simultaneously with the construction of this short road, our government should either build, or aid in building, a ship canal across the most favorable part of the strip of land lying between the Gulf of Mexico and the Pacific. Of course these works pre-suppose the procurement of the right of way, either from New Grenada, Central America, or Mexico, a matter which can be compassed either by American citizens or by our government. But I would not stop here. It is essential that the very heart of California should be reached and united with the very heart of the Union. A railroad, therefore, from some point on the Mississippi through Fremont's South Pass, if no better route exist, to San Francisco, should be constructed as rapidly as possible by the general government. It will cost some millions, but the money will not be thrown away. The investment will be a good one, viewed merely in the light of an investment. But that is not all. The great East, or rather we may now say the great West in speaking of Asia, will be brought to our very doors. Population will flow into the fertile regions of California. The resources of the entire country traversed by the road will be developed, and discoveries of the greatest importance will be made. The public lands lying along the route will be changed from deserts into gardens, and a large population will be settled along the whole line of the road, composed in part of the laborers employed in building it, to each of whom a small tract should be given. For military purposes, and also as a means of transport-ing the precious metals, and the more costly fabrics of China eastward, and of Europe westward, the value of this road can hardly be estimated. Why, then, with these and many other advantages attaching to the enterprise, should not our government proceed to prosecute it? Why do not the people call for immediate action? A few millions thus safely invested will do more to place us in the commanding and paramount commercial posi-tion we *must* sooner or later occupy, than twice the amount could effect towards that end, if expended in any other manner. Let the people of the Atlantic States, who are mainly interested, awaken the attention of Con-gress to this all-important matter.

There is another suggestion I would make, at the risk of being deemed visionary; and that is, the extension of the MAGNETIC TELEGRAPH, with all convenient speed, from St. Louis to San Francisco. A million dollars would probably pay the expense of a first-rate telegraph, with heavy wires of gal-vanized iron, as prepared by Morewood of New York. As a means of com-munication, not only with thousands of our countrymen in Oregon and California, but also with our vast and growing commerce in the Pacific and in Asia, the value of this telegraph can hardly be appreciated. It would not only be used by ourselves, but also by the agents of all nations having commercial relations with the Pacific and Asia. But it would principally benefit our own commerce, enabling us to take immediate advantage of fluctuations in the Eastern markets, and eventually to command those markets, and almost monopolize the trade of China and the East Indies.

It is not doubtful that the revenue from such a telegraph would be very great, and justify the expense of employing men in abundance to watch and repair the wires. But even if no revenue accrued beyond the expenses, the work would be of inestimable advantage to our own country, and come fairly within the spirit of that clause of the Constitution which authorizes Congress to "regulate commerce."

RETURNING TO SAN FRANCISCO, we passed through the mission of Santa Clara, the buildings of which are in tolerable preservation. As a general rule, however, the magnificent buildings and other improvements at the various missions scattered throughout California, are in a ruinous condition. At San Luis del Rey, San Gabriel, and elsewhere, it is melancholy to see what solid advantages have been lost by the poor Indians.

The first mission and Royal Presidio in Upper California was established at San Diego, in 1769, and the others were organized from time to time. The last established was the mission of San Francisco de Solano, in 1822. The priests did every thing in person at these missions, teaching the Indians agriculture, gardening and the mechanic arts. The military establishment at each mission consisted only of a *cabo*—corporal—and five privates, and they carried the mail on horseback. The infamous suppression or "secularization" of the missions occurred in 1831.

It was our good fortune to reach our ship on the 14th of June, a day memorable in the annals of California. On that day, at early dawn, a party of Americans detached from a body collected together in or near Sutter's Fort, at New Helvetia on the Sacramento, rode into Sonoma, and suddenly presented themselves in arms to the astonished eyes of the Californians, as a Revolutionary party. After seizing the cannon and muskets they found in the barracks, with such other munitions of war as could be found, they captured and carried away as prisoners, General M. G. Vallejo, his brother, Captain Salvador Vallejo, Lieutenant Colonel Pruden, and several other influential persons from whom they feared opposition. A garrison was organized from among the foreigners for the defence of Sonoma, and a messenger sent down to our ship to inform her commander that they were in arms in consequence of a proclamation issued by Castro ordering all foreigners to quit the territory within forty days under the penalty of *death*, declaring their property confiscated, and announcing his intention to enforce his threats to the letter. The messenger further stated that the insurgents intended never to lay down their arms until they had established the independence of their adopted country, to which they had been invited with promises of lands and a republican government, but instead of which they had been prohibited to occupy lands, and had been oppressed by a military despotism, &c. &c. &c.

I have now touched a part of Californian history, concerning which, although I was on the spot when the events took place, I was then entirely in the dark, as were all the naval officers of the United States, at that time in the country. The proclamation alluded to had not previously been made known even to our commander, who, as the highest American officer in the country, would certainly have inquired into such a manifest violation of our treaty stipulations with Mexico, and if necessary would have adopted retaliatory measures. But proclamation, or no proclamation, it is certain that the prisoners taken at Sonoma were carried to Captain Fremont's camp, and it is equally a fact that they were imprisoned in Sutter's Fort, and guarded in the strictest manner by a party of the revolutionists, commanded by Mr. Kerme, one of Captain Fremont's followers.* I heard also, that on the first night after leaving Sonoma with their prisoners, the revolutionists, with singular inconsistency, encamped and went to sleep without setting sentinel or guard; that in the night they were surrounded by a party under the command of one Juan de Padilla, who crept up

---

*It is now well understood that all the acts of Captain Fremont were in accordance with instructions, and however I may reflect on the unauthorized acts of others under his command, I would not be understood as in any way censuring the prompt and energetic proceedings of that gallant and accomplished officer, whose retirement from the army is a national loss.

stealthily and awoke one of the prisoners, telling him that he had a strong force of well armed rancheros, who could surprise and slay the Americans before they could fly to arms, but that he, Padilla, before proceeding, awaited the orders of General Vallejo, whose rank and standing entitled him to command. The latter being called upon so as not to awake the sleepers, immediately replied that he should go voluntarily with his guardians, that he anticipated a speedy and satisfactory settlement of the whole matter, and advised Padilla to return to his rancho and disperse his band, positively refusing to permit any violence to the guard, as he was certain it would lead to disastrous consequences, and probably involve the rancheros and their families in ruin, without accomplishing any permanent good result. This was not told to me by Vallejo, but by a person who was present, and it tallies well with the account given by the revolutionists themselves, several of whom informed me that no guard was kept by them that night, and that the prisoners might have easily escaped had they felt so inclined. The same persons also told me that when Vallejo was called out of bed, and made a prisoner in his own house, he requested to be informed as to the plans and objects of the revolutionists, signifying his readiness to collect and take command of a force of his countrymen in the cause of independence, to act against all who might oppose him—adding, that his devotion to that cause was too well known, and his opinion had been too often publicly expressed, to leave room for doubt as to his integrity and sincerity, while his position in the community was a sufficient guaranty of his ability to perform all that he promised. But the majority of the men he addressed were ignorant of the Spanish language, deeply imbued with prejudice against the Mexican race, and not knowing the sterling qualities and unconcealed political opinions of their prisoner, were naturally suspicious of his good faith in thus professing a readiness to unite his fortunes with their own. Moreover, it is not unlikely that they acted under positive orders from whoever they acknowledged as their chief; for they not only refused to compromise the matter in any way, but became suspicious of those more enlightened and sagacious men of their own number, who appeared to listen with favor to the general's appeal.

The next day a proclamation was issued by the patriots at Sonoma, setting forth their grievances, assuring the *peaceable* inhabitants of protection, and declaring their intention to establish a republican government, independent of Mexico, or perish in the attempt. A flag was also hoisted bearing a Grizzly Bear rampant, with one stripe below, and the words "Republic of California" above the bear, and a single star in the Union.

About this time I started in one of the ship's boats for the Sacramento. Leaving the ship at Sausalito, we stood up before the wind, and soon passed the straits between the opposing promontories of San Pedro and San Pablo, and entered the broad and beautiful bay which takes its name from the latter. Crossing it with a fine breeze, we made a port at Mare Island, lying just at the entrance of the Straits of Karquin, the flood-tide having carried us thus far since leaving Sausalito. The ebb-tide rushing with great violence through these narrow straits, hemmed in by the high land on either side, and consisting of the pent-up waters of the Sacramento and San Joaquim, swelled by their numerous tributaries, makes a strong current and rude sea, which it is dangerous and often impossible to stem in a boat; for the accumulated waters sometimes come rushing down like the "bores" of the East Indian rivers, forming a perpendicular wall across the straits, and of course overwhelming any open boat in their furious passage to the bay. This, with the uncertainty of the tides of the Bay of San Francisco— which, from local causes, and the frequent intervention of half tides, occurring at intervals not to be calculated on—renders the navigation of the Straits of Karquin, and the bays of San Pablo and Suisun by a small boat, dangerous to those not accustomed to these peculiarities, and especially so at night. The launch of the United States ship Warren was lost here in October of this same year with three officers and nine seamen, and a quantity of stores and specie, destined for the garrison of Fort Sacramento. She left the ship at or just before dark, with the flood-tide, and was seen to enter the bay of San Pablo; but after that, not a trace of the boat, nor the least vestige of her unhappy crew, was ever seen or heard of, although the most diligent search was made.

We went ashore and breakfasted at Mare Island; and several hours intervening before the return of flood-tide, we started out to look around for elk, of which we saw "signs." This island is famous for being the resort of a large herd of these animals, which are invariably accompanied by a *wild mare,* who has found her way thither. But although we saw the beautiful band, feeding in company with their equine friend, we could not get near enough for a shot, owing to the inconsiderate haste and wild eagerness of our sailors, who prematurely rushed forward and discovered themselves to the swift-footed and timorous game. But better than the slaughter of these innocents was the exciting and novel spectacle they presented as they dashed off under the lead of the fleet mare, and fled far far away into the low lands, stretching well towards the main, until at length they faded from sight in the morass inaccessible to human footsteps.

Passing through the Straits of Karquin we entered Suisun bay, camped at its farther extremity, just under the lofty Monte Diablo, and after losing a day in cruising about the flat submerged ground near the Sacramento and San Joaquim, we arrived at last at the Fort.

These rivers have a common delta, which actually bears some resemblance to that much-abused Greek letter inverted, the apex of the triangle being at their mouths, and their main streams forming the two sides. The intervening district is composed of low, alluvial soil, covered with a thick growth of *tulé,* a species of gigantic bulrush, the stem of which is tender and filled with air cavities. It grows sometimes fifteen feet high, and has a semi-bulbous root, fresh and pleasant to the taste, and is the food of some of the smaller amphibious animals. This district is traversed by an interminable net-work of "slues," or sheets of shallow water, (Bunyan would have said *sloughs*), nearly all of which open broadly and invitingly; but the unwary voyager who trusts to their seeming resemblance to the mouth of either river he wishes to ascend, is sure to become involved in labyrinthine mazes, and is not extricated without the exercise of some tact and judgment, the expenditure of a large stock of patience, and peradventure the consumption of all his provisions. The mouths of the two rivers, however, when once discovered, are afterwards easily recognized, and the sandbars and slight impediments to navigation are easily avoided. The whole of the *tulé* lands bordering on these rivers will doubtless be valuable at some day for the culture of rice, which will become a prominent product of California, and probably be exported to the accessible and ready markets of the East Indies. Indeed, I was struck by the resemblance which this immense tract of *tulé* land bears to the often laboriously prepared "paddy fields" of China, Hindostan, Sumatra, and the Dutch and Malayan Archipelago. In the *tulé* region of California, bounteous nature has herself prepared these fields for the industry of any who may choose to cultivate them, the quantity of land being vast and the quality unsurpassable. These lands are indeed of immense extent, comprising not only the delta of the principal rivers of California, but extending at intervals, in tracts of various areas, far up towards their sources. They are periodically submerged during the rainy season, and as the head waters of the San Joaquim communicate at that season with the *Tulé* Lakes, transportation from above may be easily effected. Emigrants from Asia will, before many years, find it for their interest to settle upon these fertile tracts of rice-bearing lands, or some of our own people may find their account in investing largely in rice plantations, which they can cultivate to great advantage by hiring coolies and other laborers at low wages. Europe pours her thousands upon our Atlantic seaboard, and Asia will yet furnish her share of inhabitants for populating our possessions on the Pacific. The industrious and imitative Chinese will not make a bad cross with our restless and inventive Yankees.

The Sacramento is a most picturesque and beautiful stream, and presents, for a great part of its extent, the remarkable peculiarity of two sets of banks, which appear to be formed of alluvial deposits—the second, or farthest removed, having been deposited by the river at the highest stage of its waters. The country beyond the banks, and the woods which line them, is rolling prairie or level plains, interspersed with groves of oak, and the soil has proved, as far as tried, extremely productive and luxuriant. The banks of the river are thickly wooded, being lined on either side by a strip of heavy timber generally about a league in breadth. The river is deep, clear of snags, and navigable to the Butes for steamers at all seasons of the year. As yet, however, no steam vessel has disturbed its solitudes. The tributaries of the Sacramento are numerous, rising in the Sierras on each side of the valley amongst timber of huge size, and their waters, cooled by the snows of these Sierras, make a delicious beverage. Nor is there any lack of water power, the sites for mill seats being almost without number. Some of these tributaries present the feature common to many of the rivers of California, of suddenly sinking into the earth and reappearing ere they disembogue into the main stream. The principal of these subterranean rivers are the *Rio de los Plumas,* known among the Americans as Feather River, and the *Rio de los Americanos,* otherwise called the American Fork. The regions washed by these streams have proved especially prolific in gold, and it may be that large deposits of this precious metal are hidden in their subterranean beds.

The Americans alone had taken up lands in this fine section of the country, and composed the sum total of actual settlers. No Californian had ventured to take out papers for ranchos here on account of the danger from Indians, and the whole region was out of favor with the Californians, and looked upon with distrust by them. Perhaps in the end they may have concluded that the Indians were not more formidable neighbors than the Yankees.

On arriving at the "Embarcaderia," (landing), we were not surprised to find a mounted guard of "patriots," who had long been apprised by the Indians that a boat was ascending the river. These Indians indeed were important auxiliaries to the Revolutionists, during the short period of strife between the parties contending for the sovereignty of California. Having been most cruelly treated by the Spanish race, murdered even, on the slightest provocation, when their oppressors made marauding expeditions for servants, and when captured compelled to labor for their unsparing task-masters, the Indians throughout the country hailed the day when the hardy strangers from beyond the Sierra Nevada rose up in arms against the "hijos del pais" (sons of the country). Entertaining an exalted opinion of the prowess and skill of the Americans, and knowing from experience that they were of a milder and less sanguinary character than the rancheros, they anticipated a complete deliverance from their burthens, and assisted the revolutionists to the full extent of their humble abilities.

Emerging from the woods lining the banks of the river, we stood upon a plain of immense extent, bounded on the west by the heavy timber which marks the course of the Sacramento, the dim outline of the Sierra Nevada appearing in the distance. We now came to some extensive fields of wheat in full bearing, waving gracefully in the gentle breeze like the billows of the sea, and saw the whitewashed walls of the fort situated on a small eminence commanding the approaches on all sides.

We were met and welcomed by Capt. Sutter and the officer in command of the garrison; but the appearance of things indicated that our reception would have been very different had we come on a hostile errand.

The appearance of the fort, with its crenulated walls, fortified gateway, and bastioned angles; the heavily bearded, fierce-looking hunters and trappers, armed with rifles, bowie knives and pistols; their ornamented hunting shirts, and gartered leggins; their long hair turbaned with colored

Sketched by J. W. Revere U. S. N.   Lith. of Wm. Endicott & Co. N. York.

SUTTER'S FORT – NEW HELVETIA.

handkerchiefs; their wild and almost savage looks, and dauntless independent bearing; the wagons filled with golden grain; the arid, yet fertile
plains; the "caballados" driven across it by wild shouting Indians, enveloped in clouds of dust, and the dashing horsemen, scouring the fields in
every direction;—all these accessories conspired to carry me back to the
romantic East, and I could almost fancy that I was once again the guest of
some powerful Arab chieftain, in his desert stronghold. Everything bore
the impress of vigilance and preparation for defence—and not without
reason; for Castro, then at the Pueblo de San José, with a force of several
hundred men, well provided with horses and artillery, had threatened to
march upon the valley of the Sacramento. Captain Fremont, who had been
recalled to California by our government, had strengthened his party by
an alliance with the patriots, and had marched at their head to the north
shores of the bay to anticipate any attack upon his party that might be
threatened—a measure doubtless authorized by our government, as well
as sanctioned by the law of self-defence.

The fame of Capt. Sutter and his fort is so extended, that some account
of that distinguished person may be interesting to my readers.

John A. Sutter is a Swiss by birth and a soldier by profession; and, like
many of his countrymen, he early sought in the service of a foreign sovereign, that advancement in the career of arms which he was unlikely to
find at home, accepting the post of Lieutenant in one of the Swiss regiments of infantry in the service of France, during the reign of Charles X.
At the period of the revolution of 1830, and the consequent dethrone-
ment of that monarch, he was with his regiment in garrison at Grenoble.
Even after the revolution was under full headway, and the tri-color flying
in the town, the brave Swiss, with their proverbial fidelity, kept the white
flag of the Bourbons displayed over the citadel; nor was it until the revolution was consummated, and Charles a fugitive, that they consented to
capitulate. On the disbanding of their corps, which took place shortly
afterwards, Sutter came to the United States, became a citizen, and after
spending several years in different States of our Union, engaging in various pursuits, and undergoing many vicissitudes of fortune, he concluded
to emigrate to Oregon, whence he went to California. With adventurous
daring he resolved to take up his abode, alone and unsupported, in the
midst of the savages of the frontier; for at that time not a single white man

inhabited the valley of the Sacramento. His first attempt to ascend that river was a failure, he having lost his way among the interminable "slues" I have already alluded to; but still persevering, he arrived at his present location, established alliances with several tribes of Indians in the vicinity, acquired a great ascendancy and power among them, took some of them for soldiers and instructed them in the mysteries of European drill, built his fort on the most approved frontier model, and boldly made war upon the refractory tribes in the vicinity. I doubt if a more remarkable instance of individual energy, perseverance and heroism, has ever been displayed under similar circumstances. This unceremonious way of settling down in a strange country, and founding a sort of independent empire on one's "own hook," is one of those feats which will excite the astonishment of posterity. In times past men have been deified on slighter grounds.

At length the influence and power of Sutter attracted the attention of the Mexican government; but as he was too remote, as well as too strong, to be punished or betrayed, they thought it their wisest plan to conciliate him. He was, therefore, made military commandant of the frontier, with full authority and absolute power, extending to life itself, within the limits of his jurisdiction. In this office he continued for several years, trading with the Indians, teaching them the rudiments of manufactures, agriculture and arms, and acquiring an extensive influence in the valley. He always, however, had a decided leaning towards his adopted country, and hospitably received and entertained, even to his own detriment, such parties of Americans as came near his retreat; and, I regret to add, that many of our countrymen made but a poor return for this kindness and liberality. Finally, the Mexicans seeing that the Americans, emboldened by his example, began to settle in the valley, and growing jealous of his influential position, endeavored to remove him, and as an inducement to give up his border fortress to a Mexican garrison, offered him the beautiful and improved mission lands of San José, near the pueblo of that name, and the sum of fifty thousand dollars; proving their eagerness to get rid of him by actually providing security for the money, a practice almost unknown in Mexican financiering, which generally consists of promises intended to be broken. But not an inch would Sutter budge from his stronghold, sagaciously looking forward, with the eye of faith, to the time when the United States should acquire possession of the country—a consummation which he devoutly hoped for, and hailed with delight when it came to pass.

The fort consists of a parallelogram enclosed by adobe walls, fifteen feet high and two feet thick, with bastions or towers at the angles, the walls of which are four feet thick, and their embrasures so arranged as to flank the curtain on all sides. A good house occupies the centre of the interior area, serving for officers' quarters, armory, guard and state rooms, and also for a kind of citadel. There is a second wall on the inner face, the space between it and the outer wall being roofed and divided into work-shops, quarters, &c., and the usual offices are provided, and also a well of good water. Corrals for the cattle and horses of the garrison are conveniently placed where they can be under the eye of the guard. Cannon frown (I believe that is an inveterate habit of cannon,) from the various embrasures, and the *ensemble* presents the very ideal of a border fortress. It must have "astonished the natives" when this monument of the white man's skill arose from the plain and showed its dreadful teeth in the midst of those peaceful solitudes.

I found during this visit that General Vallejo and his companions were rigorously guarded by the "patriots," but I saw him and had some conversation with him, which it was easy to see excited a very ridiculous amount of suspicion on the part of his vigilant jailers, whose position, however, as revolutionists, was a little ticklish, and excited in them that distrust which in dangerous times is inseparable from low and ignorant minds. Indeed, they carried their doubts so far as to threaten to shoot Sutter for the crime of being polite to the captives.

On our return to San Francisco, we heard that an engagement had taken place near Petaluma, between the Americans and Californians, in which the Americans had been victorious, driving the enemy from the field with loss. We also heard that two young Americans had been killed by the gang under Padilla, and, *per contra*, that three Mexicans had been shot for refusing to give up their arms, on whose persons were found incendiary proclamations, instigating the people to rise, on the pretence that the Americans were about to murder them, &c.

Castro was still at Santa Clara, whence the defeated party came, under the command of Joaquim de la Torre. Castro had under his command two hundred men, most of them forced volunteers and pressed men. I heard that on a feast day, when the rancheros came to the mission in their "go-to-meeting" clothes, with their wives and children, Castro seized their horses and forced the men to *volunteer* in defence of their homes, against "los salvages Americanos."

This trick reminds me of one I saw played off by the late Ibrahim Pasha, at Beyroot, in Syria. At the festival succeeding the Ramedun or Turkish lent, that worthy entered the city with a couple of regiments, ostensibly to enjoy himself like a good musselman, after his long vigils and fasting. The city was overflowing with Turks, Arabs, Greeks, Armenians, Egyptians, Jews, Gentiles, Fire-worshippers, devil worshippers, merchants, missionaries and naval officers. At the hour of evening prayer, when the faithful filled the mosques and the spaces in front of them, and were offering up their devotions, Ibrahim set a guard at the city gates, and proceeded in person to make a tour of the city. Entering each mosque with his staff, and leaving a guard at the door, he proceeded in the coolest manner to pick such men as were suitable for soldiers, and delivered them to the guard. In this way he selected two thousand able bodied troops, whom he incontinently marched off to the harbor, and, regardless of tears and entreaties —of every thing but bribes—shipped them in a couple of frigates for Egypt, with a breeze strong enough to have added seriously to the sufferings of such a crew of land-lubbers.

EARLY IN JULY the squadron, under Commodore Sloat, arrived at Monterey, with intelligence that war existed between the United States and Mexico, and the same arrival brought the electrifying news of the battles of Palo Alto and Resaca de la Palma. On the seventh of July Commodore Sloat issued his proclamation, taking formal possession of the Californias in the name of the United States, and at the same time hoisted the American flag at Monterey. Landing a strong force of marines and seamen, he garrisoned that place, and sent a summons to Castro to surrender. That perplexed personage, however, declined accepting this polite invitation, but decamped from the northern district with all precipitation, striking through the Tularé valley to Los Angeles, the capital of the lower district of Upper California. On the tenth of July, the whole northern district, including the Bay of San Francisco, was in possession of the United States, and the principal points garrisoned by our troops. All the Americans, and most of the foreigners, took up arms, and volunteered *en masse* to defend the American flag, which they regarded as the symbol of liberty, emancipation, and regeneration. Proceeding to the principal posts they offered themselves to the American officers as volunteers, without pay or emolument, each man taking with him his trusty rifle and accoutrements. It was a touching evidence of the influence of our free democratic institutions, to see these rough old trappers, whose lives had been passed with Indians and wild beasts, rally around the flag of their native land, to which they owed nothing but the accident of birth, and that abiding love of liberty and independence which is inherent in our people. Nor was the devotion of the settlers from the old world less worthy of admiration. They had sought in the far-off wilderness a refuge from oppression, and found that they had fallen under a worse despotism than they had left at home. When therefore a fair opportunity occurred for dealing a death-blow to the dominion of the mock republic of Mexico, these sons of Europe flew to arms with an enthusiasm unknown to the reluctant tools of tyrants. We could do no more than select the most youthful and hardy of these gallant men, who were hastily organized into a battalion, under Captain (since Colonel) Fremont, and marched eagerly to meet the enemy in the field. Many of these new recruits had withheld their support from the "Bear Party," which did not seem to them to possess stability.

All were now busily employed in placing the small military resources of the country in a state of efficiency, and in the course of a month the United States had virtual possession of Upper California. The courage and skill of the foreigners raised them in the esteem of the Californians, who had hitherto looked upon them as mere traders, inferior to themselves—a delusive idea growing out of the superiority in horsemanship and skill in the use of the lance and riata, possessed by the Californians. The colonial system of Spain had also taught the people to despise all industrial pursuits connected with traffic, in order that they might draw their supplies of goods from the mother country, and leave their commerce wholly in her hands.

Commodore Stockton soon took command in the place of Commodore Sloat, who returned to the United States by way of Panama. Vigorous measures were taken by the new commander for the total subjugation and occupation of the country. There being no officers of the army in the country, except Colonel Fremont, the officers of the navy and marine corps were obliged for the present to perform their duties on shore, both as officers of the newly-raised Californian battalion and as civil magistrates. It fell to my lot to exchange the quarter-deck for the saddle, having been ordered to take command of the district on the north side of the bay, garrisoned by Company B, California Battalion Mounted Riflemen. Although I had often before done duty on shore with my "charge of foot," this was the very first time I had ever served in the cavalry—and albeit not exactly a "horse marine," I found this kind of life far more to my taste than remaining on board ship, in a war with an enemy incapable of opposing us in our proper element.

On taking charge of the military post of Sonoma, I mustered my troop and found the whole force to consist of fifty men, mostly Americans, besides the usual complement of non-commissioned officers, a trumpet, a smith, and ten Indian horse boys. Our head-quarters were at the village of Sonoma, in a pleasant situation, on the line of communication with San Francisco and the Sacramento valley, being central as between those points and Bodega and Ross, on the coast. Our barracks were roomy and commodious, and we had an abundant supply of horses.

Although my men were not uniformed, they were well equipped, each having his own private arms; and they were a hardy-looking company, consisting mostly of farmers and their sons, and laborers who lived in the neighborhood, and to whom it was more convenient to serve on this station than to go South with Fremont. The greater part were dressed in buckskin shirts and leggins, fringed and ornamented in the most approved and tasteful fashion of the backwoods toilet. Several suits, made by the Sioux Indians, were very handsome, being laced with richly-dyed porcupine quills, and faced with beaver and muskrat furs. Others, again, wore suits which appeared to have been discarded from Chatham street; and one handsome young fellow, with long locks and sentimental eyes, sported a butterfly waistcoat and railroad trowsers, which, though sadly dilapidated, had figured extensively in the "social halls" bordering on our western waters—the now empty pockets having doubtless fobbed many an "ante." His very arms bespoke the fallen fortunes of a young man about town, for, too indolent or careless to bear the long and heavy rifle, which was the chief weapon of his comrades, he carried a light and handsome yager, daintily mounted with silver, and his bowie knife, although as heavy as any in the troop, was encased in a stained crimson velvet sheath. To crown all, his head was conscious of what had once been an exquisite "ventillating gossamer," but which now was reduced to the level of that peculiar description of castor, familiarly known as "a shocking bad hat."

After establishing the usual routine of the patrols, scouts, &c., I found that I should have abundant leisure to make observations, ample opportunities being afforded by the nature of my duties, which led me to visit all parts of this district of Upper California, which I consider the finest portion even of this universally magnificent country. When I first took command, anything like an organized resistance on the part of the rancheros to the forces of the United States, had entirely ceased throughout California, except at the Pueblo de Los Angeles, where Castro was encamped, in a fortified position, awaiting the arrival of a part of the American garrison from Monterey, which had been withdrawn, and embarked for a pleasure excursion to that part of the country, with a view of making a call on the Mexican hero. The roads, however, were unsafe in all directions, the expresses frequently stopped, and predatory excursions made in various directions by small parties of "hijos del pais," pretending to act under Castro's orders, and led by his ex-office-holders. These rascals annoyed the well-affected rancheros, and persons disposed to remain neutral, by stealing horses and helping themselves to cattle, farm servants, &c.—all for the sake of *"la patria."* Although the band which, under the lead of Juan de Padilla, had murdered the young men, Fowler and Cowan, had broken up and dispersed, some to join Castro, and others, less guilty, to seek their ranchos: a few of the disaffected were prowling around my district, and in pursuit of a party of these I made an excursion to the Punta de los Reyes, which extends into the sea just north of San Francisco bay. Our party of sixteen men, provided with Indian guides, started out at night from Sonoma, and making a detour to conceal our destination, bivouacked that night in the hills near the Laguna San Antonio. Early the next morning we started again, and at sunset, after a hard day's travel, by bye-paths, arrived at the rancho of Rafael Garcia. Here I found that the party I was in search of had moved off to another part of the district, having been so closely followed by some of my men that they left behind a bullock they had killed for dinner. Rushing into the house we found their hats hanging up there, which we took prisoners, as well as six loaded carbines they had left in their hot haste to be off. We also took twenty-four fine horses, which they had collected from the neighboring ranchos.

After enjoying Garcia's hospitality for the night, we found, on rising next morning, several of the neighboring rancheros, who had arrived, on their way to the Punta de los Reyes, for the purpose of hunting the elk, with which it abounds. Sending all my men, except two, back to Sonoma, I resolved to remain and witness the sport; and, getting fresh horses from Señor Garcia, we started for the point. I observed that the Spaniards had no arms; but they pointed to the riata, the unfailing companion of all rancheros, and exclaimed, *"este es el rifle del ranchero!"*—this is the ranchero's rifle. On our way, however, I observed one of the party dismount, near a small grove, and selecting a straight light pole, take from beneath his *sarape* a crescent-shaped weapon, which he fixed to the top of the pole. This instrument they call, from its shape, the "luna," and it is used for hamstringing the elk, which then falls an easy prey to the hunter.

The cool, bracing air of the morning, promised us fine sport, as the horses, on whose exertions the sport mainly depends, would not be exhausted from the heat. But, as the Irishman devoutly remarked, "Providence never opens one door but it shuts another,"—a reflection verified in the present instance, by the rising of a dense fog, which prevented us from seeing any considerable distance, and forced us to be circumspect in picking our way over a very broken and hilly part of country. Crossing a deep valley, up which I could not see for the mist, we surmounted a high hill, and I saw in a moment that we stood on an isthmus or neck of land, connecting a lofty promontory—lying right before us—with the main land. At the same time I discerned the sea on either hand, and heard the musical roar of the surf, as it tumbled ashore on the right. Suddenly one of my men exclaimed, in a low tone, "hush!" and, rifle in hand, dismounted for a shot. Following the direction of his glance, towards the promontory, I perceived a band of elk, which must have numbered not less than four hundred head of superb fat animals—the apparently cumbrous horns of the bucks thrown back on their shoulders, and the leaders seeming to hesitate whether it should be a fight or a foot race. Pacific councils, however, prevailed, and the whole body were soon in full retreat, the old bucks occasionally stopping to gaze at us, while the does and fawns made the best of their way up the slope. Our horses scenting them at the same time—for the horses of California scent large game almost as acutely as dogs—became greatly excited, and could hardly be checked from dashing forward in pursuit. The rancheros seemed to despise the stealthy advance on foot of the Americans with fire-arms, and as the game could not escape us, being surrounded on all sides by the sea, except on that occupied by our well-mounted party of six men, they planned a mode of attack, which they communicated to us.

Two of them gave their horses the rein with an "adelante!" and the noble beasts sprang forward in full pursuit of the now flying herd. At this season (August) elk are fatter than at any other, and cannot compete with the horse in speed; whereas, a couple of months later, the fleetest horse could hardly overtake them. Their speed was now inconsiderable, the rancheros soon coming up with them and scattering them in various directions. Our friend with the "luna" had hamstrung several of the poor creatures, and his companion had entangled with his riata a noble buck, which was plunging and tearing violently, the riata being at its greatest tension, and the little horse, to whose saddle it was made fast, standing stiff and stark, with eye-balls staring, and every nerve braced to meet the pulls and tugs of the elk; while the Californian sat coolly in his saddle, and addressing the elk by the familiar title of "cuñádo," (brother-in-law), pleasantly assured him that he "only wanted a little of his lard wherewithal to cook tortillas!"—a joke which the struggling victim was in no humor to relish.

From the contemplation of a scene so new to me, I was aroused by Don Egedio, (Giles) who loudly called to me to shoot; and, turning my horse, I spurred him nearer the precipice, between which and myself the remainder of the band seemed disposed to rush, on their way back to the mainland. My horse was an admirably trained animal for the purposes of hunting after the fashion of California, but he would not stand still enough for a shot from the saddle; and to have dismounted would have been to lose him, as he would have pursued the elk. But a shot I was determined to have, on some terms, and so, when it seemed to my rather obfuscated vision that I was opposite the thickest of the band, I wheeled, seized my double-barrelled gun, and pulled both triggers at a venture. My horse, unused to fire, jumped some twenty feet, more or less, and I dropped my gun but kept the saddle. My shot accidentally took effect, for when I was able to rein up, I returned to the spot and saw a poor doe lying in a reclining posture, the blood welling rapidly from a frightful wound inflicted by two heavy buckshot cartridges which had taken effect in the animal's shoulder. The unfortunate fixed upon me her large full eye, expressive at once of fright, sorrow, and reproach, and the mournfulness of the scene was heightened by the presence of a half-grown fawn, baaing and bleating around its dying mother. Sentiment, however, soon subsides on the hunting ground; and after my friend with the "luna" had coolly drawn his knife across the throat of the doe, I felt little compunction in bringing down the sorrowing fawn. In the meantime, our friends on the point had not been idle, having taken toll of two more of the flock as they passed, one of which was caught with the riata by a Spaniard and an Indian vaquero, and the other shot by one of my men. It usually requires two men with riatas to kill the animal, the object being to trip him up and then give him the *coup-de-grace;* but one man sometimes does it alone with a riata and luna, and there are rare instances where a single expert hand trips up the animal with his riata and then finishes him.

The herd had now retired to the mountains, and were dispersed among crags and precipices, almost inaccessible to horses. Our party collected and rode down the point, where we found three hamstrung animals which had wriggled and screwed themselves into the most retired places. Our friend of the luna, however, insisted with many round, full-mouthed oaths, that he had disabled nine and wounded some others in a desperate manner, with the points or horns of his iron. But these people are not to be implicitly believed, and after traversing the point in every direction, we could find but one more elk, which had fallen over the precipice and lay half his length in the sea—the vultures and sea-birds already hovering over him in great numbers, impatiently awaiting the moment when death should make him their own.

We proceeded to what was called the rancho, but on arriving found nothing but a broken down corral—passing on the way a herd of cattle so little civilized that the very antelopes were grazing amongst them. There was, however, a good cool spring of delicious water near at hand, where we made our bivouac; and the Indians now coming in numbers—like vultures, by instinct—brought in all our game, amounting to six fat elk. Our sport had "burned daylight" so fast that the sun was near the limits of the western horizon, and with our Indian assistants—but too happy to be of use where eating was in question—we soon prepared a most delicious supper of elk meat. The savory saddle, the juicy and tender haunch, the delicious rib, were all discussed in turn, and such as liked it feasted on the luscious liver—a most delicate morsel—and also on the kidney and brains. Our Indian friends were officiously assiduous in cooking the meat, and eating two pounds where we ate an ounce; and as I had fasted all day, I imitated my companions, and fairly gorged myself to such a degree that I felt much in the condition of an anaconda which has swallowed an elephant; or, like the little boy who, after his Christmas dinner, informed his anxious mother that he felt "as if his jacket was buttoned up." After joining my companions, therefore, in a comfortable drink of brandy and water "cold, without," we all wrapped ourselves in *sarapes* and blankets; and stretched out upon the ground with our feet to the fire—while the silvery moon stole over the inland mountains and bathed us in serenest light—we fell asleep. So did not our Indian visitors. They had called up their whole settlement, and were stuffing, wrangling, and gambling with jackstraws all night long. Awakened by their infernal clamor, I drove them off with a few judicious cuffs; but after they had quietly removed, they recommenced their hideous orgies ere I could fall asleep again.

The next morning I was awakened at sunrise by Don Egidio's cheerful voice, singing away as merrily as a lark, as he prepared to try out the tallow of the slaughtered elk—an object which the worthy Giles had had in view quite as much as the sport. An oval-shaped hole, about two feet deep, but shallower at one end than the other, was made in the ground, and the shallowest part of it filled with the fat and fatty parts of the elk; a fire of light sticks was made over this greasy heap, and, when well going, fed with the fatty scraps, the pure melted tallow running down into the deeper parts of the trench. A hide, doubled in the middle, and laced at the sides with thongs, was then brought, and the melted tallow dipped up and poured into it until it was filled, when the mouth of the skin was laced up, and the result was a hard bag of solid tallow. The tallow from the six elks filled two large hides, each weighing at least four hundred pounds. From the superior hardness, whiteness and delicacy of the elk's tallow, it is in much request among the rancheros for cooking purposes, and the hides are also worth something.

The Punta Reyes is a favorite hunting-ground, the elk being attracted by the superior quality of the pasture—the land lying so near the sea, that the dews are heavy and constant, adding great luxuriance to the wild oats and other grains and grasses. The elk are very abundant at this season, and more easily killed than cattle. We passed many places, on our way back, where mouldering horns and bones attested the wholesale slaughter which had been made in previous years by the rancheros of the neighborhood. I took a pair of the freshest and finest horns I could find, and put them on a led horse. They touched the ground on each side of the horse; but I was told they would not compare with some, under the arch of which—the points resting on the earth—the most profligate man in the world could walk uprightly with his hat on!

Our ranchero friends having determined to remain, and pursue their sport and profit, we took leave of them and returned to head-quarters.

A FEW DAYS after our return to Sonoma, we heard that Commodore Stockton had marched into Los Angeles without resistance; Castro, although strongly fortified, having "vamosed" with precipitation at his approach. The commodore had appointed Colonel Fremont governor of the Territory, and announced his intention to sail for the coast of Mexico, to carry on the war there. The government was partially organized, the battalion permitted to return to their homes, and the people informed that they might elect alcaldes and other municipal officers, or retain those already in office—the civil authority, however, to be for the present subordinate to the military power. The garrisons of Los Angeles, Monterey, San José and Sonoma were, however, to be retained in service, and also a small police force to protect the roads, and, if necessary, put down the Indians.

I took advantage of the seeming tranquillity in political affairs, to plan a visit to "THE LAKE," which lies north of Sonoma, the banks and islands of which, I was informed, were inhabited by numerous tribes of Indians. In the first place, I summoned such of the sub-chiefs belonging to the rancherias of the Lake as had come to work or superintend the labors of their subjects upon the ranchos at Sonoma. They accordingly appeared to the number of half-a-dozen good-looking men, some of them ornamented and armed in savage style, some in shabby shirts and trousers, and one with nothing on save the very primary article of civilized apparel. I obtained also an Indian interpreter named Santos, not a "Gentile," as those wild fellows are called who are not instructed in the language of the whites, but a "Christiano," that is, an Indian educated at a mission. These neophytes, since they have lost the wholesome restraints imposed by the excellent padres, are a vicious double-dealing set of rogues, cheating and despising their red brethren, and in return are hated and envied by the "Gentiles." As I was bound on a peaceful expedition, it was not necessary to take a large force. I detailed Serjeant Chiles, a gentleman farmer, born in Tennessee, and a harum-scarum, half-horse, half-alligator sort of genius, and withal a right good woodsman. I also took a well educated young man from that famous county of Buncombe, in North Carolina, to which so many speeches are made in Congress, and in allusion to which my friend was familiarly called "Bunk."

Setting out from Sonoma, we struck out into the rough mountain-path which leads over the ridge, dividing the valley of Sonoma from that of Napa. After a pleasant afternoon ride across the hills, in the shade of noble trees, occasionally crossing on our way some pretty upland glades, we suddenly reached the crest of the mountain, and beheld the all-beautiful Napa valley spread out at our feet. These rapid transitions are characteristic of the scenery of California. After pursuing for some time a rugged and stony mountain-path, amidst gnarled and stunted hard-wood trees, you attain, when least expected, the summit of a mountain from which you gaze with rapture—if you have an eye or a heart for nature—upon a broad and level valley, studded with clumps of verdant oaks, and dotted with herds of grazing cattle, which seem in the distance no larger than sheep. Or, emerging by a steep hill-side path, from a rocky and shaded glen, through which runs a streamlet shrouded and almost hidden by the undergrowth, the traveller is surprised by a glorious view of the bold outline of distant hills, of a rich greyish or purple hue—the middle ground of the intervening landscape being perhaps varied by a basaltic rock formation, broken into a hundred fanciful towers and battlements.

The scene now before me was one of surpassing beauty. The infinitely varied outlines of the lofty mountains lying beyond the valley; the grotesque appearance of the broken and rugged crags of basaltic rocks; the quiet river winding through the level plain at our feet, its banks distinctly defined by a long line of willows and other trees of larger growth; the gracefully undulating outlines of the smaller hills,* which, like the far-spreading plain itself, waved with a golden harvest of ripe grasses, made more golden by the "living light" of the setting sun; the scattered clumps of dark green oaks, and the miniature herds of grazing cattle—all combined to paint a landscape worthy of a country whose natural opulence is matched only by its natural grandeur.

The season had now advanced so far that the wild oats, "alfileria" (pin-grass), and burr clover, which chiefly compose the unequalled and fattening pasture of California, had dried up to straw, the spires still standing, while the seed had fallen to the earth. These seeds are very large and nutritious, and serve for food both for the cattle and the Indians. At this season the cattle grope along the ground for the seed, and are fatter than at any other time of the year.

Napa Valley is said to be the finest portion of this part of California. It is about thirty-six miles in length, and extends nearly north and south, the lower part lying on the Bay of St. Paul, from which a navigable estuary sets up and receives the waters of the Napa river, which traverses the whole length of the valley. It is bounded on each side by lofty Sierras, broken into every variety of Alpine scenery, the ravines of which are filled with the finest timber, and very probably contain gold. At the lower end of the valley the Sierras are six or seven miles apart, but the ranges gradually approaching each other meet at the upper end, a bold, well-timbered, serrated mountain lying directly across it and terminating the prospect in that direction. In the plain, at the foot of this mountain, are the "*Aguas Calientes*," the most famous of the many hot-springs in California, which possess powerful medicinal properties. The soil is of almost incredible fertility, the yield of wheat being as high as a hundred-fold, while corn and vegetables of all kinds, including the finest potatoes I ever saw, flourish most luxuriantly. The fruits of the temperate zone thrive here side by side with those of the tropics. Peaches, pears, apples, melons of all kinds, and rich luscious grapes, may be seen growing in the same garden with sugar cane, dates, figs, and bananas, leaving no room for doubt that all the other productions of tropical climates would, if introduced, flourish equally well. There is reason to believe that Californa will hereafter be dependent on

---

* Lomas.

no other country for the necessaries of life. She can grow her own tea, coffee, rice, vegetables and breadstuffs, and not only grow, but manufacture, her own wool, cotton, hemp, and flax. Her supplies of animal food are boundless, and the salt is at hand to preserve them. Indeed, it is difficult to name any product of the earth, whether it be to eat, drink, or wear, which California cannot yield, while her mineral wealth excites the astonishment of the world. The Napa Valley early attracted the notice of the first settlers on the north side of the bay, and was among the first grants made by the Mexican governors. The best lands, uniting *every* advantage, such as grazing, fertility, easy transit by land or water to market, fresh water, and a healthy and pleasant situation, are now taken up, the owners being Mr. Fowler, Dr. Bale, Mr. Yount, (owner of "Caymus"), Don Salvador Vallejo, (owner of "Napa" and "Los Francas"), Señor Higuera, and Don Gaetano Xuares, (owner of "Toluca"). The ordinary Spanish and Mexican measure of land is by the square league, a single league being equal to about five thousand acres. The lands of the Napa Valley are granted in tracts varying from one to four square leagues, the ranchos being wider or narrower according to the varying spaces between the Sierras. Don Salvador Vallejo is the largest proprietor, owning two adjoining estates, which make together six square leagues, a snug little farm of thirty thousand acres of the best land in the world. The climate is a perpetual summer, and the atmosphere is not obscured by the "neblina," (fogs), which prevail nearer the sea. In the rainy season ('t were treason against nature to call it winter) the rushing and picturesque cataracts descend from the Sierras on either side, over beds dry at all other times of the year, swelling the river Napa to its fullest dimensions. The exquisite views which abound in every direction, the complete seclusion of the spot, bounded at the broader end by the waters of the bay, and at every other point by jagged mountain crags, realize the ideal of a "Happy Valley," divested of the inconveniences attached to that inhabited by the Prince of Abyssinia. It is a characteristic of this neighborhood, that the sides of the Sierras abound with elevated table-lands, which are several degrees cooler than the plain, and are admirably adapted for sheep farms. The large estates will gradually be divided, and even before I left California, some of the ranchos in the Napa Valley had been sub-divided into smaller farms, to meet the wants of emigrants from the United States.

On the north side of the bay there are valleys similar to that of Napa, having ranges of mountains on the sides, and extending to the bay, which receives the waters of their streams. Among these are the valleys of Sonoma, Petaluma, Novato, and San Rafael; none of them, perhaps, so fertile or so beautiful as Napa, but all famous in the legends and traditions of the Indians.

We stopped for a night at the hospitable mansion of Mr. Yount. This old man had led an adventurous and chequered life, in the course of which he had fought under Jackson at New Orleans, and in the Seminole war, had been taken prisoner by the Indians, and actually bound to the stake. He had been a hunter and trapper, and Indian fighter at large, in the heart of the continent, until his combative propensities were gratified—and he finally found himself one day at the "jumping-off place," and made his first attempt at ocean navigation on the bosom of the broad Pacific. In the unpretending skiff of an otter-hunter, often unaccompanied save by his trusty rifle, he coasted the shores and islands of California, in search of the pelt of his valuable prey. While employed one day (in the year 1836) in his regular pursuit, he chanced to steer his skiff into the navigable creek or estuary of Napa, rightly judging it a place of resort for his furry friend. The valley was then inhabited by none but Indians, and he made his way up to a beautiful spot, a few miles from his boat, which had been selected for a rancheria by a tribe called the "Caymus." Here he sat down to rest, when suddenly there flashed upon his mind, like a gleam of light, a long-forgotten prophecy of an old fortune-teller in his native state. He declares that the Sybil had predicted the spot of his future residence in terms exactly answering to the description of this valley, including all the accessories of grove, plain, mountain, river, and even "medicine-water," as the Indians call the springs. The old man pondered over this prophecy, counted his gains, which had been considerable, and philosophized over the vicissitudes of human life—not forgetting, however, to examine the valley more carefully. On his next visit to Monterey, he became a citizen of California, and obtained a grant of land embracing the charmed spot indicated by the western witch. He then came and settled it, purchasing cattle with his gains in the "lower country." But the happy valley then swarmed with Indians, jealous of white men and constantly fighting among themselves, so that this elysium was turned into a pandemonium by their screams and war-whoops. But an old hunter and trapper who had passed his life in the wilderness, alternately fraternizing and fighting with Sioux, Crows, Black-feet, and Camanches, had not come thus far to be either frightened or outwitted by the more peaceable, simple, and indolent Indian of California. He quitted his skiff, formed an alliance, offensive and defensive, with the rancheria of Caymus, erected a log-house after the manner of his ancestors in the days of Daniel Boone, (who was *supposed* to have settled in the *far* west,) and with his faithful rifle—the only fire-arm in the valley—not only stood and repelled the attacks of rival rancherias, but attacking in turn, exterminated the unruly, sustained the wavering, and, single-handed, bullied the whole valley into submission. Many a weary and anxious and watchful night did he spend ere this result was achieved; but once accomplished, his sovereignty remained undisputed; the conquered became his servants, and the allies of Caymus remain to this day his laborers and farm-hands.

Early the next morning our whole party came together, and we rode at a moderate pace up the valley. The party consisted of myself, one sergeant, two privates, one Indian interpreter, six Indian chiefs, and three vaqueros. We formed rather a grotesque procession. Being on an official visit, I had surmounted my "calzoneras" (riding suit) with my epaulettes and sword; the other white men wore a mixture of the Mexican and Rocky Mountain costume, and the vaqueros were clad in the cast-off clothing of persons who had already worn it threadbare. As to the chiefs, they had changed their apparel and appeared *en grand costume*, in the simple garment introduced into Paradise by father Adam, with the ornamental addition of a large quantity of feathers stuck in their heads—a style of dress to be preferred perhaps to the costume of our State of Georgia, which is said to consist of a shirt-collar and a pair of spurs.

Just before noon we arrived at the rancho of Mr. Chiles, my sergeant, who was one of the first Americans that came to this country. His farm is a pretty, secluded spot, situated in a valley between the high "serrania" or mountain range, which forms the eastern wall of Napa valley, and the opposite chain which separates his land from the broader and more extensive lands of the western slope of the valley of the Sacramento. He saw this place a year or two since while hunting elk, and being struck with its advantages, obtained it from the governor, who, by the laws of Mexico was authorized to grant lands to actual settlers, under certain conditions, to the extent of eleven square leagues. These conditions were that the settler should reside on the land with his family, plant fruit trees, stock it with cattle and horses, fence some part of it, and build a house on it. Failing to perform these conditions the land absolutely reverted to the government. But these requirements were not strictly enforced, being manifestly too rigorous in the unsettled state of the country; and the titles of the grantees who had not complied with them were considered perfectly good, it being indeed doubtful whether a single rancho in the territory has literally performed all the conditions.

A CALIFORNIAN RANCHO or farm, of the first class, is about equal in extent to a German principality. While some are content with one, two, or three square leagues, (not miles), others luxuriate in a domain of eleven square leagues, which, according to Californian measure, is nearly three times the size of a township of our public lands. About the homestead a rancho presents a singularly primitive and patriarchal appearance. Job himself, after his sorrows were ended and his wealth doubled, hardly possessed more extensive herds of wild cattle, (*ganado bronco,*) which are usually seen on the outskirts of the rancho, but betake themselves to the woods or the ravines among the hills at the approach of a stranger. They seem to have a vague apprehension that you intend to drive them to the *rodea,* where they are driven to be counted on particular days, or perhaps to the *matanzas* or shambles. As you advance nearer the house, you fall in with the *vacas chichiquas* (tame milch cows) and *menadas,* (brood mares and colts) guarded by their *garañon,* (stallion) who starts fiercely from his pasture, and regards with jealous gaze the animals of your *caballada,* keeping a wary eye, the while, on his seraglio; still approaching, you meet large herds of sheep, attended by little half-naked Indians; and when close to the house your ears are saluted with the yelping of a regiment of curs, whose melodious notes are always at concert pitch. And now you reach the *milpa,* or kitchen garden, a horticultural appendage which is sometimes rudely fenced with brush, "dumped" around it without an excessive regard to quantity or symmetry; but oftener boasting no better enclosure than a small troop of Indians, who, with loud cries of questionable melody, warn off the profane flocks and herds which would fain trespass upon its sacred precincts. Nor is it by day alone that these aboriginal moveable and musical fences perform their functions; for during the season when the "sarse" is ripening, the remorseless rascals bivouac near the "milpa," making night hideous with their excruciating melodies, and gambling with their *parientes* (relations) when the ranchero permits them. The house is usually a rude edifice of *adobes,* (sun-burnt bricks), with the usual farm offices around it, patched on as may be most convenient; and it is invariably flanked by a *"corral,"* (a circular fence for enclosing cattle), or by several corrals, according to the size and consequence of the rancho. Of course these houses vary in splendor and magnitude, as one star differeth from another in glory; but the best of them are not remarkable in these respects. The family is generally pretty large—consisting, first, of the head of the household, usually a bland, jolly-looking old gentleman, resembling Corcuelo, and next, of his handsome sons, appareled in the becoming Mexican riding dress, and accomplished in all the arts and mysteries of the *campo,* such as managing and lassoing the wildest cattle and most intractable horses. Then come the women, mother and daughters, comely and buxom, and reasonably tidy, but less delicate and more robust than their Mexican sisters. The rest of the family consists of "vaqueros," and servants, male and female, of Indian blood, who inhabit the "rancheria," or small Indian village, built of rush wigwams, near the house. Although these worthy rancheros have few superfluities to offer, besides beef and mutton, the wayfaring stranger is always sure of a hearty and unaffected welcome amongst them. Hospitality is inherent in Spanish blood. As the poorest shepherd of the Sierra Morena, or the Alpuxarras invariably offers a part of his humble dish of *"gaspacho"* to a stranger, so the honest ranchero of California places everything at his disposal; and while an offer of remuneration is received with a constrained politeness, indicating wounded sensibility, it is always met with a decided negative. How long this will be the case remains to be seen. As civilization advances it is not unlikely that putting every thing "at your disposition" will mean as little in California as in Castile; and the only mortification evinced at an offer of remuneration will result from the insufficiency of the guerdon. The world is advancing; and California must keep pace with it.

The ranchero prefers the month of March for the "fundacion" or establishment of his farm. In the first place, he builds a house of boughs, a mere sylvan bower, which, for the next seven months, answers all the purposes of a more substantial lodge, besides enabling the occupant, however poor, to keep open-house. During these seven months he enjoys, without interruption, the most charming summer weather, the skies being almost without a cloud, and occasional mists and constant dews supplying the place of rain. In this part of California thunder and lightning are unknown, but at rare intervals thunder is heard in the neighborhood of Los Angeles. Taking possession of his primitive mansion with his family, the ranchero proceeds to improve his estate. He purchases about one hundred head of cattle, at least thirty or forty horses, and usually adds a flock of sheep and a quantity of poultry. When the breeding of cattle is properly attended to, the increase in this country is astonishing. The kind of cattle most suitable for a rapid increase are "vaquillas," (heifers), the usual proportion being one hundred heifers to half a dozen bulls. To one "manada," (herd), consisting of thirty or forty mares, a single stallion is added. On a well-regulated rancho, the increase of neat cattle may be safely calculated at thirty per cent. per annum, allowing for casualties. Thus one hundred head, properly selected, nearly double by the end of the third year, at which time the first year's calves begin to produce, making, I believe, a greater ratio than is known in any other country. This estimate, however, is exceedingly moderate, fifty per cent. and even seventy per annum having been obtained under favorable circumstances. This is probably due to the favorable climate, the unequalled pasture, and the state of nature in which the animal lives.

When the ranchero procures his cattle and other animals, until they are "carenciado," or accustomed to the farm, they are driven every day or two round and round some convenient spot, by the shouting "vaqueros." Both the place and the act of driving are called "rodea," and this practice renders the cattle comparatively tame and peaceable, habituating them to the control of man, and exerting a great influence upon their increase. A "rodea" is usually held, in a well-regulated district, one day in each week, and upon every rancho alternately, the neighboring rancheros attending to reclaim their stray cattle. The several owners recognize their animals by their peculiar *"fierro"* or brand, and by the *"señal"* or ear-mark, which differ on each rancho. The brand, which is registered according to law, is usually the initial letter of the ranchero or his rancho, but is sometimes a merely arbitrary sign. The ear-mark is a peculiar slit or hole, or a combination of both. These marks are made on the young calves, and at least once a year they are renewed. To effect this, the animals must be thrown down, which feat is performed by two horsemen with their lassos. The usual time for marking is at the annual "matanzas," or slaughter, in the month of August. The cattle are then driven to the corral, or circular farmyard, and the doomed ones slaughtered; the hides are pegged out in the sun, the meat cut into strips and hung on trees and poles to dry, and the tallow, after being melted down in large try-pots or kettles, is packed in skins sewed up with thongs. The hides and tallow are the only parts exported, the dried beef being consumed in the country as well as the finer quality of tallow or "manteca," made from the fat of the intestines. The heads, horns, hoofs, bones, &c., are utterly wasted and thrown away; and, indeed, until within a few years, immense numbers of cattle were slaughtered for their hides alone, the entire carcass being left to corrupt, or to feed immense numbers of wild beasts and large vultures, which were thus greatly encouraged and augmented. I shall have more to say of the matanzas in another chapter. Stabling for any kind of animals is entirely unknown, the nearest approach to it being a sheep-fold. A "mayor-domo" or steward, usually a white man, but sometimes an Indian, superintends a whole rancho; a couple of vaqueros are necessary to look after the cattle and horses, and an Indian family attend to the sheep and do "chores." The wages of the Indians are moderate, and are always paid in merchandise, a dollar in money being sometimes thrown in on a feast day.

A rancho is thus soon established, and if the owner be industrious and provident, he secures not only a competence, but, by cultivating his fields —which in the valleys produce one hundred bushels of wheat to the acre, and other crops in proportion—his fortune is made. In no other country was it so easy to acquire an independence. I say *was*, because the new order of things will probably raise the price of land, and prevent the occupation of such large tracts by individuals. Still, for many years to come, industrious farmers can undoubtedly become opulent on small means, without troubling themselves about gold mines. A league of land on most ranchos will support one thousand head of neat cattle, besides horses, sheep, hogs, &c. Of these, after the third year, three hundred can be killed, annually, without prejudice to the increase of the stock at a handsome rate, the females being mostly reserved from slaughter. These will yield, on an average, $10 per head; say $3,000. If the rancheros are not rich, it is owing partly to the oppressive, plundering system, pursued by their late government, but chiefly to their own good-for-nothing habits. Laziness, carelessness, gambling, a low state of civilization, and a community of goods, (of which hereafter), are not calculated to produce thrift, and it is not strange that their condition has been less comfortable than that of day-laborers in the Atlantic States. As an instance of their improvidence, I will state that, although cattle are so abundant, milk, butter and cheese, can scarcely ever be procured at a rancho. They will not trouble themselves to tame cows for milking; but this rule is not invariable, a few milch cows (*vacas chichiguas*) being sometimes found about a rancho. All the Californians care to eat is bovine and cereal food, and they are good judges of beef and tortillas.

The trade of this country has been mostly monopolized by a few Boston houses, and Boston is better known among the natives of all kinds than any other part of the United States. These houses despatched to their agents assorted cargoes of plain cottons, prints, handkerchiefs, shoes, hats, coarse woollens, hardware, fancy goods, and, in short, specimens of all the cheapest fabrics of Lowell, Lynn, and Marblehead, and a plentiful supply of the auction trash of Boston. All these "notions" arriving at Monterey, a bargain was struck, as in Mexico, with the Governor, "Commandante General," "Administrador," &c., to lump the duties, with a sovereign contempt of the Mexican tariff, and without regard to what was contraband or non-contraband. The vessel received her permit, and forthwith opened a retail shop on board, peddling the goods from port to port at most enormous profits, justified to the awfully-shaved purchaser by well-salted invoices, and monstrous duties paid to the honest officials. Now the ranchero purchaser was already in debt to the merchant and had no money; but his credit stood high, and he took more goods on a fresh "trust," at prices which no man without a caoutachouc conscience could ask, and which no man without a naked family would ever agree to pay. Thus a piece of coarse Lowell "manta," or unbleached muslin, costing at home not over three dollars, was spared to the ranchero for twenty dollars, and other things in the same fair proportion. But the benevolent dealer sold his goods without money, if not without price, contenting himself with the note of his easy customer. Had this been the end of the joke, the ranchero would have been perfectly satisfied. But that most awful day in the calendar—pay-day—was yet to come; and the Scripture tells us that, "Where the carcass is, there shall the young eagles be gathered." So our Boston adventurers were seldom out of the way when the "matanzas" were going on. Then, or shortly afterwards, the "cuerreros," (hide-seekers), and the "cuerreritos," (the little ditto, or clerks), were on the alert, and incontinently set about riding to the ranchos, and riding down the rancheros, with urgent and fervent dunning exhortations to the effect that they would be pleased to "poney up." Various were the shifts and devices resorted to by the hard-pushed debtors —who emulated their brethren in more enlightened communities—to avoid "coming up to the Capting's office to settle." Their cattle had not yielded the expected increase, the wild Indians had proved uncommonly thievish, and a hundred other dilatory pleas were interposed. But the persevering Yankee never relaxed his efforts, never ceased to dun, dun, dun, until he had worried the debtor out of the requisite number of hides at moderate prices. Hence, perhaps, the expression common to baffled creditors, "I will take it out of your hide." Well, the hides went to Boston, and in due time a few of them came back in the shape of dressed leather and pegged shoes, which were disposed of to the original owners of the raw material at a "ruinous sacrifice,"—each pair of the latter probably stripping only one bull of his hide. Since the time when Queen Dido came the hide game over the natives at Carthage, it is probable that there has been no parallel to the hide-and-go-seek game between Boston and California. I will conclude this sketch by remarking, that the Eastern gentlemen employed in this business are greatly addicted to talking through their noses, and the Spanish language spoken with this peculiar twang produces effects never contemplated by the founders of the sonorous and euphonious Castillian.

AFTER HIS WIFE and children, the darling objects of a Californian's heart, are his horses. In this respect he is not surpassed by the Arab. His whole ambition centres in his horses; his livelihood depends on them; and they are the chief ministers of his pleasures. Dismount a Californian, and he is at once reduced to a perfectly helpless state, and is of no use in the world. He can neither take care of his farm, nor hunt, nor move from place to place; and is, to all intents and purposes, a wretched cripple. Even his work is done on horseback, when ingenuity can make that possible; and an American carpenter, residing in the country, assured me that an apprentice left him because he could not "shove the jack-plane" on horseback. If the Californian wishes to visit his next-door neighbor, even in town, he mounts his horse; and I have been told of a skilful and celebrated vaquero, who having occasion to walk from a gambling-house to a dram-shop across the street, and from insuetude in this mode of progression having impaired the beauty of his countenance, indignantly exclaimed upon picking himself up, "Zounds! this it is to walk on the ground." ("*Caramba! esto es cammiar en la tierra*.")

The lineage of the Californian horse is undoubtedly of the purest and highest. The domestic horses of the country, as well as those immense herds of wild horses which range the vast plains of the Tulares in their primitive freedom, all derive their descent from the Andalusian horses, which so materially aided the redoubtable "Conquistadores" to subvert the Aztec empire and the throne of the Montezumas. This stock of course gives them a pure Arabian descent. How far they have retained the excellence of their blood, it is not to be supposed that a sailor can judge; and yet I should know something of the Arabian horse, having seen and mounted the noblest of the race in the stables of Mohammed Ali, Viceroy of Egypt, and his son Ibrahim Pasha, as well as those belonging to other potentates in Syria, Egypt, and Barbary, besides choice specimens of the Persian stock in British India, and the real Nedjids of the Imaum of Muscat. The accident of travelling in an official capacity introduced me to those splendid studs, and gave me opportunities which I could not otherwise have enjoyed. To my eye, the Californian horses possess most points in common with those of the East, being of small size, but full chested, thin flanked, round in the barrel, clean limbed, with unusually small heads, feet and ears, large full eyes, expanded nostrils, very full flowing manes and tails, and shaggy rough coats as compared with our breed—while in color they are seldom dark, but usually white, all sorts of greys, spotted, cream color, and dun, the proportion of piebalds being very great. The white and black horses are generally preferred.

There still remain vast numbers of wild horses in California, but they have greatly diminished within a few years. As lately as ten years ago, it was customary to corral large numbers of wild and half-wild mares, and slaughter them with the lance, merely to check the rapid increase of the equine race, which the rancheros feared would make pasture scarce for the neat cattle, which were far more profitable than horses; and owing to this abominable practice, it is said that good horses are more rare than formerly.

In the plains of the Tulares natural corrals exist, formed by glens in the sierra, which are surrounded by precipices, up which a goat could hardly climb. To these the people of the settlements proceed *en masse,* and surrounding a large caballada of wild horses, pursue them through the narrow inlet to the selected glen or dell, the entrance to which they speedily close with branches previously collected by their vaqueros, or the neighboring Indians, the latter being always on hand on such occasions—not to get horses to ride, but to eat. The rancheros then enter the natural corral on horseback, with the ready riata, and selecting such a horse as suits their fancy, he is speedily noosed, and despite his struggles and plunging, is led out, and delivered into the custody of the vaquero. Suddenly the wild and trembling animal is thrown rudely to the ground, and in a trice is bridled, and bitted with the formidable Spanish bit, capable of breaking the jaw of the most refractory beast. The Californian immoveable saddle is then lashed on his back, and he is forthwith mounted by a rider equipped with the rowels. A scene of contention for the mastery then ensues between the man and horse; but the former, aided by his powerful machinery, invariably comes off victor of the field. The horse submits like a sensible and generous foe, tacitly acknowledges the superiority of the man, and never requires a second lesson. Sometimes a corral is made on the plain itself, but this is rare, as it is "mucho trabajo." A more common way is to give chase to a caballada on the open plain, the pursuit being maintained by well-mounted cavaliers, until the colts and weaker horses of the herd give in, when they are successively lassoed as fast as overtaken. Mares are seldom ridden, and are so abundant in the wild state, that horses must always be plentiful in that glorious country.

The tame horses are colts taken from the manadas, on the ranchos of the proprietors. They are broken to the bit and saddle in the same rough manner as the wild horse, and after being once subjected, they may be ridden by almost anybody. Often, however, they are gradually broken while yet little colts, by the children of the ranchos. The value of a horse is proportioned to his adaptation to the various operations of a cattle-farm, his courage, skill, and fleetness in the pursuit of wild cattle, and his familiarity with their subjugation and management. The severest test of these qualities is his behavior in attacking a bear, a feat often undertaken by a single ranchero, without other aid than his horse, his inseparable friend the riata, and the accustomed knife worn in his garter. Thus equipped, he will lasso the largest and most ferocious bear; and, drawing the brute to a tree, and taking a turn or two around him, will despatch him with his knife, while the sagacious horse keeps the riata fastened to the saddle at its fullest tension. The bear, indeed, is immensely stronger than the horse, and if lassoed by the fore-paw, could, by merely standing on his hind legs, draw up several mounted men united by their riatas; but skill and intrepidity accomplish what mere force could never effect; and I have seen the fiercest and wildest mountain bull attacked and overcome by a single skilful vaquero, who carried him off as peaceably as if he were a puppy led by a string. On such occasions the horse exhibits the wonderful sagacity of his nature, his sense of his own importance, as the trusty ally of his master, and a degree of excitement and pleasure at least equal to that of his rider. The intelligence of the animal then most nearly approaches human reason, and his large expanded nostril, his reeking coat, his cautious approaches to the foe, around whom he lightly careers, like a boxer in the arena, the stiffness of his muscles when he plants and braces himself for the sudden and violent jerks of his antagonist, far more powerful than himself, and above all, the careful and jealous watchfulness of his piercing and regardful eye, form a picture of equine sagacity and attitude which would delight a Horace Vernet. And when the bellowing and raging bull, at length overcome in the struggle between strength and skill, falls heavily to the earth, cowed and conquered at the feet of the victor, it is surprising to see the apparent scorn with which the noble beast looks on the catastrophe, and how—guiltless of the meaner passion of revenge—he seeks only to recruit his exhausted strength for the next conflict.

No stabling, no grooming, no farriery, no shoeing, no docking, no clipping, no jockeying, are connected with the care of the California horse. After a hard day's journey he is unbridled and unsaddled, and suffered to roam at large until he is again wanted by his master. The manadas, once put under the care of their garañon, require no farther management than merely to drive them back from a neighbor's rancho, to which they may have strayed. The sultan garañon keeps a jealous eye over his harem, and should one of them attempt to stray from her "carencia," or to encourage the advances of a neighboring sultan, not only does the injured husband, with war-like neighs loud-sounding, attack the seducer with hoofs and teeth, but the luckless odalisque is sure to receive a severe punishment.

The horse in California probably attains his greatest age, owing, perhaps, to his living in a state of nature, and having abundance of food. General Vallejo has horses in his possession which he has owned upwards of twenty-five years, and I have been assured that this age is not uncommon. They are subject to none of the maladies of our horses, that I could ever see or hear of. The few that are broken to harness work well. Such a thing as storing food is almost unknown, although sometimes a little barley is put away for the use of a favorite horse during the rainy season. The season of scarcity, however, which begins about the first of October, is brief, as pasture or grass seeds, and wild oats, are abundant nearly the whole year.

With the earliest showers in October or November, the alfileria (pin-grass), the bunch-grass, or tussock, the burr clover, and even the wild oats, spring up spontaneously throughout the whole country, and nature begins to put on that verdant garment, which, by Christmas, becomes a beautiful carpet, enamelled with wild flowers of a thousand tints and hues. The tender blades which first shoot up, cause the animals to purge, and they consequently become weak and lose their flesh; but soon the riper food grows plentiful, and as you journey moderately with your horse, allowing him his regular night-feeding, he begins to pick up, and soon waxes fat, although, unlike Jereboam, he does not kick. In the early spring months the cattle revel in the most luxuriant and abundant pasture, and this continues until September, when, it is true, the grass dries up, but the earth is covered with its seeds, which, as I have before mentioned, possess the most nutritious qualities, and are collected for food by the Indians. The seed of the alfileria and burr clover are about the size of our flax-seed, and bread is made from them by the Indians. The cattle, and large wild animals, grope for these seeds; and at this season the whole animal creation, even the countless little marmots, squirrels, &c., are revelling in fat, and beef and game are deliciously juicy and tender. Then ensues a season of comparative scarcity, and, before the rain sets in, the earth is parched as hard and dry as an adobe; the streams have retired altogether from their beds, or run in a slender thread, or sometimes leave only a water hole here and there; the leaves of the trees fall off; the ground is sparsely covered with the dried grass, upon which the cattle barely subsist, with the addition of the long fresh tough grass, growing in the most inaccessible mountain retreats, to which they retire in a moping and melancholy mood. The game, too, now gets lean; the bucks commence running with the does, and a shabby bluish colored coat supersedes the lively fawn-colored uniform they have been wont to wear. As few rancheros ever lay up even a moderate store of barley or fodder for their caballadas, the tame saddle-horses pine away, and show in their meagre, Rosinante condition, how severely they feel the loss of their accustomed food. The only animals which appear in fair condition are the manadas, which, accustomed to a free and roving life, are led forth by their garañons to a sort of rustic retirement and privacy, amidst the romantic glens and dells of the most remote and secluded part of the rancho, where they pass away the time very pleasantly. At length the first showers descend; the thirsty earth greedily drinks up the moisture, and is revivified; the murmuring brooks again appear on the surface, along the whole length of their beds; a thousand rills and little cataracts leap from the mountains; the trees put forth fresh foliage, the "sere and yellow leaf" being often immediately replaced by the springing bud. And now nature everywhere dons her green mantle, embroidered with an infinite variety of flowers, and thus the new year divides the autumn from the spring.

The only enemy of the horse in California, is the "leon," or puma, an animal of the same species, but larger and more ferocious than our panther. They are armed with long, sharp claws and teeth, and destroy many young colts, but seldom attack a full-grown horse.

Notwithstanding the great variety in the colors of horses, the language of Spain is so admirably adapted to a cattle-breeding community, that a horse of any shade may be so accurately described, in a few words, that a Californian will not fail to recognize him in the most numerous caballada. There are names for the primary colors, and combinations of these are used to describe any intermediate shade, however minute. Thus, *"pinto"* being the specific name for all piebald horses, a *"pinto colorado"* is a piebald horse on which the spots are reddish, and so *"bayo blanco"* is the designation of light cream color. The various shades of roan, for which we possess that single term, are here distinguished by innumerable combinations, as *"bayo picado,"* a roan with dark spots, *"bayo colorado,"* &c. The bays are classified with the same minuteness, as *"saino,"* *"saino prieto,"* *"saino colorado,"* &c.; and a horse with four white feet receives the addition of *"cuatro alba."* Any peculiarity the animal may have, such as an excrescence, deformity, or mutilation, is likewise pithily brought in when describing him. There are also arbitrary terms, such as *"champurrada,"* a horse of the color of gruel and chocolate mixed; a *"retinto,"* a horse of the color of the wine of California, and many others "too tedious to mention." I have often described horses in this way, which the vaquero whom I addressed had never seen, but which he recognized as a "caballo conocido"—a well-known horse. The far-reaching vision, too, of these fellows, is extraordinary; for they can distinguish the horse much sooner than the rider, or select a horse from a large caballada, or manada, at distances which, if mentioned to the uninitiated, would appear enormously stretched.

I think that a cross of the Californian mare with the American horse would produce a superb animal. The garañons of California are generally heavy-moulded and unsprightly, while the mares are precisely the reverse. The foal of a Californian mare, sired by a genuine blooded horse from Virginia, would probably be the perfection of horseflesh. The Californians take no pains to cross the original stock, although none are greater admirers of fine horses; and it is desirable that some gentleman of the turf should emigrate with a few choice male specimens of the American stables.

AFTER PASSING a few hours in resting our animals in anticipation of the rugged road we should now have to travel, and in viewing the improvements of Mr. Chiles, we all started again on our journey. After a pleasant ride, through a broad valley, we again ascended the serrania by a most excruciating road, which, however, was well atoned for by the bold mountain scenery and the huge pine-trees, whose cones were often larger than a man's head. Our route lay over volcanic masses of basaltic fragments, and conducted us to the rancho of Greenock, the frontier settler on this side. Here we remained all night, and starting next morning at sunrise, our Indian guides conducted us over the last pass of the sierra, and we entered a country of beautiful uplands, broad savannahs, and shady glades, containing much excellent timber. After riding leisurely all day, diverging occasionally to get a shot at a deer, we suddenly emerged from our mountain-path upon a level and extensive plain, and saw the Lake, or rather a portion of it, in its narrowest part, the border being fringed with plains of tulé, and the dim outline of the distant and mountain-bounded horizon, indicating that either the Lake or the plain was very extensive. Nearer to us was a huge mountain jutting like a towering promontory into the Lake, to the base of which we directed the course of our jaded horses.

While we are toiling on to reach our destination, I will mention that "Bunk" this day made a most astonishing shot. A single elk was browsing on the side of a hill, the space between him and us being covered with undergrowth of a considerable elevation. He stopped grazing, and appeared to watch our movements with great interest, but without apparent anxiety on his own account. Bunk dismounted and took a careful and deliberate aim, making allowance, as he afterwards told me, for the fall of the ball in its flight. The crack of his rifle was followed by the disappearance of the animal, as suddenly as if he had sunk into the earth. The Indians of our company, (who only could have done it), plunged into the undergrowth and soon towed the elk to us tailing on to a horse-rope. Mecate! he was a noble buck, with enormous antlers, and almost as weighty as a bullock. His death-wound was caused by a bullet striking on the shoulder and passing directly through the spinal vertebra; and the blow must have stunned him as if it had been an electric shock, which accounted for his sudden fall. The distance seemed so great that I had it carefully measured with a riata, exactly three yards in length, and the result was one hundred and six lengths of the riata, or three hundred and eighteen yards—about two hundred and fifty on an air-line!

We reached the base of the high sierra, which is here laved by the waters of the Lake, a little before sunset, and encamped in an oak grove, opposite a pretty little islet, about four hundred yards from the tulé-fringed margin. After some shouting to the people of the island in their own language by our Indian guides, a tulé-boat was launched and approached our camp.

The Indians at first supposed that we had come on a hostile expedition, and were seen from the main-land running around the island, apparently calling to arms, while a signal was made from its conical summit, in answer to which several tulé-boats that were out fishing in the Lake approached the islet, and some Indians drawing a net in front of the village, stopped work to observe us. The poor wretches had good cause to suspect us. The Californians often went on a foray in quest of servants, and this species of kidnapping, practised up to the time the United States acquired possession, is one great reason why the Indians hate the rancheros. A number of these "hijos del pais," desiring servants, or farm hands, would club together, being well armed and mounted, and attended by their allies, the "Christiano" Indians, who, like all mercenary apostates, love to oppress those from whom they have separated. As no man is so low as not to imagine he has inferiors, so these "Christianos" like no better sport than to show their superiority to the "Gentiles" in the art of war, while at the same time they gratify that propensity to *hunt something* which is inherent in the nature of man. These marauding parties went forth to the Indian country, and suddenly coming upon a village, made an attack when least expected, killing such as resisted, and carrying off to the settlements such as they thought best suited for servants. Sometimes these infamous expeditions were planned by the Mexican officer or Alcalde of the District, who called in the aid of volunteers. These war parties were much dreaded by the Indians, and hence their selection of places like this islet, which could not be approached by surprise. But perhaps the controlling reason for founding a village on this particular site was the facilities it afforded for catching fish, an occupation much less troublesome than hunting. An advantage of this kind is a God-send to the Indian of California. If there is anything he hates and dreads it is labor, or anything that has the name or semblance of labor of any description. If he hunts in this game-stocked country, it is not because he loves hunting, or because, like our more northern Indian, he may profit by selling skins; but solely because he is pushed to the last extremity for food, and can no longer obtain the miserable apology for it upon which he is accustomed to subsist.

I crossed to the islet in a tulé-boat, which consists of two bundles of dried tulé lashed up like a hammock in the shape of cigars, and bound together at the ends. They float very lightly, are dry and secure, drawing, with a heavy load, only an inch or two of water, which is due to the extremely light and cellular character of the rush. They can be made in an hour or so after the tulé is cut, and exactly suit the lazy habits of the Indians, who could hardly be induced to build a wooden boat. I found a village of low conical tulé huts, arranged in a sort of street, running parallel to the shore of the lake, and every one of these wigwams was—

> —"like the sweet South
> That breathes upon—the banks of Newfoundland—
> Stealing and giving *odor*."

The two or three hundred inhabitants appeared very anxious to see us, some of the women and children having never seen a white man. Whether they thought the sight worth seeing after all, I am not able to say. The old chief was as ancient in his aspect as fish-like in his smell, and his want of resemblance to Mr. Forrest in the classic tragedy of Metamora, was very striking. In fact, this venerable chief had nothing whatever to say about "the Great Spirit," was utterly silent on the prolific theme of the "red man and the pale faces," and apparently ignored "the hunting-grounds and graves of his forefathers." As to his "wigwam," it was there, and there was no escaping it; but he did not brag of it; and, in short, if the naked truth must be told, he was for all the world like any other Indian nudity squatted on a mat, except that he wore around his neck a polished pearl-like shell, as a badge of authority. The quality of his perfumery might have been cavilled at by those who imagine that their own musks and pomatums are more endurable than the aroma of stale fish; but, for my part, I inhaled the nosegay with perfect composure, inwardly exclaiming, however,

"O! his offence is rank!—it smells to heaven!"

I think I may with great propriety congratulate my countrymen upon the enlistment of many thousand representatives of this true "Democratic stock," under the banner of our "free institutions." If they only possessed votes, the future demagogues of California could fraternize with them to their hearts' content.

But I am neglecting the ancient piscatorial chieftain. This worthy disciple of Massaniello received with apparent satisfaction, the intelligence that the United States had taken possession of the country, but like a wary old diplomatist, he would not commit himself or his "isleñas" to any decided course at present. In policy, indeed, he was a wily old fox, and his mind seemed made up not to take sides until it was apparent which side was strongest. It was evident, that the dread inspired by the Californians, who two years before had harried his rancheria and carried off numbers into servitude (my interesting Christiano interpreter Santos making one of the nice party), weighed heavily on the old man, and made him cautious of compromising himself with foreigners, whom he knew only as a race of roving hunters, totally inferior to the rancheros in numbers and civilization. Still, it is not to be supposed that he thought us at all on a level with his own race; on the contrary, these people possess more of that Christian grace called humility, than most of the eloquent preachers who regularly recommend it once a week to their congregations, and of course are themselves meeker than Moses. These Indians, however, are so positively humble, that many persons of eminent piety might profit by their example.

The chief seemed much astonished that a person of "reason,"—all whites are called "gente de razon,"—should visit his rancheria on any other errand than to make captives. When he accompanied us to our camp, he was evidently very proud of the slight condescension on the part of the "razons," the Californians being accustomed to treat the Indians, chiefs and all, with sovereign contempt. The preparation of supper excited a most intense interest among the natives, each man of our party having brought along a choice piece of venison or elk-meat. It was quite evident that the Indians of the rancheria had become tired of fish, a party having already started off on the back track to secure what was left of the elk, whose remains we had left some twenty miles in the rear. We had plenty of volunteer cooks, and spread out a most abundant supper. The preparation of tea was the most exciting topic of the banquet, our guests having never before heard of that exhilarating beverage. Upon asking my dragoman, Santos, why he laughed so loudly, he told me that the old chief had at last found out that the tea was tobacco, which the generous white man had prepared in a new form with hot water as an agreeable refreshment, which wonderful discovery the shrewd old savage was communicating to his astounded auditors.

The next morning our road lay around the Sierra facing the islet, on the mainland side or neck of the promontory, which was too precipitous to admit of going around on the lake side. We crossed a wide plain, sterile and dreary, covered with fragments and large blocks of obsidian, a sort of black volcanic glass. Towards afternoon, however, we came into a beautiful diversified country of pleasant glades, broad meadows, and rich level savannahs, again catching a view of the far-expanding lake. Towards sunset, we arrived at Sacred Town, one of the largest rancherias of the Laguna Indians. Here were excellent enclosed fields of corn, calabashes, &c., and riding through the rancheria, we stripped saddles in a fine oak-grove near the border of a pretty stream, well removed from the filth and smell of the "sacred" precincts. Though it was late, I held a conference with the principal chiefs, who, having been informed by our Indians of our peaceable intentions, brought us a supply of vegetables, fruits and other refreshments. This was the home of the six sub-chiefs who had accompanied us, and here we left them.

I announced a grand council for all the head men of the rancherias in the vicinity, and as we intended remaining here a few days, I spent the intermediate time in acquiring information respecting the Indians.

THERE IS NO DOUBT that a numerous and wide-spread Indian population exists in Northern California, in the vicinity of the Bay of San Francisco, and the valleys of the Sacramento and Russian rivers. I think it would be safe to compute their numbers at between forty and fifty thousand, not including those living as far north as the Roque river region, and the country of the Shaste Indians. These latter savages are fierce and warlike, attacking all who enter their territory, and especially white men, who should not venture among them in parties of less than eight or ten well-armed men. They cannot properly be classed with the Californian Indians with whom I am acquainted, and concerning whom I am about to make a few observations.

When the missions were secularized and plundered in 1831, Upper California was supposed to contain a population of 4,500 "gente de razon," (whites,) and about 50,000 Indians of the Presidios alone. Of the latter it is said that 22,000 were more or less Christianized, the majority of the Indian population being composed of Gentiles, or wild Indians. Notwithstanding the ravages of smallpox and other diseases among them, I am inclined to think that *all* the Indians of Upper California, including those above excepted, may be safely estimated at sixty thousand. It should be remembered that many of them live in retired and secluded retreats, wholly unknown to the whites, and that the sea-coast north of the settlements, the country north of Ross, and the almost unexplored valley of the Roque river, are, according to the reports of the few hunters and trappers who have lighted their solitary camp-fires in those regions, inhabited by great numbers of Indians.

The Laguna Indians are a fair specimen of the California aborigines. They are docile, mild, easily managed, and although lazy and unthrifty, will work tolerably well for short periods at making adobes, getting in crops, and doing farm-work generally, taking in payment, with great avidity, beads and toys of the cheapest kind, handkerchiefs, cottons, and other common dry goods. On the other hand, they are roguish, ungrateful, and incorrigibly lazy unless closely watched, and occasionally punished corporeally. They are not at all revengeful, and are cowardly and cringing towards the whites. They are thorough sensualists, and most abandoned gamblers in their small way. They have some rude games of chance with bones, resembling dice, and with something like jack-straws, at which, as I know to my cost, they will sit up all night, playing for articles of little value, literally "making night hideous" with such awful noises as would do credit to an amateur concert of rooks, jackdaws, magpies, and bullfrogs. They have but little idea of differences in value, and will give large odds merely for the sake of playing. Thus one will wager his shirt worth two dollars against a small piece of tobacco worth sixpence, and if he had ten dollars he would readily wager the whole sum against a dollar's worth of beads, or even a single string. All the gold they may acquire will undoubtedly fall into the hands of sharpers for a twentieth part of its value. They are physically an inferior race, and have flat, unmeaning features, long, coarse, straight black hair, big mouths, and very dark skins, of a temperature lower than those of the whites, and to the touch something like a frog's.

The Gentiles go in the extremest "model artist" style of costume, except a mantle, which they make of rabbit skin, or a "feather blanket," so called, curiously wrought of feathers from the breast of the wild duck. They are offensively dirty in their persons, and also in their habitations, which are conical wigwams of tulé, bountifully stocked with industrious fleas. Their food is principally bread, made of acorns, which are very large and plentiful in California, and are pounded into a paste in a wooden mortar, and baked in a rude oven. This bread looks and tastes like coarse black clay, strongly resembling the soundings in Hampton roads, and being about as savory and digestible. They also make "mansanita" bread of a small red berry, borne by the tree of that name; and convert burr-clover seeds, wild oats, and all sorts of roots which they dig up, into the "staff of life." They also eat fish—to that I will swear—and dry it for winter use. They ingeniously entrap and ensnare the smaller animals, descending even so low as field-mice; but their great performance is hunting deer, which they approach with a buck's head and horns fastened to their own noddles, groping along stealthily in the high grass, until the genuine and deceived animal is within range of their arrows. They also are fond of horse-meat, and when hard pressed with hunger will occasionally steal a bullock. They are wretchedly improvident, and seldom lay up stores to last through the rainy season, which it is absolutely necessary to provide against, as the country cannot then be travelled, and all the animals retire to the fastnesses of the mountains. Like all the family of man, even these spiritless people have their warlike propensities, and maintain armories to make their bows, and arrows, and lances. The bows are beautifully made of light and elastic wood, stiffened, and made more elastic by sinews, strongly braced, at the back of the bow. The arrows are neatly fashioned from a peculiar light, strong, straight twig, and are tipped with barbed obsidian heads, and winged with feathers. The head is tied on with sinew, and the shaft is ornamented with rings of the distinguishing paint of the owner's rancheria. Their knives and spear-points are made of obsidian and flint. They are dexterous in the use of their weapons, especially the arrows, which are of two kinds, one short and light for killing game, and the other a war-shaft, measuring a cloth-yard in length. These are carried at the side, in a quiver made of the skin of a bear's cub or fox, stripped off whole. The bow-strings are made of the wild flax of the fields.

When going to war with a neighboring rancheria, the *casus belli* is usually trifling, such as a trespass on lands in acorn time, the stealing of girls, &c. On coming in sight of the enemy, they form in an extended line, something like light infantry, and shouting like bacchanals, dance from side to side to prevent the foe from taking deliberate aim. They do not scalp the slain like other North American savages, which is a trait indicative of the native gentleness of the Californian Indian. They paint their bodies with cinnabar, ochre, charcoal, pipeclay, or anything else that comes to hand. Besides their weapons and feather blankets, they manufacture from pingrass very excellent baskets, called "coras," of all sizes, generally of a conical shape, and so finely worked that they hold water. They sometimes ornament the smaller ones with beads, pearl-shell, feathers, &c., so that they present quite an elegant appearance. They also make a sugar of the root of the tulé.

Their religion appears to be polytheistic, their deities being both numerous and multiform. They frequently carry with them an assortment of pocket-gods, which they worship. Those I have seen were rude images of bears, otters, beavers and other animals, carved in wood or bone, and were usually worn with a string around the neck. I once saw in a rancheria of Sacramento Indians the handle of an "Arkansas tooth-pick," composed in equal parts of horse, alligator and snapping-turtle, which was probably the spoil of one of my erratic countrymen, and enjoyed a high degree of sanctity. A Supreme Being, however, is evidently acknowledged by them, and to Him they address their humble petitions for favor in war, hunting, crops, food, and the like. On important occasions they employ women, who have a peculiar "call" for worship, to go forth into the solitudes of the woods, where they sit on the ground for hours, and cry loudly in monotonous prayer, nothing interrupting them when engaged in these devotions. Whether the petitions which ascend from costly temples, "made with hands," are most acceptable to the Most High than these lowly and simple supplications of His poor Indian children, is a question for theologians to solve.

These unsophisticated people do not appear to be very strongly attached to their own religious opinions, and so little are they tinged with sectarianism or bigotry that they are easily induced to embrace the white man's faith, especially the Catholic.

Their patriotism exhibits itself in clanship; and while they will get all they can out of a white man, they will share, with reckless generosity, to the last morsel, with their "parientes," kindred and friends.

The Indian rancherias are situated in pleasant, well-selected spots, near the banks of a stream and remain in the same spot until it suits the fancy or convenience of the nomadic proprietors to "pull up stakes." They possess no title to any land whatever in the country, the Indian titles, even to the mission property, having been extinguished by the laws of Mexico, and the lands granted to Mexican citizens resident in California. By the laws of that country the Indians were deemed "minores y pupiles"—minors and pupils—and were at first placed under the tutelage or guardianship of the ecclesiastics at the missions; and after the missions were suppressed by the Mexican Congress, they were turned over to the hard guardianship of the military and civil authorities, who were authorised, under certain restrictions, to cause them to be employed among the white population. They were likewise forbidden to vagabondize about the country, in the exercise of those roguish propensities for which they are notorious.

Numbers of half-educated Indians, formerly of the missions, are scattered among the untutored masses, and the "Christianos" possess great influence over the "Gentiles," although they are cordially hated by the latter. Although the Indians seem stupid and are naturally lazy, they are easily taught, and those of the missions were adepts in various trades, as well as agriculture, and some of them became priests, after receiving an education.

Deprived of the beneficent instructions and wholesome restraints to which they had become accustomed, it is not surprising that many of those who were once the best of Indian Christians are now the very worst of horse-thieves, on the same principle that a relapse is more dangerous than the original disease. The most debased among them once proudly styled themselves "Californios del Presidio"—Californians of the mission—and they gloried in the guardianship of the good priests and the King of Spain. These missions would have been productive of immense good had they been preserved, and they have at least demonstrated that the Indians are susceptible of great improvement, and possess much aptitude for acquiring knowledge. The good fathers were earnestly devoted to the welfare of their docile pupils; and, although like all missionaries, they were fond of making proselytes, and sometimes used means to that end not entirely justifiable, still their conduct compares—perhaps I might say contrasts—most favorably with that of missionaries elsewhere, even those from our own country, boasting a faith which assumes to be more enlightened. From observation and inquiry, in every missionary country which I have visited, I have no hesitation in saying that the efforts of the Catholic fathers have been far more successful than those of any other Christian denomination in the work of ameliorating the condition of uncivilized man, and the

A "PUI" DAY.

Sketched by J. W. Revere U. S. N.

Lith. of Wm. Endicott & Co. N. York.

number of their converts—if that proves anything—is certainly greater than that of all the Protestant sects combined. I think I have seen enough of the world to know that religious intolerance and arrogance are peculiar to no sect, but depend upon the facilities for putting them in practice—and I have seen more stringent despotism exercised by Protestant than by Catholic missionaries. It is earnestly to be hoped that some time prior to the general conflagration, Christian sects will be at peace with each other, and that men will no more think of quarreling about speculative opinions in theology than about the cut of their noses. Men of the highest intellect, the purest morals, and the utmost honesty of purpose, have differed and will differ in matters of religious opinion; and men and women of no intelligence, full of sanctimonious pretensions and unreasoning bigotry, will consign the great lights of the age to the good offices of the Gentleman in Black, with as little ceremony as they would order a chicken to the gridiron. In the end, the mass of mankind will probably conclude with the Catholic poet, Pope, that

"He can't be wrong whose life is in the right."

Of course, it will never answer for our government to restore the mission property, or to have any, the remotest connection, with church matters; but now that all sects are at liberty to settle in California, on equal terms, it would be good policy on the part of the white population to encourage the return of the worthy padres to their shepherdless flocks.

Polygamy is practised only by the chiefs, and seldom by them; but wives are repudiated and exchanged among them. They are much kinder to their women than most savages, and do not expect them to do much drudgery. Rape exists among them in an authorised form, and it is the custom for a party of young men to surprise and ravish a young girl, who becomes the wife of one of them. Nothing more clearly proves the native purity of woman, than the dread these poor creatures have of this horrid orgie, and it is to be hoped that the law will prevent and punish this most atrocious custom.

A remarkable peculiarity of these Indians is their use of the "Tamascal" or sweat-house. It consists of a conical mound of earth, supported from the inside, and prevented from falling in, by rough beams and posts; and having but a single aperture which serves for an entrance. Every rancheria has one or more of these singular pyramids, according to its population; and no collection of even twenty or thirty Indians, is without its tamascal. It is generally situated near a pool or stream, and those who use it, rush from the tamascal into the water. These sweat-baths appear to be used as luxuries, are always resorted to on "Pui" or feast days, and by a singular superstition, are connected with their religious sentiments. They are also employed in the celebration of rites of a peculiar nature, analogous to those practised by the ancients in the mysteries of Pan and Apollo in the cave of the Parthenon. Men, women and children, of all sizes and ages, collect in a state of nature, around the smouldering embers, in the centre of the tamascal; and, closing the entrance, remain shut up together an incredible length of time, sometimes chaunting a low and monotonous strain. When the rite is concluded, the entrance is opened, and the whole congregation rush into the open air and make for the water, into which they promiscuously plunge in a state of profuse perspiration. After cooling off, they retire to their huts, and, rolling themselves into balls, remain torpid for hours. The use of these sweat-baths is prescribed for many diseases, and I have heard Californians say, that they derived benefit from a moderate sweat without the water-bath, in cases of neuralgia and rheumatism. All agree, however, that the immoderate use of these baths by the Indians, cause many diseases of a rheumatic character.

The most wretched of mankind have their pastimes, and like other savages, the Indians of California have their dances, and the extent to which the men dress their heads in plumes for a "pas de deux," gives them the appearance of having been picked clean of their feathers everywhere besides.

The Indians of the Sierras of the Tularés, stretching nearly the whole length of Upper California, are said to be the most numerous in the country. They are also about the greatest rogues that infest it, stealing numbers of tame horses from the white settlers on or near the coast only to use for food—the Indian generally making no other use of the horse. When the theft is discovered, the predatory band are immediately pursued, and if overtaken, which they generally are, the lives of the whole gang pay the forfeit for this offence, which in the eyes of a Californian, is of a most heinous nature. As the Americans are generally more prompt than the Californians in the pursuit of their stolen animals, the marauders generally prefer the horses of the latter, well knowing the superior energy of the

Yankee settler, and that on these occasions he is apt to be quite as remorseless as the rancheros.

The indifference to death which prevails among the pacific Indians of California is very remarkable—the more remarkable because they *are* pacific, and easily overawed and conquered. Like most savages, they reason with a rude but true philosophy, that the loss of a life so hard and precarious as theirs is little to be regretted. I have inquired after Indians employed at the port of Sonoma, whose leave of absence had run out, and have been answered that they were *dead*. At first I supposed they were keeping out of the way, and had got up these reports to deceive me; but afterwards I have found that they were really dead. Not the least emotion was ever shown by those who communicated the information to me, but the laconic announcement was made in a tone as indifferent as if the subject were a dead dog. "Es muerto"—he is dead—that was the whole story; and if the cause of death were inquired into, the reply was the everlasting "Quien sabe? Es muerto."—Who knows? He is dead. And, indeed, if familiarity with death can disarm it of its terrors, well may these poor wretches laugh in the face of the King of Terrors. Wherever they come in contact with the white man, they rapidly melt away under the effects of his diseases; and, like their eastern fellows, they will now have to contend with the white man's poisonous liquors. General Vallejo told me, that when he first came to Sonoma, in 1836, that valley was inhabited by twenty thousand Indians, and there were as many more in the neighborhood. Twenty thousand of them were carried off in a single year by the ravages of smallpox, and the tribes of Sonoma have now been swept from the face of the earth—mowed *down,* as I said to a friend—mowed UP, as he beautifully replied. When it is remembered, that smallpox is not the only desolating disease which follows in the wake of the white man, and that his rum has proved among our Indians as fatal as his natural disorders, it is very clear, that unless measures be promptly taken to protect and preserve the inoffensive natives of California, the present generation will live to read the epitaph of the whole race.

Taking into consideration that the Indians of California are pacific, tractable, and useful to the white population; that they have no national character—each rancheria being an independent and isolated community, claiming only the little land on which it stands; that we find them nevertheless upon their native soil, to which they hold an equitable title derived directly from the Almighty; that they have been already partially civilized by the missions; that many of them have learned something of the customs of the whites; that if removed to the sterile border region, they would become a tribe of horse and cattle thieves, and drag out a wretched and precarious existence in the midst of the savage "Digger" tribes, a warlike and cruel race, subsisting on snails, roots and larvae,—their preservation and regulation becomes a question of great moment to the governments of the United States and of California, worthy the serious attention of just and enlightened statesmen. As I have already stated, their numbers must still be very large, their rancherias extending throughout California, and enjoying various degrees of prosperity. When I have inquired as to their numbers in various parts of the country, the answer has always been, that in such and such localities there were "miles de Indios"—thousands of Indians. To give them civil rights, on an equality with the whites, would be more absurd than to grant such rights to children under ten years of age. The elective franchise, in such hands, would be both a farce and a curse. But to extend over them the protection of just statutes, devised for their advantage; to make them equal with the white population before the law, so that the atrocities heretofore practised by kidnappers should be restrained by the remedies which the civil and criminal law extends to white persons; to secure to them the right of trial by jury, and the right to hold land in limited quantities—would be measures not only righteous in themselves, but expedient, in point of policy, and creditable to the humanity of the United States.

I COULD LEARN no other name for the immense body of water, on whose shore we were encamped, except that of the "Laguna," or "THE LAKE," from which I inferred that there was no other lake of any magnitude in that district of country, which, by the way, is probably the best watered of any in California.

"Hopitse-wah," or "Sacred Town," is the principal rancheria of the Laguna; and the aged chief of that fragrant metropolis luxuriates in the name of "Hallowney," which has such a decidedly Hibernian sound, that the antiquarian is at liberty to infer that he is descended from that wondrous Phenecian stock, which peopled the Green Isle, and made it the abode of civilization, while England was yet a howling wilderness.

It was through old Hal that I summoned deputations from the neighboring rancherias of Gentiles, he having despatched runners for that purpose; and on the third day after our arrival, we held a council in the grove of old oaks, where we had established our head-quarters. Although the bill of the performance was made as attractive as possible, the attendance was not large, the poor fellows at a distance having suffered severely from the incursions of the rancheros, and feeling shy and uncomfortable in the company of white men. I could almost fancy one of these remote chiefs answering my summons with a significant gesture, and the usual

Timeo Danaos et dona ferentes,

which, with "E Pluribus Unum," has probably penetrated the Indian country by this time. But although our council was not large, it was very select; and those who shall read my "eloquent remarks" on the occasion, may perhaps declare the "audience fit, though few."

A circle having been formed, and the preliminary pipe having gone gravely round—that being the last ceremony these people would omit—I arose, and, through my dragoman, Santos, addressed the assembled wisdom of the various tribes, substantially as follows:

"I have called you together to have a talk with you. The country you inhabit no longer belongs to Mexico, but to a mighty nation whose territory extends from the great ocean, you have all seen or heard of, to another great ocean thousands of miles towards the rising sun. The country inhabited by that nation, is called the United States, and its millions of people are called Americans. I am an officer of that great country, and, to get here, have traversed both of those great oceans in a ship of war which, with a terrible noise, spits forth flames, and hurls forth instruments of destruction, dealing death to all our enemies. Our armies are now in Mexico, and will soon conquer the whole country. But you have nothing to fear from us, if you do what is right. Our magnanimous government will protect you, and make you a happier and better people than you now are, if you are faithful to your new rulers. A stop will be put to the oppressions of the rancheros; for ours is a country of laws, and we do not suffer the crime of kidnapping to go unpunished. We shall do what we can to better your condition, and we shall expect you to do all you can to help yourselves. Your ancestors have roamed the plains, and mountains, and forests of California for centuries; but they have accomplished nothing. We come to prepare this magnificent region for the use of other men, for the population of the world demands more room, and here is room enough for many millions, who will hereafter occupy and till the soil. But, in admitting others, we shall not displace you, if you act properly; but we shall be glad to see you advancing in civilization side by side with the white man. You can easily learn, but you are indolent. I hope you will alter your habits, and be industrious and frugal, and give up all the low vices which you practise; but if you are lazy and dissipated, you must, before many years, become extinct. We shall watch over you, and give you true liberty; but beware of sedition, lawlessness, and all other crimes, for the arm which shields can assuredly punish, and it will reach you in your most retired hiding-places."

When my harangue was ended a perfect silence prevailed, and it became a matter of doubt with me whether its effect had been impressive or soporific. At length, the venerable chief Hallowney got upon his legs and delivered himself of a "talk," in a guttural but not unpleasant tone, and seemingly with considerable energy, as he jerked the words out as if he were spitting some fiery substance from his mouth. He spoke nearly in these words:

"I am glad to see you, and so are my friends and neighbors. We know your people and respect them. They do not maltreat us like the Californians, who hunt us down and steal our children from us to enslave them. They are always ready to wage a war of extermination against us, but they never have sent any one to talk to us about such good things as we have heard this day. They think words would be wasted on miserable Indians, and many of my neighbors cannot yet believe that you have come to talk soberly and justly to us. We are sensible of your condescension, and we think well and thankfully of your visit. We desire nothing more than to be allowed to live in peace like our ancestors. If we are not molested in our far-off forest retreats, we will not only refrain from stealing your cattle and horses, but will detect and deliver up all thieving Indians. We will also work in harvest-time for your farmers, and do what we can to better our own condition. All we want is just treatment, and you may tell your people that we will requite it."

In the evening, after the council had broken up, we had a visit from a party of Indians, both male and female, attired in head-dresses composed of the black feathers of the large Californian vulture, which fell down their backs. The men were painted all over with stripes and spots, and the women wore kilts or short petticoats made of flax or hemp hackled out and fastened round the waist, but so fashioned as not to impede the motions of their limbs. They wore besides, various articles of savage finery on different parts of their persons, and all were masked. We followed this motley party to the lawn near the tamascal, where were seated on the ground several chiefs and medicine-men of the rancheria, some of whom had whistles or double flageolets of reed, which were stuck into their *noses*. Their musicians sung, in a monotonous tone something like a recitative, with a nasal flageolet accompaniment, while the men and women paired off into couples, and danced or rather trotted around, the men keeping time and singing, and at the same time rattling a small dried calabash like a child's rattle.

Great preparations had evidently been made, but I soon got tired of an exhibition so absurd and unmeaning, and not thinking it necessary to stand upon ceremony with my unpolished entertainers, I took French leave. After dark, I strolled in the same direction, and some of our party told me that the Indians had stripped off all their finery, and had bundled promiscuously together into the tamascal, where they were enjoying a stew.

The next morning we started at early day-light, and riding through the rancheria found it nearly deserted, the Indians being in a torpid state, and sleeping off the effects of the night's debauch. The old chief, Hallowney, however, came out of his lodge, and on my giving him a plug of tobacco and a red handkerchief, presented me with a pretty cora or Indian basket, and offered to send me any number of warriors in case I wanted them.

It was quite apparent that the Indians had become better convinced of the superiority of our countrymen, a result contributed to not a little by the skill of our party in the use of fire-arms, of which they had seen memorable instances during our brief visit. Our rifles were indeed a perfect God-send to the poor fellows, who were almost starving in the midst of plenty. Within a mile or two from the sacred village we found elk and deer in abundance, and we astonished the natives by keeping them supplied with these delicacies.

After leaving the rancheria, we travelled along the line of the Lake, at a distance of a mile from its margin, through a broad plain, which Mr. Chiles, a practical and knowing man in such matters, pronounced equal to any land he had ever seen for farming purposes. This fertile plain was principally prairie, but relieved by occasional strips of timber. We rode on it until noon, when we dismounted in a pleasant dell, by the side of a cool spring, ate a repast of venison, and enjoyed a glorious siesta until the sun began to decline from the meridian. Again we mounted, feeling like giants refreshed, and leaving the Lake to the right we began to ascend, for now we had to surmount the Sierra lying between the Lake and the valley of the Russian river—"Rio de los Russes."

We had reached the first plateau of the Serania, and were riding leisurely along, when a shout from the foremost of our party, the instant dismounting of the white men, and their rapid advance to the front and a cover, apprised me that a fight was brewing. I was left entirely alone, and several arrows fell near me, while my ears were saluted by the yells of the contending parties, and the warning shout of Chiles, which rang like a clarion. He was stationed behind a "madron," a tree, whose smooth bark and hard wood render it an excellent fence for the farmer, as well as a capital screen for an Indian fighter. I caught a glimpse of naked figures dancing about among the trees, and saw the vaqueros securing the deserted horses, and heard the inspiring music of our riflemen. My Christian friend and interpreter, Santos, was badly frightened, and could not raise a shout; but a deputation of Hopitse-wah Indians who had accompanied us, now interfered in the capacity of heralds, and after a vast amount of bawling, made the hostile party understand who we were.

Being assured that we would not injure them, the assailants came in, one of their party being badly wounded by a rifle ball. It appeared that they were from a rancheria towards the western end of the Laguna, on a warlike expedition, to revenge the trespass on their grounds perpetrated by the "Isleñas" or Islanders, the injury consisting in picking acorns. They mistook our party for an expedition of rancheros, in pursuit of servants; but had they known we were Americans they would not have troubled us, —their dread of the rifle, seldom used by the rancheros, imposing a salutary restraint. The young man who was hurt took his wound very coolly, although it was a severe one, the ball having entered under the shoulder-blade and made a hole directly through to the left breast, where it came out. I examined the wound and gave directions to keep the hole open at the breast, but as the poor creature said it pained him to cough or to breathe hard, I concluded that the lung was injured, and it is probable that the reaction which ensued carried him off. It was getting late, and having neither medicines nor surgical instruments, which, indeed, in our hands would have been of no avail, we left the sufferer to his fate. His friends seemed to think it a matter of little consequence, as there was no present pain, and said they would take him to a rancheria where there was a fine tamascal, which, with the Indians, answers all the purposes of "Dr. Brandreth's grandfather's vegetable universal pills," among some civilized people.

Here was another instance of the indifference to death which happily prevails among the Indians. If, with the white man's diseases, they acquired his terror of death also, they would be miserable indeed. But it is an alleviation of their misery, and not a small one either, that their minds are never troubled about death—that grim Apparition who haunts the living in Christian countries up to the day of his final visit. It is one design of Christianity to destroy "the sting of death;" and yet it may be doubted whether the votaries of any other faith look with half so much horror and dread upon dissolution. I have heard it stated from the pulpit, by a very eminent preacher, that the Greeks and Romans had a more awful fear of death than we of the Christian faith; but I can find no proof to sustain the assertion, the argument to be deduced from my limited reading demonstrating decidedly the reverse of that proposition. The cause of this dreadful awe of death, of this constant presence of the ghastly Spectre, in the imaginations of thousands of Christians, is not to be found in the system itself, but in the defective manner of its inculcation by those entrusted with that duty. Children are taught, from their earliest years, to fear nothing so much as death; and the very elaborate manner in which they are taught the great cardinal doctrine of a devil scarcely inferior in power to the Deity; and when turning for relief to the good Creator, are shown an awful Being, with three wrathful features to one of mercy, or even of justice, as understood among men—these are circumstances, which, taken in connection with the eternal fires of hell, are little calculated to make the future life attractive. I insist upon it, that if children are to be frightened to death by dreadful pictures of the devil and of hell, as their probable portion forever for trivial offences, they should at least be permitted to find refuge, when they seek it, in a Being *all* love, benevolence and mercy. I defy any man, however exemplary in his conduct, who has been bred under the influence of a stern relentless theology, and has once "believed and trembled," ever after wholly to divest himself of superstitious and most appalling fears on the subject of death. It is in vain that reason and revelation seek to dispel these dark visions which clouded his childhood— it is in vain, that when in health he discards the whole doctrine of terror, and leans with hope and confidence on the unfailing mercy of heaven—it is in vain that in his calmer moments, he recognizes in death a process as natural as sleep—that he feels how surely the same hand which upholds him here, will shield him hereafter. Let sickness come, and the pale Phantom rises up before him and mingles its hideous features, with the dregs of the bitter cup which he drinks at the thought of leaving unprotected those whom he dearly loves. An undefined terror creeps over him which he cannot dispel—an evil spirit is raised which he cannot exorcise unless he have grown a very Pharisee. Better be the thoughtless and indifferent Indian than the terror-stricken Christian—but better far to be the *true* Christian, trusting implicitly in the love and goodness of a Being who has created us for some beneficent end, and whose mercy literally "endureth forever."

Under the lead of our Indian guides, we pursued our journey over a scarcely perceptible Indian trail, directly up the steepest part of a huge mountain. We preferred this rugged route to one easier and longer, as it shortened our journey across the Sierra, and opened to us new scenes. After scaling precipices accessible to few animals, save a goat or a California horse, climbing along the sides of yawning chasms, which seemed to invite us to "step in" sociably, and draggling through dense thickets, abhorred by horses, composed of a thorny, bushy, prickly, crooked undergrowth, called "chemisal"—probably from its propensity to tear the very shirt off your back—we attained the summit of the mountain just at sunset. My first glances were cast to the farther side of the Sierra in the direction of our intended route; and as I gazed upon the wild and rugged descent, forming the foreground of this magnificent picture—the faint blue outline of the gigantic and undulating mountains of the Russian river range towering in the dim distance against the horizon, blending earth with heaven—and the broad valley lying between, enveloped in mist, whose subtle tenuity, mingled and combined with the more subtle prismatic rays of the setting sun, producing atmospheric phenomena of endless variety and ravishing beauty—I thought the scene sufficiently compensated the toils of the day's journey. But if this landscape filled the spectator with rapture, what could be said of the peerless scenery which met the eye on turning to the right, and which burst upon me so suddenly that I could scarcely realize I was standing upon the surface of this much-abused earth. I gazed on this glorious spectacle in speechless astonishment, and had I been an enthusiast, my first impulse would have been to bend the knee in adoration. There, spreading out seemingly from our very feet, but far, far below the elevated point on which we stood, lay the expansive Lake, its broad mirror illuminated by the last rays of the setting sun, and its numberless splendid features borrowing enchantment from the last fond smile of the dying day. I feel that it is not for me to attempt a description of such overwhelming grandeur and beauty, and I gladly avail myself of a life-like picture of the scene, drawn by the hand of the wizard limner of Scotland:

> And thus an airy point he won,
> Where, gleaming with the *setting sun,*
> One burnished sheet of living gold
> Loch Katrine lay beneath him rolled.
> In all her length, far winding lay,
> With promontory, creek and bay;
> And islands that, empurpled bright,
> Floated amid the livelier light;
> And mountains, that like giants stand,
> To sentinel enchanted land.
> High on the South, huge Benvenue
> Down on the lake, in masses, threw
> Crags, knolls and mounds, confusedly hurled,
> The fragments of an earlier world.
> A wildering forest feathered o'er
> His ruined sides, and summit hoar;
> While on the North, through middle air,
> Ben-an heaved high his forehead bare.
>> *Lady of the Lake.*

Few white men have visited this magnificent Laguna. According to the best authorities, it is between fifty and sixty miles in length, the width varying at different points; and it contains several inhabitable islands, on which are established populous rancherias, with plantations of corn, calabashes and tobacco. In the course of time it will become famous, and perhaps the "tired denizens" of the Atlantic cities may yet make summer excursions to its glorious shores.

Descending the western slope of the Serrania, we descried a fire in the valley below, and, making for it, we arrived about nine o'clock at the rancho of Don Fernando Feliz, the sentinel on the outskirts of civilization on this side of the mountains. The old gentleman received us with great kindness and hospitality, and we concluded to spend the next day at his rancho to recruit our horses, which were rather "used up" by the difficult passage of the Sierra.

This enterprising ranchero's history is somewhat singular; or rather, his motive for moving so far away from white settlements sounds strangely. It is well-known that some of our western squatters move off in quest of "elbow room," whenever a new settler approaches within the uncomfortable distance of twenty miles. But Don Fernando did not object to the vicinity of society, but wanted more land for his own use. The same American settler would probably occupy only two or three hundred acres, and think that a "mighty smart chance" of a farm; but Don Fernando was in despair because he had only fifteen thousand acres, and could not get more adjoining it. He had been the owner of the magnificent rancho of Novato, on the bay of San Francisco, which I know to be one of the very choicest in California. It contains three square leagues of land, is intersected by a navigable creek, coming to the very door of the house, and into this creek runs a beautiful clear stream of fresh water, which irrigates the rancho; it abounds in excellent pasturage, is of unsurpassed fertility, in the midst of a safe and settled neighborhood, and remote from the wild Indians, who are utterly abhorred by the Spanish Californians. And yet Señor Feliz assured me, that, being a poor man with a large family, he could not manage to get along at Novato, and had been constrained to come thus far, in the very midst of the detested wild Indians, that he might have eight leagues of land—or nearly of forty thousand acres—to say nothing of the declivities of the Sierras on each side of the valley.

Having spent a day with this extensive landed proprietor, it was arranged that his son should accompany us on our journey; and the next morning, bright and early, we prepared to start. An amusing, good-humored altercation here ensued between father and son with respect to the horse the young man should ride. The latter wanted a horse broken to the bit and saddle; but the sagacious senior, perceiving a capital chance of making his boy useful, endeavored to persuade him that he would be much better accommodated on a "potro," or wild colt, which an Indian vaquero was leading. Finally the youth gave in, and, after a short contest, conquered his untamed charger, and we proceeded, in gallant style, down the valley of the Russian river.

This stream flows into the sea between Bodega and the presidio of Ross, the most northern part of settled California. It is probably a subterranean outlet of the Laguna, as all fresh lakes have an outlet. At the upper end of its beautiful valley it sinks into the earth, but soon comes to the surface. The lofty Sierras, which almost lock one end of the valley in their embraces, gradually diverge, until that on the north is merged in the Serrania of Napa and Sonoma, while that on the south-east extends into the vast plain of Santa Rosa, which contains abundance of excellent land, and several valuable ranchos. The river abounds in romantic and secluded spots, where the Naiads might love to disport themselves in the cool, clear wave, and it also affords the more matter-of-fact advantage of water-power for mill seats.

A certain Indian chief, named Pinole Colorado, made one of our party, and as we leisurely "pricked on the plain," the old fellow rode on before to display his finery. One of our men had shot a large bald eagle, which Colorado had stripped of its feathers to decorate himself withal. The feathers

Sketched by J. W. Revere U. S. N.

Lith. of Wm. Endicott & Co. N. York.

A RANCHERO FEAT.

were stuck about his head, the claws adorned his neck, and the ghastly head dangled from his top-knot. His naked skin was daubed with red paint, (whence his name), and he was preparing to make a warlike entrance into his rancheria, where he expected his chaste and elegant attire would create a sensation. Coming to a thicket he suddenly stopped, and made signs to me to do the same.

The reason of this was soon apparent; we had come unawares upon an illustrious stranger, whose reception of us might perhaps have proved unpleasant had we stumbled against him. He was a huge bear lying on his back, and so entirely ignorant of our approach that he was in the most unceremonious and at-home sort of manner playing with his paws, which were sportively elevated in the air. Stringing his bow with the rapidity of lightning, old Colorado shot two arrows up to the feather into the recumbent and unsuspecting foe, and hastily retreated, while I discharged the contents of my holster pistols into the monster as he made towards me. It was no time to stand on a point of honor, so I promptly gave my horse the spur, and he, like a well-trained beast, stood off with a spring to one side. The rest of the party soon came up, and an active, well-mounted, half-breed vaquero, named Hidalgo, whirled his riata with a whiz around the head of the enraged animal, and he was soon despatched, after a sharp and unbearable conflict with the whole party. He was indeed a "rouser." His skin was of a light yellowish brown, grizzled all over with black and white hairs; and he measured seven feet from crown to tail, and nine feet across the hams, the claws and paws being in proportion. The track of this huge plantigrado measured twenty-two inches in length, and eighteen inches across the ball, and had much the appearance of the footprint of a human giant, the ball, sole, heel, and toes, being in the dust like those of a man.

We treated the conquered foe with as little respect as Achilles did the lifeless body of Hector—cutting off his fore-paws, which are excellent eating—being very tender and gelatinous—and robbing him of his grizzly hide. There was a mighty fuss among the horses when we made a disposition of the latter trophy; but we finally tied it to a mare that ran with our caballada, which put the poor beast in coventry, causing her to be avoided by the other horses as if she were the veritable bear in person.

We passed the site of an old rancheria, in a beautiful and celebrated spot by the river's side, which we distinguished by the raised earth where its lodges had once stood. Colorado informed me, that the Spaniards had killed or carried into captivity all its inhabitants. Palmyra and Thebes have left more lasting memorials of the desolating fury of man, and the names of Aurelian and Cambyses have been made famous by their ravages; but in the records of eternal justice the wrongs of the wretched Indian are as legibly written as those of the proudest nations—and his oppressors, however obscure among men, are not unknown to that dread tribunal which shall judge alike all the persecutors of the human race.

Arriving at the rancho of Piña, and that being the centre of an Indian population, I deemed it necessary to hold another talk. A stormy scene ensued. It appeared that old Colorado had accompanied me thus far to make use of my authority to reinstate his tribe in their rancheria and territory lying in the very centre of Chino Piña's rancho. But as the latter had a grant of the land from the Mexican government, and as I had no jurisdiction in the matter, even had I been disposed to interfere, I of course declined complying with the demands of the chief. At this, Colorado laid all the blame of my refusal to young Chino, and insulted him before my face; whereupon, to avoid bloodshed and establish discipline, I had him taken into custody by one of my men, with orders to make him ride on before, and if he attempted to escape, to shoot him. He did escape, however, by diving under his horse and making off in the bushes. Bunk fired at him, but the Indian made good his retreat, owing no doubt to the clemency of the marksman.

Coming to the rancho of Sotoyomé, belonging to Mr. Fitch, an American, we found the matanzas going on, and had a fine chance to witness a complete exhibition of this important operation. Mr. M. Carson, a brother of Kit, the celebrated mountaineer, is the *mayor-domo* of this rancho, which contains eight square leagues of land and ten thousand head of cattle, besides sheep, manadas, &c.

The wild cattle were driven to the *rodea*, a number of half-tamed bullocks called "cabristas," turned among them, and the whole herd—surrounded by vaqueros dashing around them, and urging on the refractory and lazy—were driven towards the corral. Thus, amidst clouds of dust, through which might be caught indistinct glimpses of agitated horns, fierce-rolling eyeballs and elevated tails—an occasional wild-looking, naked Indian vaquero, with his hair and top-knot streaming out, or a Californian vaquero, known by his fluttering *sarape*—the bellowing, rushing herd approached the corral. And now the cabristas, appointed to lead the herd, were loudly called for by the vaqueros with "corral! corral!" "adelante cabristas!"—and the trained animals, quickening their pace, rushed to the front of the herd and towards the opening of the corral. Duped by their leaders, as many a herd of wiser animals have been before, the wild cattle blindly followed, and the whole were snugly secured within the walls of the corral. The vaqueros then entered on horseback—for who should venture in on foot would be instantly gored to death—and, swinging their whizzing riatas, entangled such as were doomed to die. They also threw down young bulls, which were lashed by the horns, through holes bored for the purpose, to tame draught bullocks—an operation called *"mancuerno,"* designed to prepare the animal for working purposes. Proper measures were also taken to prevent the number of bulls from exceeding their due proportion to the gentler sex.

A place was selected near the river—the Russian—and convenient to the corrals, of which there are several large ones—where the operation of skinning, trying out tallow, cutting the flesh into strips to be dried, and all that sort of disgusting thing, was carried on by half-a-dozen "hijos del pais" as superintendents, and any number of Indians as drudges.

The remarks I made concerning the adaptation of the Spanish language to the raising and management of horses, applies with equal force to the case of cattle. If the Spaniards are good for nothing else, there can be no question that they are not excelled as managers of cattle and horses, and to this vocation they are generally devoted wherever they are found. The training of the Californian horses, their unmoveable saddles to which the riata is attached, and their severe bits, are all adapted to this end. I have often witnessed man and horse, made fast to a wild ferocious bull, dash at full speed down a fearful precipice which a practised pedestrian would have hesitated to descend.

It was the month of September, when the bears come down to the plains in search of the ripe acorns which fall to the ground, and which hereafter will furnish food for innumerable swine. We were promised a fight between a bull and bear, but had not time to remain to witness this edifying exhibition of "the noble science of self-defence."

This is a sport often enjoyed by the Californians. The bear being lassoed by the vaqueros is carried to a corral, and the other end of the riata being made fast to a bull, the amiable couple are allowed to fight it out together. A hempen rope of equal size would not bear the severe tension of the horse-hair cord of which the riata is made; and nothing tries its strength more thoroughly than these death-tugs between a bear and a bull. The bear sometimes climbs upon the fence of the corral, but is pulled back again by the bull, and they never abandon the conflict until one or the other is killed. It would seem incredible that the largest and most savage bull could be a match for the crushing force, the terrible scythe-like claws, and the dreadful jaws of a full-grown grizzly bear; but the knowing ones of the California fancy say that it is about an even thing between them, the victory inclining as often to one side as the other. However, I would give odds on the bear.

It is somewhat singular that this system of matching the same kinds of ferocious beasts in deadly conflict, prevails extensively in the more enlightened Atlantic cities, especially in the city of New York. The practise is said to have been borrowed from the people of London, who were ever famous for their pugnacious propensities and their love of cruel sports. And what is quite as remarkable, is the fact that the results of these battles are about equal in California and New York. I have been struck, while reading the newspapers, with the ever-varying fortunes of the field contested by these combatants. One day, I have noticed that the bulls were victorious, and the very next it was announced that the bears were having it all their own way. Sometimes the bears appeared to be keeping the upper-hand for weeks together, and I have sympathised with the unfortunate bulls—when suddenly some very powerful animals of the bovine race appeared to come on the field, and for a succession of weeks to rout all of the ursine breed that ventured to show their noses. It seems a great scandal that these cruel exhibitions should be kept up in the midst of a boasted civilization, and it is respectfully suggested that the civil authorities should interfere and prevent these savage encounters between irrational beasts, which destroy each other to the great moral and pecuniary detriment of the community:—for, of course, where such spectacles prevail, there must be more or less gambling, extending far and wide among the people, producing a lax state of the public morals, and inflicting much misery upon innocent women and children.

When I arrived within two miles of Sonoma, in the plain of a hot-spring, near which the caballada of my troop were accustomed to graze, I was told by the horse-guard that important news had arrived from the officer in command of Fort Sacramento. On reaching my quarters, I received a letter, stating that the Sacramento valley had been invaded by a force of one thousand Wallawalla Indians, the advanced guard of which, consisting of two hundred warriors, had encamped on *Rio de las Plumas* (Feather river), within a day's march of the fort. It therefore became necessary that I should immediately respond to the call made upon my command for assistance.

THE PROSPECT of an engagement with a strong force of warlike savages, at a time when we were threatened with a most tedious tranquillity, was extremely welcome and cheering, especially in view of the fact that the enemy were the aggressors.

The Oregon Indians more nearly resemble those east of the Rocky Mountains than they do the Pacific tribes or families which inhabit California. Instead of being broken up into small communities, they exist in a state of nationality, and consequently are enabled to make, comparatively, powerful warlike demonstrations. They are animated by a more martial spirit than their feeble and indolent southern neighbors, and are capable of overrunning their villages, and exterminating them with very little effort. They also possess, in common with the north-western Indians east of the mountains, much of the spirit of traffic, and devote themselves to hunting, both for the sake of obtaining food, and to procure furs for the purposes of trade. In every physical point, they are a superior race to the Californian Indians, but they do not excel the latter in pursuits requiring the use of intellect, trading excepted. Indeed, there is no reason to doubt that the docile natives of California acquire the arts of civilized life far more readily than their ruder brethren of the north.

In comparing the northern and southern savages who inhabit the Pacific side of the North American continent, the student of history will not fail to hatch theories and arrive at conclusions suggested by the history of Europe, which, after all, *may* not be properly called "the old world" by comparison with America.

The traces, nay the positive evidences, which exist, of an era when the south-western Indians had attained a high civilization—except in their religion, which appears to have been of the lowest grade of idol-worship, polluted by human sacrifices—lead us to inquire into the probable causes of their relapse into utter barbarism. The Indians of Mexico, even at the date of the Spanish conquest, possessed an extensive and powerful empire, and still retained a degree of civilization very far above what is now known among their descendants. To account for their subsequent decline, is simply to know the familiar history of their wrongs. The outrages practised upon them by the conquerors were sufficient to have degraded and broken the spirit and nationality of a people much more hardy and advanced. The descendants of the victors themselves rapidly degenerated when transplanted to that magnificent country, and it is not surprising that the oppressed should sink lower and lower in consequence of the degradation of their oppressors.

But who shall say what point of advancement had been reached by the Mexican Indians centuries before the day of Montezuma?—Even then they preserved the shadow of greatness. Their temples were still remarkable structures, evincing great knowledge of architecture. They possessed national archives, written in hieroglyphic, which are supposed to have carried back their history to a remote antiquity, and which were brutally destroyed by the bigoted priesthood, under the influence of religious fanaticism, or suppressed by the civil authorities for the purpose of removing the last vestige of Indian nationality. Who shall say that the Mexican Indians, in the days of Montezuma, were not infinitely inferior to those who, ages before, had possessed the country? When we remember the stupendous structures, whose scattered remains fill us with astonishment, and almost superstitious awe; when we bear in mind that indubitable indications still exist of vast cities, covering many square miles of territory, filled with sculptured relics of an unknown order of architecture; and when we take into consideration that these ruins must date centuries beyond the era of Cortez—we become bewildered and lost in the mazes of antiquity, and almost shrink from the task of accounting for these vestiges of an earlier world. Still we cannot avoid conjecturing that here was the seat of a powerful empire; and this conviction forces itself so strongly upon our minds, that we cannot help speculating upon the character of the wonderful people who built those extensive cities, whose desolate ruins appeal to us from the gloomy solitudes of ancient forests, which have sprung up in their long-forgotten highways, and, by the simple power of vegetation, have overturned their gorgeous temples and palaces.

Looking far beyond the day of the Spanish conquest, we are constrained to believe, that a comparatively civilized people inhabited Mexico, and in endeavoring to solve the mystery of their disappearance, nothing has seemed more probable than that the *northern* Indians swooped down from their mountains and forests, and overran the effeminate children of the south, sunk in luxury and sloth. When Rome subdued Greece, the Greeks in their turn are said to have vanquished their conquerors, by imparting to them the arts and refinements of civilization. At that time, however, the Romans themselves were making advances in arts as well as arms, and were in a fit state to receive the softening influences of Grecian culture. But when the barbarians of the north overwhelmed the Roman Empire—then the seat of art, literature, and learning—the result was the reverse of that which followed the subjugation of Greece. Barbarism was in the ascendant, and not only rejected all alliance with the humanities, but nearly overwhelmed civilization, which for centuries lurked only in bye-places, while the bulk of Europe was wrapped in the dark pall of ignorance, and governed by the brutal law of physical force, but little improved by the influence of religious superstition and intolerance.

And now for the point of this profound disquisition. Why should not the northern tribes of Indians have overrun Mexico centuries ago, and mingled with the civilized people who built those ancient cities, without wholly destroying them? Why should they not have become inseparably intermingled with the more luxurious southern race, as the conquering Tartars have done with respect to the original Chinese? Why may it not have been that Montezuma flourished at a time when the ancient and almost forgotten arts were in process of restoration, and the people in a transition state, and on the eve of a revival of learning? My theory supposes that the ancient inhabitants were completely merged in the invaders, and that their institutions became extinct, or existed so faintly as to be scarcely perceptible; yet that in process of time a decided improvement took place in the condition of the descendants of the invaders, the feeble light flickering from the Past shedding a dim ray over the dawning Future. But what has this to do with the Indians of California? It has everything to do with them. I will not stop to argue that a country so admirably adapted for the abode of man has been, for many centuries, inhabited by the human race. I will assume thus much, and leave the antediluvians to dispute the postulate if they dare. Now, upon the hypothesis that the savage Northmen penetrated the continent as far south as Mexico, it follows that they passed through California, then perhaps inhabited by a large tribe of Indians, possessing a national character, and having some acquaintance with the arts, but immeasurably behind the mysterious builders of those ruined cities in Mexico and Central America. California, being on the route to the principal seat of conquest, shared the fate which usually attends intervening countries lying on the conqueror's road,—the people being massacred and plundered without mercy. Its proximity to the northern tribes probably subjected it to constant incursions, until its people were so incessantly harassed and persecuted that their bond of union was violently sundered, and they were compelled to seek safety by breaking up into scattered communities, and like the nomadic tribes of Arabia, to shift their habitations from place to place.

Theories are day-dreams, and at the best are scarcely more than "airy nothings." While, therefore, a theorist has no right to plume himself upon his sagacity, the public have as little right to find fault with the exuberance of his fancy. I have stated *my* theory, and any one is welcome to invent a better.

It now became my duty to repel an invasion of the descendants of those desolating conquerors, who ages before had perhaps overrun the Pacific coast, and subverted the empire of the mystic builders of those mighty cities, whose sculptured ruins excite the admiration and amazement of the present generation.

Messengers were despatched in every direction, to raise the entire population of my district, and this levy *en masse* included not only Californians, Americans, and Foreigners, but also Indians. They were directed to report themselves with all convenient speed at Sutter's Fort, it being necessary that I should push forward to the place of rendezvous with all expedition.

Starting without delay with my own troop of "regulars," I bivouacked the first night in the western serrania of the Sacramento Valley, and the next afternoon arrived with my men and caballada on the banks of the great river.

Those who are curious in military matters may like to have a description of a Californian *ponton*. We had no boats, no water equipment of any kind, and yet we crossed the Sacramento with perfect ease and safety, without wetting any of our arms or luggage. We stripped saddles, and all hands went to work cutting the tulé which abounds on the rivers of California. We lashed these monster bulrushes together with our horse-ropes, making them into bundles shaped something like segars, and with these bundles we constructed a raft, upon which we deposited our arms, accoutrements, saddles, and horse-furniture. The floating mass was then paddled over with the greatest ease, the air-chambers of the tulé, as well as the lightness of the material itself, rendering it extremely buoyant.

For the purposes of emigration, the tulé will prove of the greatest utility. On the occasion to which I allude, we could without difficulty have carried artillery across the river, and by making large rafts, any number of men could be ferried across with perfect ease and safety. Horses should be made to swim over, as their cumbrous weight would render it necessary to make very large rafts, while their restiveness might make it exceedingly difficult to float them over on such a fragile bark. The emigrant, however, can, by means of the tulé, cross the river dry-shod himself, and also carry his provisions, wagons, &c., at the expense of a little time spent in constructing a raft. It would be well for those intending to settle in the interior of California, to come prepared with a good supply of rope for the purpose of lashing the rushes together. After a little experience, it will not be considered any thing of a feat to cross rivers in this simple manner. I would also suggest, that the first man who takes pains to build one of these rafts in a workmanlike and substantial manner, and gets possession of a point on the Sacramento where there is a considerable amount of travel, will be able to amass a handsome fortune by carrying over emigrants, and those returning from the mines, with their horses and luggage. A raft built as near as may be in the shape of a scow, covered with a plank floor, and surrounded by a secure railing, would probably do an immense business at any frequented crossing.

Before the tulé was floated, the horses were surrounded by my men, and by dint of shouts and noises of every imaginable description, were forced, greatly against their wills, to take to the water and swim over.

On reaching the opposite bank, a few of them were caught by a party stationed there for the purpose, and the vaqueros mounting them, were enabled to drive the rest to a tongue of land nearly surrounded by the river, where they were secured, and equipped again as easily as if they had been in a corral. The whole operation did not last more than half an hour, and the entire company, caballada, arms and equipments, were, in that brief space, passed safely across a broad and deep river.

We were warmly welcomed at the fort, where preparations were going on for an energetic defence, and such was the alacrity of the inhabitants on the north side of the bay, that, within twenty-four hours after my arrival, I found myself at the head of a force of one hundred and fifty white men of all descriptions, and nearly three hundred Indians, all well armed, and all the whites well-mounted. This was a flattering proof of the estimation in which the United States government was held by the Californians and foreigners of that district.

A hostile visit had been expected for about a year, from an Oregon tribe of Indians, called Walla-Wallas, to avenge the death of a young chief called Elijah, a protégé of the missionaries of that country, and like too many of their proselytes, uniting the vices of the white man to those of the Indian. It was proved to my satisfaction that he was killed by Mr. Cook, an American, residing in California, in a private quarrel, in which he was the aggressor, and that he had previously put one of his own tribe to death for a trifling cause.

The Americans of my party were all armed with rifles; the Californians with lances and riatas; the Indians with bows and arrows, lances and knives, the lance-heads, arrow-points and knives being made of obsidian. The whole party were encamped on the borders of the American Fork, and I immediately proceeded to organize our forces.

The Californians certainly deserved great credit for turning out in such numbers, and showed themselves worthy of becoming citizens of the United States. They brought along a large supply of excellent horses which were of the greatest service, and they took the almost entire charge of the caballada, and of all things pertaining to the horses. With proper drilling, and with officers of the right kind, there is no doubt that the rancheros would make excellent cavalry, for they are by no means deficient in courage, and in the management of their animals are not surpassed by the Cossacks or Mamalukes.

Captain Sutter had called in all his savage Indians, and by way of a caution to evil disposed persons, the gateway of the fort was ornamented with the scalp of an Indian, the long black hair hanging dejectedly down, as if mourning for the death of its late proprietor. I speak lightly of this scalp because it had been the property of an Indian who had been sent since my last visit—it was said by Castro—to burn the wheat crop of New Helvetia, and if possible to kill Captain Sutter himself. In endeavoring to put his nefarious purposes into practice he had met with his death, and his scalp was nailed to the outer-wall to deter others from engaging in similar undertakings.

My arrangements were now entirely completed, and it was extremely gratifying to review such a gallant body of men gathered together at such short notice in a country which a few days before had belonged to a nation at war with our own. I flattered myself that if we came across an enemy we should give a good account of ourselves, and the amphibious position I occupied added zest to the sport in prospect. But accidents will happen in the best regulated families—screws will get loose in the most perfect machinery—there is no use in counting chickens before they are hatched—and there's many a slip between the cup and the lip,—all these philosophical reflections came over me like a wet blanket, when, just as we were about to mount, I was surprised and confounded by a visit from old Yellow-Bird himself, the head-chief of the Walla-wallas, accompanied by other chiefs of his nation. It was very annoying, and I could have wished that the old fellow was farther off, at the head of his Indians, in battle array, while I was leading a most terrific charge into the midst of his warriors. The propensity of men to practice their profession is very striking. The soldier hates to miss a battle; the sailor is furious when he cannot come to an engagement; the lawyer abhors the settlement of a suit which he is cocked and primed to argue, with resistless eloquence and consummate science; and, for aught I know, the doctor secretly regrets the sudden recovery of a promising invalid. I have noticed that boys at a fire look with regret upon the successful efforts of the firemen to extinguish the flames, and absolutely consider themselves defrauded of their rights when the conflagration ceases. Such was my first impulse at being disappointed in my reasonable expectations of a fight with the Indians; but, of course, such unholy regrets very soon vanished.

Old Yellow-Bird and his party came up to the fort on excellent horses, and they were entirely unarmed, well understanding that their weakness would be sure to protect them. He had come to have a "talk;" and as his request to that effect was reasonable, and my military occupation, for the present, in abeyance, I did not hesitate to gratify this highly respectable savage. After the usual preliminaries, he spoke, with commendable brevity, as follows:

"I have come from the forests of Oregon with no hostile intentions. You can see that I speak the truth, because I have brought with me only forty warriors, with their women and little children, and because I am here with few followers, and without arms. We have come to hunt the beasts of the field, and also to trade our horses for cattle; for my people require cattle, which are not so abundant in Oregon as in California. I have come, too, according to the custom of our tribes, to visit the grave of my poor son, Elijah, who was murdered by a white man. But I have not travelled thus far only to mourn. I demand justice! The blood of my slaughtered son calls for vengeance! I have told you what brought me here; and when these objects are accomplished, I shall be satisfied, and shall return peaceably to my own country. When I came to California, I did not know that the Boston men had taken the country from the Spaniards. I am glad to hear it; for I have always been friendly to the Boston men, and have been kind to those who have passed through my territories. It must be plain to you that we did not set out on a hostile expedition against your countrymen."

Having had some experience in making speeches to the Indian aristocracy, I replied to the address of Yellow-Bird without much embarrassment. Those curious in such matters, are welcome to a sketch of my brief remarks:

"I am glad to hear you disclaim hostile intentions. If you continue on friendly terms with our people you will not regret it; and I hope you will let the chiefs in Oregon know that any hostile movement will be severely punished by the powerful nation who possess that territory. You came here to ask vengeance upon the man who killed your son; but you must remember that he was killed before the United States had conquered California. I doubt if our tribunals can properly interfere with offences committed while Mexico owned the country; but I will take the matter into consideration, and if I think it right to interfere at all, I will make the case known to the civil authorities, who will do what is right. It is certain that I cannot take cognizance of it. Proceed with your traffic; visit the grave of your son; and depart in peace to your own country."

As soon as I had concluded these remarks the council broke up, and the old man visited the grave of his son, which was not far off from the fort. Having performed this pious rite, he returned to his camp on Feather river.

The settlers in the valley had become alarmed at the reports of an Indian invasion, and the rumors of war lost nothing by circulation and repetition. As, in the olden times, the feudal vassals flocked, at the first approach of strife, to the strongholds of the bold and doughty barons, so now did the settlers on the Sacramento gather for safety in the fort at New Helvetia. Nor did they give credence to the plausible story of old Yellow-Bird, but imagined that danger was lurking in the movements of the wily savage.

Although I was inclined to believe that the valley was safe enough, the occasion seemed favorable for making a demonstration of our strength to overawe the local Indians, who were sometimes disposed to be troublesome. Not requiring, however, the entire force under my command, I dismissed a portion of the recruits, and proceeding up the valley of the Sacramento as far as the Butes, we encamped in their vicinity. The Butes consist of several remarkable hills, which rise, like pyramids, from the broad bosom of the plain. They are thickly covered with forest trees, and form a striking and agreeable feature in the landscape. In the rainy season, the bears and other animals take refuge in the coverts of these primeval pyramids, which reared their verdant heads heavenward, ere Cheops and Cephrenes were known to fame, and will survive the very memory of the massive piles, which the Egyptians believed would be sempiternal. When the rains are uncommonly heavy, the whole plain is deluged, and the water is sometimes of sufficient depth to be navigable for canoes. The settlers say that the hunting on the Butes is unsurpassed; but, owing to the abundance of the grisly bears, is apt to be attended with danger. These animals are more abundant in the Sacramento valley than in any other part of California; or, probably, than in any section of the continent of America. The great influx of gold seekers to that auriferous region, will doubtless have the effect of very sensibly thinning the ranks of the grisly monsters.

The valley of the Sacramento is still populated by numerous tribes or families of Indians, who live like all California Indians, in independent rancherias. They inhabit various spots along the whole length of the main river, and branch off along the borders of its tributaries. They resemble very closely their brethren of the Laguna and other portions of the Territory, in manners, customs, language, and nastiness.

Before starting on my expedition to the Butes, I had despatched a party of old Indian hunters as scouts, with instructions to scour the entire valley up to the Cañon, or head waters of the Sacramento. These men returned to me at our camp, on a creek near the head of Feather River, to report the result of their reconnoisance, and their account agreed with the facts I am about to relate.

The Walla-wallas had arrived at night-fall at the cabin of the remotest settler, with their whole caballada, which, from the nature of their expedition, was very numerous. The solitary settler was taken all aback, and his fears were not diminished by the fact, that he had some time before been advised that the Walla-wallas contemplated a hostile visit to California. Expecting to obtain authentic information from his wild unbidden guests, he inquired of the head-chief whether there were more warriors behind. Yellow-Bird, understanding neither English nor Spanish, was compelled to resort to signs, and by way of intimating that there were "a few of the same sort left," held up nine of his digits, intending to convey the idea that there were only the same number yet to come in. In fact, he had left on the road nine of his men, who had been wounded in an encounter with a party of the Ishmaelitish Shaste Indians, their wounds being too serious to admit of traveling. The terrified settler—a man by the name of Sill—was exactly in a frame of mind to magnify everything which tended in the least to confirm his fears, and jumped at once at the conclusion, that his visitors were a mere advanced guard, and that the main body of nine hundred fierce warriors remained behind, and were then marching on the trail of the supposed vanguard. Taking counsel of his fears, he seized the first opportunity to slip away from his ill-boding guests, leaving them in undisputed possession of his premises and property; and hastily saddling his fleetest horse he rode as if the fiend were at his heels directly to the Fort. Arrived at a place of safety, he was not slow in justifying his consternation and precipitate flight. He announced, with all the assurance of one who deals with certainties, that the Walla-wallas had at length arrived in force, to harry the farms and carry off the cattle of the settlers, for the purpose of avenging the death of the young chief, Elijah, and that a thousand savage warriors were on their way, breathing nothing but death and desolation, and resolved to make war to the knife upon all the whites who came in their way. From this apocryphal story originated the fearful rumors which were flying through the country, and rousing the peaceful population to take up arms to repel the savage onslaught.

My spies reported that they had scoured the country and could find no trace of any more Walla-wallas besides the little party which had come up to the fort, and they assured us that it was absurd to suppose Yellow-Bird had come with hostile intentions, inasmuch as his band had brought along their women and children.

The effect of this intelligence was quite depressing. My men had hoped to the last that they would have a brush with the Walla-wallas; and one queer fellow, a Canadian Frenchman, named Gendron, proposed that we should now, in view of the unfortunate turn of affairs, exterminate a rancheria or two of the inoffensive Indians of the Sacramento. I regret to say that this humane and equitable proposal was applauded by some of the American settlers, who were bent on having a fight on some terms.

As the more civilized of our party, including myself, did not exactly approve of the views of these respectable gentlemen, on the subject of going to war, I was inclined to march back to the fort, not knowing to what lengths my undisciplined troops might see fit to go if they remained in the wilderness.

Those not familiar with the lawless spirit and brutal insensibility of some of the old backwoodsmen, may suppose that the atrocious proposition of the Canadian was not meant in earnest. But never was a plan of operations more seriously advised in a council of war. The fact was that several of the settlers desired to take advantage of the armed party under my command for the purpose of obtaining Indian servants according to

—"the good old rule,
— the simple plan—
That they should take who have the power,
And they should keep who can."

The Canadian Gendron indeed did not hesitate to admit his desire to gratify an amiable weakness of his lady-love, who was a huge Nez Percé woman, and had followed his rugged fortunes over half the continent. This strapping squaw officiated in our camp as a sort of vivandiere, and made a very creditable "fille du regiment" for the backwoods. She was, indeed, a female of irreproachable character, and her personal attractions were so very peculiar that she might easily have passed through the world with the reputation of a vestal, had not her charms overcome the sensibilities of the amorous Canadian. But this lovely creature had her little foibles, and, among others, was a strong desire to obtain a *fille de chambre*. It was with a view to obtain this appendage of civilized life, that the Canadian had proposed to sack a rancheria; and I could not help laughing at the droll humor and impudence of the fellow when he divulged to me that such was his desire. The bare idea that a semi-barbarian, who had passed his whole life under no better shelter than a few boughs, or at best a skin tent, and who never spent even his winters in a house, should take a fancy for a female attendant—not for himself, but for the fascinating wife of his bosom—was so intensely ludicrous, that I could not rebuke his barbarity so sternly as I meant to do.

Having become satisfied that there were no Walla-wallas in the neighborhood, except those encamped on Feather river, and becoming assured that I could control the evil passions of the few men who had a hankering after Indian captives, I resolved to march to the encampment of old Yellow-Bird. He received us very courteously, and I found most of his party sick, owing to the unhealthy situation of their encampment. The site they had selected was in the bend, just where the Feather river falls into the Sacramento, and a more unhealthy spot could hardly have been chosen.

Most of my men, both whites and Indians, as well as myself, caught the ague and fever from this visit up the Sacramento valley, from which I infer that this meanest of all diseases may be apprehended wherever the tulé lands border the river. The decomposition of the short-lived tulé upon these lands when they are overflowed, generates a miasma which produces that universal malady of new countries. The uplands sloping towards the Sierra, on each side of the tulé plains, are supposed to be comparatively exempt from the prevalence of the curse; but until the country becomes more settled, I should prefer to give the lands, which are periodically over-flowed, as wide a berth as possible.

The settlers in the Sacramento valley, however, pay little regard to the ague and fever. There is nothing like habit in such cases, and the old bel-dame who insisted that eels thought nothing of being skinned, because they were used to it, might not have been so far out of the way after all.

The upland slopes on the side towards the Sierra Nevada are extremely beautiful, and must soon attract the attention of settlers. The waters of the streams proceeding from that Sierra, such as the American Fork, the Co-sunmes, &c., are as clear and as cold as the purest and coldest spring-water. The most admirable locations can be selected, combining many advan-tages, among which are a salubrious climate, fertile land, water-power, and such scenery as ought to soften the natures of the most reckless adven-turers. Mill seats may be found in great abundance; and the quantity of timber on the spot, ready for the axe and saw, is almost inexhaustible.

Returning from my visit to the Walla-wallas, I very foolishly mounted an American mare, instead of a Californian horse, and the beast not only fell with me, but adding insult to injury, saw fit to roll over me. Unfortu-nately, I fell with the guard of my sabre under me, and the weight of the mare caused it to make a very disagreeable impression on my ribs, from the effects of which I did not recover for several days. At this time, my forces had been reduced to my usual command at the garrison, and I now dismissed them, and sent them to Sonoma. I followed after in about a week, but had another attack of fever and ague when I reached Napa val-ley, from which, however, I rapidly recovered, under the genial influence of the exquisite climate, which prevails in that abode of bliss.

THE NEW YEAR (1847) found most of the ships of the Pacific Squadron, lying at anchor in the harbor of San Diego, which town was garrisoned by our forces. Next to the splendid harbor of San Francisco, that of San Diego is the best in California; and it is so graphically and accurately described by Mr. Dana, in his excellent book, entitled "Two Years before the Mast," as to render any further description superfluous.*

From what has been already said, it might be inferred that all the Californians were well satisfied to live under the government of the United States. But such was not the fact. It is a singular trait of human character, that men will adhere to governments to which they are accustomed, even though they be extremely oppressive. So in the matter of religion, the popular faith is maintained by the masses, with a tenacity and fanaticism proportioned to its absurdity, intolerance, and tyrannical administration. Patriotism or loyalty, appears to be inherent in all races of mankind; and in colonies, the mother country—notwithstanding the most monstrous

---

*I would here take occasion to remark, that the encomiums bestowed upon that record of a merchant sailor's life, are richly deserved by the accomplished author, whose description of the sea-coast and harbors of the Pacific, are of unsurpassed excellence. It is much to be regretted, that an opportunity was not afforded to a writer so competent, to describe the glorious scenery of the interior, and also the manners and customs of the people of California.

tyranny—is upheld against all foreign enemies, unless the colonists have come to an open rupture, and violently sundered the chain of sympathy.

California was substantially a Mexican colony; and, although her people groaned beneath the oppression of their feeble step-dame, and had actually driven away the viceroys sent to plunder and harass them, many of them, and perhaps the majority, still preferred her to a power with which she was at war. They were ready at any moment to declare themselves independent of Mexico, but they were not prepared to aid another nation to wrest their province from the mother country. It was the same old story of the quarrel between man and wife, the meddling outsider standing a fair chance of drawing the fire of both parties.

Although I had mingled so much among the rancheros, and was treated by them with so much kindness, I was not surprised to learn that the Californians had risen in arms against our authority. Their leader was a certain Flores, a Mexican officer, holding the rank of captain in the army. This scoundrel, in common with most of the Mexican officers in the country, and many of the most influential Californians, had not scrupled to violate his sacred parole of honor, and place himself at the head of a revolutionary movement. The pledge of neutrality had been exacted by our officers immediately after the hegira of Castro, and after the dispersion of his forces this easy commutation for imprisonment had been eagerly and gratefully accepted by the very men who were now taking the lead in a miserable and ridiculous attempt to drive our forces from California.

It is only just to say, that but comparatively few of the more respectable and wealthy rancheros, openly participated in this futile revolt, although it is probable that the great majority, even of that class at the South, might have done so, had they not been deterred and restrained by prudential motives. But, on the other hand, some of the better class were sincerely desirous that our government might remain in possession of California, and they proved this preference, not by mere words, but by actually enlisting under our banners, to fight against their deluded countrymen. The whole movement was set on foot by discontented Mexican officers, both those belonging to the military establishment of Mexico, and those who had held civil stations under the late provincial government. The subordinates were chiefly composed of vaqueros, landless and dissipated sons of rancheros, and loafers in general, too lazy to work, who came from the neighboring Mexican State of Sonora, with a single eye to the flesh-pots of California.

I am aware that some enthusiastic persons will applaud the devotion of those who, under Flores, sought to throw off their allegiance to the United States, and will bitterly condemn the brave men who joined our standard. While I shall not quarrel with their admiration for the graceless vaga-bonds who rose up against us, I cannot avoid saying a word in behalf of those who adopted the opposite course. If their motive had been base and mercenary, I should freely join in condemning them; but it is my firm opinion that they acted under the influence of principle, and adopted the course which they deemed most beneficial to their country. They had no love for Mexico, and stood in the position of revolted colonists. It is true, they had never come to blows with the mother country, and, indeed, had a forcible collision, which could be called a civil war, ever occurred, it is probable that every inhabitant of California would have received us as cordially as we received the French during our revolutionary struggle. But the rancheros who took sides with us were capable of understanding that Mexico had oppressed California, and their hatred of the tyrants did not require to be baptized in blood. They saw clearly that the destiny of California was indissolubly interwoven with that of the United States, and that no better fate could be in store for her. They saw that annexation to the United States would secure to them true liberty and equal laws, while they had nothing to hope from continuing under Mexican domination, or from the erection of a feeble and sickly sovereignty, on their own account. Their position was one which called forth the exercise of the highest moral courage; for not only did they contend against their countrymen, but also against their kinsmen, the whole white population of California being allied to one another, either by the ties of blood or by intermarriage.

The sudden uprising of the insurgents had been succeeded by the capit-ulation of the garrison of Los Angeles, and a party of the rebels had driven back to their ships, with some loss, the crew of the frigate Savannah, who were stationed near that town.

LIEUTENANT COLONEL FREMONT was on his march to the south with the battalion of Californian volunteers, whose numbers had been swelled by recent emigrants, a large body of whom had entered the country, and eagerly enlisted under the flag of the United States.

About this time the late GENERAL KEARNY arrived in San Diego, after a most toilsome and remarkable march, from Santa Fé, in New Mexico, which was hardly surpassed by the famous expedition of DONIPHAN. Near the former place his slender forces, worn out by the fatigues and sufferings of a long and painful march through a wild and desert country, came to an engagement with the Californians. Notwithstanding that his loss was severe, in proportion to the number of his troops, he was enabled to bring off all his wounded, and was relieved from all apprehension of a further attack, by a detachment of troops sent from the garrison. The following is General Kearny's report of the affair of San Pasqual:

HEAD QUARTERS, ARMY OF THE WEST.
SAN DIEGO, Upper California, December 13, 1846.

SIR:—In my communication to you of yesterday's date, I brought the report of the movements of my guard up to the evening of the fifth instant, in camp near a ranche of Mrs. Stokes, (San Maria), about forty miles from San Diego. Having learned from Captain Gillespie, of the volunteers, that there was an armed party of Californians, with a number of extra horses at San Pasqual, three leagues distant, on a road leading to this place, I sent Lieutenant Hammond, First Dragoons, with a few men, to make a reconnoissance of them. He returned at two in the morning of the sixth instant, reporting that he had found the party in the place mentioned, and that he had been seen though not pursued by them. I then determined that I would march for and attack them by break of day; arrangements accordingly were made for the purpose. My aid-de-camp, Captain Johnston, First Dragoons, was assigned to the command of the advance guard of twelve dragoons mounted on the best horses we had; then followed about fifty dragoons under Captain Moore, mounted, with but few exceptions, on the tired mules they had ridden from Santa Fé, (New Mexico), one thousand and fifty miles; then about twenty volunteers of Captain Gibson's company, under his command and that of Captain Gillespie: then followed our two mountain howitzers with dragoons to manage them, and under the command of Lieutenant Davidson of the regiment: the remainder of the dragoons, volunteers, and citizens employed by the officers of the staff, &c., were placed under the command of

Major Swords, (quartermaster), with orders to follow on our trail with the baggage, and to see to its safety. As the day (December 6th) dawned, we approached the enemy at San Pasqual, who was already in the saddle, when Captain Johnston made a furious charge upon them with his advanced guard, and was in a short time after supported by the dragoons, soon after which the enemy gave way, having kept up from the beginning a continued fire upon us; upon the retreat of the enemy, Captain Moore led off rapidly in pursuit, accompanied by the dragoons mounted on horses, and was followed, though slowly, by the others on their tired mules. The enemy, well mounted and among the best horsemen in the world, after retreating about half a mile, and seeing an interval between Captain Moore with his advance and the dragoons coming to his support, rallied their whole force, charged with their lances, and on account of their greatly superior numbers, but few of us in front remained untouched; for five minutes they held the ground from us, when our men coming up, we again drove them and they fled from the field not to return to it, which we occupied and encamped upon. A most melancholy duty now remains for me: it is to report the death of my aid-de-camp, Captain Johnston, who was shot dead at the commencement of the action; of Captain Moore, who was lanced just previous to the final retreat of the enemy; and of Lieutenant Hammond, also lanced, and who survived but a few hours. We had also, killed, two sergeants, two corporals, and ten privates of the First Dragoons; one private of the volunteers, and one man engaged in the topographical department. Among the wounded are myself, (in two places), Lieutenant Wamer, Topographical Engineers, (in three places), Captain Gillespie and Captain Gibson of the Volunteers, (the former in three places), one sergeant, one bugler, and nine privates of the dragoons; many of them receiving from two to ten lance wounds, most of them when unhorsed, and incapable of resistance. Our howitzers were not brought into the action, but coming to the front at the close of it, before they were turned so as to admit of being fired upon the retreating enemy, the two mules before one of them got alarmed, and freeing themselves from their drivers ran off among the enemy, and was thus lost to us. The enemy proved to be a party of about one hundred and sixty Californians, under Andreas Pico, brother of late governor. The number of their dead and wounded must have been considerable, though I have no means of ascertaining how many, as just previous to their final retreat they carried off all excepting six. The great number of killed and wounded proves that our officers and men have fully sustained the high character and reputation of our troops, and the victory thus gained over more than double our force may assist in forming the wreath of our national glory. I have to return my thanks to many for their gallantry and good conduct on the field, and particularly to Captain Turner, First Dragoons, (A. A. A. G.), and to Lieutenant Emory, (Topographical Engineers), who were active in performance of their duties, and in conveying orders from me to the command.

On the morning of the seventh, having made ambulances for our wounded and interred the dead, we proceeded on our march, when the enemy showed himself occupying the hills in our front, which they left as we approached till reaching San Barnardo, a party of them took possession of a hill near to it, and maintained their position until attacked by our advance, who quickly drove them from it, killing and wounding five of their number, with no loss on our part.

On account of our wounded men, and upon the report of the surgeon that rest was necessary for them, we remained at this place till the morning of the eleventh, when Lieutenant Gray, of the Navy, in command of a party of sailors and marines sent out from San Diego by Commodore Stockton, joined us. We proceeded at 10 A.M., the enemy no longer showing himself, and on the twelfth (yesterday) we reached this place; and I have now to offer my thanks to Commodore Stockton, and all of his gallant command, for the very many kind attentions we have received and continue to receive from them.

Very respectfully, your obedient servant,

S. W. KEARNY,
Brigadier General U. S. A.

Brigadier General R. JONES,
Adjutant General U. S. A.

The eminent services of COMMODORE STOCKTON, at this most important and critical juncture, can hardly be too highly extolled. While the party-press at home were making free with his proclamations, and denouncing the decided course which he had taken the responsibility to adopt, those who were at the seat of war regarded him as the sheet-anchor of their hopes, and were able to see that his whole conduct was suited to the emergency which had arisen. To his gallantry, wisdom, sagacity and prudence; to his timely and energetic measures, the people of the United States are chiefly indebted for the rapid and final suppression of the Californian insurrection, which, at once and forever, sealed the destiny of the most magnificent and opulent territory in the world.

In the existing state of affairs, the Californian movement, although ultimately hopeless, possessed the elements of temporary success. Their forces were easily kept on foot—for the Californians are a hardy race, and will undergo any amount of fatigue, so long as they are well mounted. In their own climate they are regular Cossacks, so far as regards sleeping at night in the open air, and subsisting on the country people, whether friends or foes. They are the best fellows in the world to send on foraging expeditions, and they will be sure to quarter themselves on somebody. They had the advantage of a perfect knowledge of the country, and possessed the secret sympathy of many of the rancheros who took no active part in the rebellion. They thus enjoyed a monopoly of the horses; and all the beef, tortillas, and other articles of the commissariat which they required, were to be had by them everywhere. They had a persuasive way of their own for obtaining everything they stood in need of; and not the most lukewarm or miserly of their countrymen dared to make a complaint, well knowing that death would be the consequence of withholding or begrudging supplies. Thus their riatas fell with impunity on every man's cattle; these lawless appropriations being made in the name of "La Patria"—a cause which recognizes no "vacas agenas," or cattle of other people. It is impossible to tell where this system of patriotic brigandage would have ended, had it not been for the prompt and energetic measures adopted at this crisis by the Commander-in-Chief.

Few men, holding the rank of Commodore Stockton, would have ventured to assume the responsibility which he took upon himself on this occasion; and, perhaps, nothing short of imperative necessity, would have justified the boldness of his measures. Without delay or hesitation he caused his ships to be abandoned by their crews, and as soon as these brave tars were landed, they were immediately converted into an effective force of infantry and artillery. Jack is amphibious. He will fight like a lion amidst the waste of waters in defence of the wooden walls, and when on shore he will pitch, pell-mell, into the enemy, or march up undaunted to the cannon's mouth.

Although the American residents in the country had turned out in considerable numbers, and with great alacrity, to defend their homes, and sustain the supremacy of their dear native land, they were very indifferently organized, having but few officers of the regular service to teach them discipline and tactics. Most of their companies were commanded by officers elected from their own ranks—brave and hardy yeomen, it is true, and men of excellent character, but almost totally uneducated, and wholly unskilled in civilized warfare, their stock of military knowledge having been acquired in border warfare with the Indians. There was not a bayonet to be found among them, the whole party being armed with rifles and hunting equipments, with the usual allowance of revolvers and bowie-knives.

The Californians had complete possession of the principal points, and possessed great advantages from their superior skill in horsemanship. Their good-understanding and persuasive arts with the rancheros, and their facilities for driving cattle, placed the American forces in a quandary for supplies of provisions, which were not to be obtained without active effort. The American settlers were more annoyed in this particular than the Tarpaulin regulars; for, while the former were forced to depend on their own skill and good-luck for food, the sailors could fall back on their salt-junk, bread, and whiskey.

After being drilled and equipped as thoroughly as was possible, under the circumstances, the American forces, consisting of one company of United States dragoons, the sailor artillery and infantry, one company of San Diego volunteers, under the command of Captain Santiago Arguello, and Captain Gillespie's company of rifles—in all about five hundred men—marched out of San Diego, and took the road to the Angelic capital.

On the eighth day of January, 1847—the anniversary of a day famous in the annals of our country—the river San Gabriel was crossed by this gallant little band, in the face of the enemy's artillery and cavalry. On the ninth, a skirmish took place, with a trifling loss on our side, and without materially impeding the march of our forces. On the tenth the American troops entered Los Angeles, and the stripes and stars once more supplanted the conquered flag of Mexico. The following is General Kearny's report of the actions of the eighth and ninth:

HEAD QUARTERS, ARMY OF THE WEST,
CIUDAD DE LOS ANGELES, Upper California, Jan. 12, 1847.

SIR:—I have the honor to report, that, at the request of Commodore R. F. Stockton, (who in September last assumed the title of Governor of California), I consented to take command of an expedition to this place— the capital of the country—and that on the twenty-ninth of December, I left San Diego with about five hundred men, consisting of sixty dismount- ed dragoons, under Captain Turner; fifty California volunteers, and the remainder of marines and sailors, with a battery of artillery. Lieutenant Emory (Topographical Engineers) acted as assistant adjutant general. Commodore Stockton accompanied us. We proceeded on our route with- out seeing the enemy till on the eighth instant, when they showed them- selves in full force of six hundred mounted men, with four pieces of artil- lery, under their Governor Flores, occupying the heights in front of us, which commanded the crossing of the river San Gabriel, and they ready to oppose our further progress. The necessary disposition of our troops was immediately made, by covering our front with a strong party of skirmish- ers, placing our wagons and baggage train in rear of them, and protecting the flanks and rear with the remainder of the command. We then pro- ceeded, forded the river, carried the heights, and drove the enemy from them, after an action of about one hour and a half, during which they made a charge upon our left flank, which was repulsed; soon after which they retreated, and left us in possession of the field, on which we en- camped that night.

The next day (the ninth instant) we proceeded on our march at the usual hour, the enemy in front and on our flanks, and when we reached the plains of the Mesa, their artillery again opened upon us, when their fire was returned by our guns as we advanced; and after hovering around and near us for about two hours, occasionally skirmishing with us during that time, they concentrated their force and made another charge on our left flank, which was quickly repulsed, shortly after which they retired, we continuing our march; and in the afternoon encamped on the bank of the Mesa three miles below this city, which we entered the following morning without further molestation.

Our loss, in the actions of the eighth and ninth instant, was small, being one private killed, and two officers (Lieutenant Rowlin of the Navy, and Captain Gillespie of the Volunteers) and eleven privates wounded. The enemy, mounted on fine horses and being the best riders in the world, carried off their killed and wounded, and we know not the number of them, though it must have been considerable.

Very respectfully, your obedient servant,

S. W. KEARNY,
Brigadier General U. S. A.

To Brigadier General R. JONES,
Adjutant General U. S. A., Washington.

LIEUTENANT COLONEL FREMONT was, in the meantime, advancing from the north with a body of five hundred men, provided with artillery, and on his way, fell in with the scattered forces of the Californians, and concluded with them a treaty of peace. He then proceeded on his march, and joined the commodore at Los Angeles.

All parties now seemed to have ceased hostilities, and perfect tranquillity ensued on the re-capture of Los Angeles. The Californians, tired of war's alarms, had quietly dispersed and gone back to their ranchos; the Mexican leaders and other vagabonds, "sloped" in the direction of Sonora; the American settlers returned to their farms; the sailors marched in triumph to their ships; and what finally became of the detachment of regular troops who entered California, via New Mexico, under the efficient command of Colonel Cooke, of the United States Army, I do not at this moment remember.

The only other action of any moment—besides those of the eighth and ninth of January, and the affair at San Pasqual—which occurred during the conquest of California, was a skirmish between the party of rifles, led by Mr. Burrows, and a superior force of Californians, who were, however, routed, with a loss of several killed and wounded. Poor Burrows, while gallantly charging, far in advance of his men, having discharged his pistols and rifle, and while continuing the unequal conflict with the latter weapon clubbed, was shot dead by a pistol fired by a Californian. He was a gallant young man, and greatly esteemed by all who knew him. Peace to his ashes.

Of the unhappy differences which existed between Commodore Stockton and General Kearny, it hardly becomes me to speak; much less is it within my province to comment upon the more serious disagreements which sprung up between the General and Colonel Fremont. The whole controversy is familiar to the people of the United States, and to their deliberate and impartial judgment, it may safely be submitted. My own opinion is, of course, made up, and it is not difficult to determine the side to which I lean; but I am restrained from dwelling on these little troubles —which will happen in the best regulated service—not only from respect for the memory of the dead, but also, from an earnest hope, that those unpleasant passages may be forgotten, and justice be done to the gallantry, good conduct, and honest motives of all who were engaged in the conquest of California. Although no engagement took place which could be dignified by the name of a battle, still there are laurels enough to be divided among all who planned the operations, and who led the troops and tars of our country to victory.

The people of California make admirable partisan soldiers, and if led and disciplined by competent officers, would probably make as good cavalry as any in the world. It was generally admitted by the officers who saw them under probation, that they were remarkably steady under the galling fire of the squares at San Gabriel and the Meza, but not understanding how to charge "en escadron," they could not penetrate the squares.

Their officers, instead of encouraging their men, by leading them on in person to the conflict, were generally the most arrant cowards, as the Californians themselves admitted. Their chief anxiety seemed to be to keep out of harm's way, and they much preferred backing their friends to fronting their foes. Just imagine a set of fellows in epaulettes, keeping *behind* their men, and urging them forward with cries of "Anda! vete muchachos!"—"go ahead, boys!" From this valorous practice they acquired the name of "animadores," or animators—a title bestowed in derision. I have met with instances of similar officers, in other parts of the world, and the most notable case was the following:

On the east coast of Africa, there is a place called Mombus. It is a good harbor, with an island lying at the mouth of it, on which stands a castle commanding both the entrances from the sea. The possession of this place being coveted by Syeed Bin Sultaun, Imaum of Muscat—although owned by the Portuguese—who maintained there a strong garrison—he blockaded it with his ships, and took along with him a large land force. The Imaum's troops are his own slaves, but the Mussulmen are excellent masters, and liberate their bondsmen on the easy condition of their embracing the religion of Islam. The blacks of that part of Africa lying in the dominions of the Imaum of Muscat, south of Cape Guardafui, are hardy and valiant troops. Their sole arms, however, consist of a light javelin and a long, straight broadsword. The latter is their favorite weapon, and is invariably accompanied with a small conical target or shield, of rhinoceros' hide, about fourteen inches in diameter, which will resist a musket-ball. The Imaum's people in Zanzibar and other places, strut about with their long swords hanging from the shoulder to the heel; the shield being tied by a thong to the scabbard, and balanced on the wearer's breast. I have been struck with the martial appearance of these colored gentlemen when thus arrayed, looking like living statues cut from ebony, their bodies being wholly unclothed and well greased with palm oil.

Well,—to return from this digression within a digression,—the Imaum finding the Portuguese obstinate in holding out their town and fort, in spite of his blockade, hit upon an ingenious plan to possess himself of both. Standing in with his ships at night, just out of gun-shot, he manned all the boats of the squadron, and ordering into them five hundred of these "sword and buckler" men, he shoved off with muffled oars. Pulling close under the walls, he disembarked these men silently, and immediately pulled off a short distance from the beach. The Imaum now assuming the character of an "animator," addressed the men in person from his gig, in a tone too low to be heard by the enemy's garrison, amidst the plashing of the waves. In a few words, he appealed feelingly to their courage and fidelity, and throwing to the intrepid eunuch who led the party his blood-red flag, concluded his remarks to his astounded auditors in these words: "I am resolved to possess that fort by morning, and I command you to hoist that flag on the castle before to-morrow's light. If you remain on the beach the enemy will probably exterminate you at the dawn of day; but if he foolishly spares you, and that flag is not floating from the castle by day-light, I will open *my* fire, not on the walls of the fort, but on *you*." He then coolly left the bewildered negroes to their fate, and regained his ship. How many of this devoted forlorn hope were slain I know not; but when the first gray streaks of day visited the castle of Mombus, that blood-red flag was streaming from its battlements, the garrison had passed beneath the edge of the sword, and the Imaum's ships soon standing in with the morning sea-breeze, the town and its dependencies capitulated. How men so slightly armed succeeded in this wonderful exploit is one of those military mysteries which I shall not try to unravel, but it is certain that, like the Californians, they had the advantage of a capital "animator."

HAVING HAD OPPORTUNITIES to become acquainted with the characteristics, manners, and customs of the native Californians, both of the Upper and Lower Provinces, I will attempt to give some account of these people at large. Hitherto, I have spoken of the rancheros or landed proprietors, but they are far from including the entire white population of Spanish descent.

The people of the southern portion of Upper California, and those of the Lower Province, resemble the inhabitants of Mexico, with whom the reader has been made pretty well acquainted by means of the late war. But, although the resemblance is strong, it is not to be denied that even the more southerly Californians are physically far superior to the Mexicans. They are a larger, more robust, more manly looking race, and this superiority is probably owing partly to the salubrity of their climate, and partly to their food, which consists principally of beef. The diet of the Californians, indeed, is so nearly confined to animal food, that the church grants them a dispensation on her meagre or banyan days. A dispensation to the Mexicans would be little better than a farce, as they are in a state of comparative starvation all the year round, and do not probably fast much more during Lent than at Christmas.

In energy of character, and in point of courage, the Californians far surpass their southern neighbors. That the former are by all odds superior as rancheros and herdsmen is admitted by the Mexicans themselves; nor do I believe it possible, that any people could surpass the Californians in horsemanship, or excel them in the masterly use of the riata or lasso.

Gambling is a universal practice among all classes of Spanish Californians, and it is with them an absorbing and ruling passion, to the indulgence of which they devote their whole energy. Their favorite game of cards is "monte," and when the rancheros and other classes get fairly started at this exciting game, they "go it with a perfect looseness." The recklessness with which they will stake all they possess on a deal of cards is perfectly astounding, and this seductive vice, if persisted in, will ultimately prove ruinous to hundreds of the "hijos del pais."

In connection with this profligate habit of gambling, it is proper to allude to a remarkable social peculiarity of the Californians. They are not Fourierites; for every married man lives in his own house with his own family, and every married woman rocks her own babies and cooks her own dinner. Nor are they communists; for every man has a distinctive title to his own goods, and disposes of them just as he pleases. And yet it may be almost said, that no man really owns what is nominally his, and is liable to be stripped of his possessions without his consent by the mere force of public opinion. Let me explain.

The Californians are nearly all related or connected in some way or other, the principal families being few in number—their branches, offshoots, and ramifications extending in all directions. A single family name will have a thousand representatives—all derived from the same stock. The clanship of Scotland, and the cousin-ship of New England, are not more remarkable than the kinsmanship of California. The larger the family circle the more important the family, and the Californians therefore take the greatest pride in owning their numerous relatives, and esteem it a sacred duty to succor them when in distress. From this extensive family connection and family feeling has grown up a public opinion more despotic than any law ever devised by the wit of man. Burke has remarked, that ancient chivalry, in taking leave of the world, has left behind it the "point of honor." This valuable legacy has of late years been rejected not only by civilians, but by some military men of unsullied reputation. But

the "point of honor" in California is something very different from the
duello. It consists in honoring, to any practicable extent, the drafts of
thriftless and vicious relations. The payment of a gambling debt is nominally a "point of honor" everywhere; but in California it is "*the* point of
honor," not only with the loser, but with all his relatives and friends. If a
worthless vagabond is unlucky at cards, he does not scruple to involve his
family connexions in his own ruin, and the kinsman, however remote, who
refuses to pay a "draw" for a gambling debt, is looked upon with sovereign
contempt by his countrymen. No matter how great the inconvenience, it
is expected that the man who is able to pay, shall extricate his most distant
connexion from the weight of an obligation incurred by gambling. Other
debts are of little moment; they will be put off to the last, and avoided
altogether if possible; but a gambling debt admits of no subterfuge or
delay, but bears on its face a valid and confidential consideration.

The foreign sharpers are well aware of this generous failing in the Californian character, and are not slow to take advantage of it. On a feast day,
they are to be seen encouraging the unlucky ranchero—stimulated with
aqua ardiente and wine—to play deeply, and they eagerly supply him with
ready-money, knowing that their benevolent loans partake of the sacred
character of the gambling debt they are intended to pay. If the money is
not convenient, the heartless speculator furnishes the victim with an order
for goods, at extortionate prices, provided the winner will accept that as a
substitute for the cash. In return for these little accommodations, the lender
takes on the spot an order for cattle, horses, and hides, and sometimes carries the joke so far as to take a conveyance of the poor fellow's rancho.

But if the loser at monte has nothing of his own, he does not hesitate to
give an order on some unlucky kinsman for the amount of his losses. Nor
is this resource confined to connexions by consanguinity. In addition to
the ties of blood and wedlock, is that of "compadre" or gossip, which is
still looked upon as a paternal connexion, and is established merely by
consenting to be godfather to a child. Thus, if one of the "hijos del pais"
goes to a fiesta at the mission of San Juan, San Luis or elsewhere, and, when
under the influence of wine, is unlucky at monte, he first stakes his cattle,
horses, and other property on his rancho, next his horse, saddle, and bridle,
with which he came to the feast, and finally his very wearing apparel. If
the cards still run against him, he does not scruple to give an order on a

"tio," or uncle, or a "prinio," or cousin, for the needful quantity of horses and cattle. After running through with his next of kin, he brings up with the luckless compadre; and after he is victimised, if the cards are still adverse, the broken gambler coolly walks off to the nearest ball or fandango, and dances "dull care away."

The unlucky and unconscious relative or gossip, who is perhaps, quietly attending to the affairs of his rancho, and striving to support a needy family, is suddenly aroused to a sense of the situation of his graceless spendthrift kinsman and to his own misfortune, by the presentation of the order, which he *must* pay, or incur the displeasure and scorn of the whole community, and be everywhere pointed at as a mean contemptible fellow, regardless of honor, and faithless to all generous and Christian principles. If the victim venture to expostulate with the author of his calamity, and request him never again to get both parties into such a sorry scrape, the reply is invariably, "Oh! my friend, our relations to each other are confidential!"—and with this powerful argument the obligation is cancelled.

This absurd and vicious custom speaks favorably for the amiable and affectionate disposition of the people, but it almost prevents the accumulation of any property which the ranchero can call his own.

It is a melancholy fact, that the wealth of many foreigners has been acquired by taking advantage of the peculiar passions and weaknesses of the rancheros and their relatives; but I would not be understood as intimating that *all* the foreigners are willing to engage in these nefarious practices. Many of them are industrious, hard working men, who live wholly by honest means. All the mechanic occupations are in their hands, and they monopolise the whole traffic of the country, the Californians being naturally averse from attending to any other business than that of raising cattle and horses. From this circumstance, the Californians have fallen into a habit of underrating the capacity and character of foreigners, and look upon them as a sordid race, good for nothing but money-making. They look upon the "cuereros" and "cuereritos" as fair game, and consider it a feat indicating "mucho talento" to weather them.

I will mention one or two instances of the practise of gambling away the property of others, which have fallen under my own observation.

I once knew a young man, after losing at gambling all that he possessed in the world, to stake a vineyard and garden belonging to an aged female relative, who was at the time absent from her little property. She had no other dependence for a livelihood, but derived from this little possession a scanty but certain subsistence. The cards were against the heartless gambler, and the poor woman's humble home was lost. She gave it up, and never retrieved it, and was thrown upon the charity of the world for the remnant of her miserable days.

I personally knew of another case of a young ranchero, who staked at monte, the cattle and horses of his compadre. But it so happened, that in this instance the worthy gossip was a foreigner, and when the order was presented to him, he laughed in the face of the bearer, and sent him off with a flea in his ear. He was ever afterwards looked upon as a miserable, miserly, scurvy fellow; but he bore the pressure of public opprobrium far more philosophically than he would have done the loss of his property. Like the miser in Horace, he could say,—

> "—Populus me sibilat, at mihi plaudo
> Ipse domi, simul ac Nummos contemplor in arco."

During my travels in the valley in the Russian river, a story was related to me which has some bearing upon the gambling customs of the Californians, and as I may not find another opportunity to repeat it, I will insert in this place the

STORY OF RAMON AND DOLORES

One beautiful day, when I was out on a hunting excursion, I came to a lovely glade in the valley of the Russian River. At a little distance a smoke arose, and making towards it, I perceived the ruins of a house, which a young man was apparently surveying with melancholy interest.

It was, or rather had been, an adobe house, similar to all the rancho houses of the country, and its ruined and desolate walls bore marks of the ravages of fire. The young man was evidently a Californian. His "dolman" (jacket) was handsomely embroidered, his "calzoneros" (riding trousers) were trimmed with a profusion of little dangling silver buttons, and he wore on his head a handsome broad-rimmed sombrero. His whole appearance evinced that he was a person of the better class of the "hijos del pais." I accosted him, and in reply, he politely touched his hat, with the native courtesy of all Californians, and invited me to alight and accompany him to his temporary encampment. It was near at hand, and consisted of a sylvan bower of a picturesque form, and made of boughs; its leafy shade making it quite a pleasant residence during the dry season. Being pressed to remain all night, I consented to do so, with many thanks.

Our supper was cooked by an old lady, the mother of the young man whom I had met at the ruined house. Early the next morning, while the old lady was preparing breakfast in the absence of the young man, who had gone with three or four Indian servants to the ruins of the house to commence cleaning up the rubbish, and get ready for rebuilding—my curiosity being excited by the strange spectacle of Spaniards coming apparently to establish themselves in a part of the country so distant from their compatriots, I questioned my good hostess concerning their history, and as delicately as possible inquired why the young man appeared so downcast and unhappy?

"Ah! señor," said she, "my poor Ramon has good reason not to love this valley, although it looks so beautiful; and if it were not that he has papers taken out for this tract of land, and that his brothers and he cannot agree on the family rancho near the lower Pueblo, we should never have come to this distant and solitary place."

She then, with many "gritas" (bewailings), and with frequent pauses—being interrupted by agonising emotions of grief and anguish—related to me her sorrowful story, pretty nearly as follows:—

"I am the widowed mother of nine living children. Three years ago, Ramon Sepulveda, my son, whom you see at work yonder among the adobes of the ruined house, came of lawful age. Although he is the third of my sons, he was always my favorite. My two eldest boys, though handsome and dashing fellows enough, and brave besides, as well as excellent vaqueros and skilful rancheros, were reckless gamblers, and thriftless in their management of our paternal rancho, which was the sole dependence of our numerous family. They frequently spent in a single week, when started on their course of dissipation, all our means for the whole year. We relied for support on the hides and tallow produced on the rancho, and those were sufficient to have made us independent with the least frugality.

"Ramon, on the contrary, who was steady and prudent, would remonstrate with his brothers, and beg them to remember that our rancho was much in debt through their extravagance and waste, and that the cuereros, when they came to the rancho at the time of the August matanzas, were pressing for the payment of their debts. The elder brothers would often listen to these wise counsels, and for a few days, or even weeks, be more industrious, and seem anxious to do better. I would fondly imagine that all was going on right again at 'Los Alizos'.* But at length, getting weary of work, and giving way to their evil propensities, they would ride off to the Pueblo, pretending that they only wanted to rest for a while and see their relations. But very soon they would be enticed away and take to drinking and playing monte, forgetting that 'the best throw at dice is no throw at all', and finally come back to me stripped even to their clothes and saddles, and much in debt besides.

"At length, in consequence of frequent expostulations, my dear Ramon, the only support and comfort I had among them, began to be regarded as a mean-spirited fellow and a sneak, who had not the spunk to go to town and drink and gamble among the 'caballeros'.

"Thus matters went on, until one day after the feast of Santa Clara, Juan and Antonio returned from the Pueblo. After hanging around sheepishly for a day or two, evidently conscious of guilt, and hardly looking either Ramon or myself in the face, they mounted their horses and rode off, as they said, on a visit to Santa Barbara, where a ship, with goods, was lying. They said they were going to purchase a few pieces of 'manta', (coarse cotton,) for Indian shirts, and to propitiate me they took advantage of a wish I had expressed a day or two before, to have some of the same goods.

"The very next day after their departure, an American came to the rancho and put into our hands a 'libranza', (draft or order,) for one hundred head of vaquillas, (heifers,) and two horses, one of them a noble iron-gray, a favorite of my son Ramon, and an animal which he prized above any other horse on the rancho. And why should he not? That horse was his familiar friend. He had frequently lassoed bears with him single-handed, and used him exclusively in any feat among the cattle on the place requiring great dexterity. Indeed, 'El Rey' knew his duty better than many men, good vaqueros too, dumb beast though he was. No wonder then that Antonio and Juan kept out of the way, for the horse was 'un caballo conocido', (a well-known horse).

"Ramon was in despair at this last, most ungrateful, unprincipled blow, dealt by brothers for whom he had vainly toiled; and, although he took

---

* "The Sycamores,"—the name of the rancho.

pains to conceal from me his dissatisfaction, I could see very plainly how keenly he suffered.

"The custom of the country made it necessary to acknowledge the order, signed as it was by my two eldest sons; and Ramon gave the necessary orders to our mayor-domo to drive the cattle up to the corral to be ironed with the mark of sale ('venta') on the shoulders; and he himself mounted El Rey for the last time, to see in person that his orders were properly executed. Custom, señor, forbade the non-payment of the debt, for all our relatives in the country would have scouted us for not assisting those of our own blood with the last vestige of our means.

"On the return of my prodigal sons, I complained bitterly to them for depriving me, a widow and their mother, of my little support, at a time when we were in debt already far beyond our resources, and I dwelt particularly on the turpitude of their robbing poor Ramon of his favorite horse. They seemed ashamed and penitent for a short time; but before many days, they openly expressed their regret that they had not procured more money while they were about it. In fact, they had not received for the cattle and horses which they sold, more than a third of their real value. It is, indeed, ever so with the bargains of the avaricious foreigners, who are always awake to the faults and follies of our young men, and are greedy to advance them money when they get excited by play and drink, as my sons were in this instance. Although they are your countrymen, señor, you know as well as I do that this is the case in California, and that they enrich themselves by administering to our evil passions, and taking advantage of them to our ruin.

"Well; Ramon came to me one day after this last occurrence, and said, 'Mother, I have resolved to leave this part of the country, and go to the north side of the Bay, and I am going to the capital to-morrow to get out papers for a rancho there. Every one who has been there says it is a much finer country than this, and I would go anywhere rather than live here any longer, exposed to the dissipated and gambling habits of my brothers. I have asked Dolores if she will marry me and go along with me, and the dear angel has made me strong and happy by saying that she will accompany me to the world's end'.

"Maria de los Dolores, and her sister Anita, were the two beautiful daughters of Don Fernando Soto, who owned the next rancho of San

Nicolas, and was an excellent old man. Ramon had loved Dolores for two years, and her sister was engaged to José Antonio, my second son; but, owing to his scape-grace habits, they could not be married, and old Don Fernando was trying to break off the match altogether.

"Ah! señor, you should have seen the beautiful Dolores at this spring-time of her life, when she gave her warm heart and willing hand to the son of my hopes, and was ready to follow him joyfully to the ends of the earth. She was very beautiful, too beautiful for this wretched earth. She was taller than most women, but lithe and graceful as the willow. When she came into a room, the grace and cordiality of her salute, went directly to one's heart. She was just fifteen, which, with us, is a mature age for marriage. In the dance she moved like a celestial vision, and ravished all who looked upon her. She was not dark, like most of our maidens, but her skin, as soft as any satin, was almost a pure white, with just enough of a faint flush of the olive mingled with the rose, to relieve it from any sickly look. You should have seen her hair, so long, so thick, so glossy, and so jetty black, and hanging around her lovely neck and shoulders, in a thousand raven ringlets. Her great almond-shaped eyes were as blue as yonder heaven; and the long black lashes gave them a strange and more than mortal expression. I never saw such lips—so full, so fresh, so ripe, so rosy red. And when she smiled, what sight could be more beautiful than her white and even teeth, more radiant than pearls, every one of which appeared to laugh at you. Why should I speak of her admirably rounded arms, her exquisite feet, her beautiful neck and swelling breast?

"Her dress was always light and careless, but everything she put on, seemed to borrow beauty. Everybody that saw her said she must have lived abroad, because her manners were so perfect and easy. The very hide seekers, who have no souls, were awe-struck in her presence, and treated her as if she had been a superior being. And so she was, señor. All those exquisite outward charms were only baubles and dross compared with the soul within, and which seemed to shine out in all her personal attractions. She had learned to read and write, and knew more than any other maiden I ever saw. But I did not think much of that. It was her angelic disposition, her heavenly purity, which bound me to her as strongly as if she had been my own child. Ah! señor, it breaks my poor heart to think of dear Dolores, as she looked when she so freely gave her hand and heart to the only man I ever knew that was worthy of her!"

After a few convulsive sobs, checked by a strong effort, the old lady continued:

"The thought of ever quitting 'The Sycamores', in which I had been living so long and quietly with my dear husband and family, had never entered my head, and I gave Ramon a positive refusal. He went, however, to Monterey, saw the governor, and visited the land he intended to occupy, with which he was well satisfied. You may see for yourself, señor, by looking around you, that he might well be satisfied with the land—for it is here. He came back to Los Alizos with everything arranged, both for leaving our hitherto pleasant home, and for his marriage with his adored Dolores.

"When I saw that my chief dependence was about to leave me—for he managed everything about the rancho—my heart sank within me, for I felt as if Ramon was about to desert me for ever. In my distress, I applied to José Antonio, Juan being away, to know if he would manage the rancho, for I had determined not to leave it, as, among other reasons, this place was at that time inhabited very sparsely, and no white man lived nearer than ten leagues. The idea of going to live among the 'Gentiles', without the near support of 'gente de razon', was very horrid to an old body like me, and at this time the Gentiles were much worse than they are now, and had been known to kill white men who had gone amongst them to settle.

"However, I did not offer any objection, but even encouraged Ramon, when I saw he was bent on going, for I knew he would have the sweet society of a young wife, who could make him happy in any situation. Besides, he had his way to make in the world—for Los Alizos would not always hold us all—and so I made matters up in the best way I could, trusting always in the protecting power of the blessed Virgin, and her Almighty Son. Ramon and Dolores were accordingly married, and the day after their marriage they started for the North, with the benedictions of all who knew them, the reverend padre Ambrosio, with upraised hands, commending them to the good keeping of all the holy saints the adorable mother of God.

"Pues, señor!" (well, sir!) continued the old lady, wiping her eyes, "when they rode off, and I saw our sweet Dolores mounted on a pretty 'blequita', (little mare) which had been broken for her use by her own Ramon; their Indian boys, and Indian woman, driving their caballada; and my gallant Ramon following them on a fine horse, with his lance in hand, and its pennon fluttering in the breeze, my heart failed within me; and when I turned to go in, I felt desolate, forsaken and broken-hearted.

"José Antonio, however, promised well, and I endeavored to console myself in the best way I could for the loss of Ramon. We went on in the old course for two years. Ramon made us one or two visits during that time. His darling wife had become the mother of two children, and was in good health; but, owing to family cares, she seldom left the rancho. At the end of those two years, which had brought nothing but happiness to Ramon and his Dolores, some of the rancheros, who lived near the settlements, made up a party and went into Ramon's neighborhood, ostensibly to catch horse-thieves, but really to obtain servants by capturing the Indians. They attacked in the night-time a populous rancheria of Gentiles living near Ramon's rancho:—you may have seen the place, señor, just where the Russian River makes a bend, forming a deep pool. It is a charming bathing place, with an old 'tamascal' near its banks, and is surrounded by beautiful forest-trees. The poor, persecuted Gentile-men fled, after losing several of their number, leaving behind their women and children. The inhuman marauders and assassins, after selecting such of these as they wanted for servants, cruelly tortured, and barbarously murdered some of the women and children, who could not be driven off. The Gentiles who had fled came back, but not to attack the numerous and well-armed body which had sacked and pillaged their rancheria. But, sir, the very worm will turn when he is trodden on, and these poor ignorant Indians, giving way to their outraged feelings, took vengeance on the settlers in the neighborhood, who had indeed no connection with the marauders, but were sacrificed to the blind fury of the Gentiles, to atone for the crimes of their guilty compatriots. One ranchero, who was Ramon's next neighbor, was found murdered in his bed. But how shall I be able to proceed? Alas! sir, the house of my inoffensive, kind hearted son Ramon, was attacked; his wife, the heavenly and angelic Dolores, and her two infant children, brutally murdered; and Ramon himself, after performing prodigies of valor, and slaying with his lance several of the Indians, escaped by the excellence of his horse to Sonoma, dragging at the end of his riata an Indian prisoner, whom he had lassoed in the fray.

"General Vallejo was at that time, *Comandante General*. He raised a party, and with Ramon, visited this scene of terrible disaster. They attacked the savages, and wreaked a most awful vengeance; but Ramon's cattle had all been driven away, and the bodies of his little family lay buried in the blackened ruins of his once happy home. Poor, poor Ramon! Bereft at a single blow of wife, children, and property, the unfortunate returned to the paternal rancho, having lost heart to go on with his own,—his old neighbors also declaring he should not go back and expose himself to the barbarity of the Gentiles. Affairs remained thus until last year, when Ramon, again discouraged by the conduct of his elder brothers, we resolved to come back to this melancholy but lovely spot. My two other sons have left California—José Antonio went off to Sonora with Castro, and Juan is now in the field under that little Mexican blackguard, Flores. Ramon would not join them, but proposed to me to come up here and settle anew, which I consented to do, because many of your valiant countrymen have settled in this vicinity, and the neighborhood is much safer than it formerly was. Next week, Ramon will receive his cattle which are coming here from 'Los Alizos', and we hope to be comfortably settled by next year, for we rancheros require little, as you know, señor. But my poor child is not the blythe and frolicksome young cavalier he was before his sad bereavement. He has grown pensive and melancholy, and vainly tries to hide from me the grief which consumes him by day and night. Sometimes I will steal upon him unawares, and my heart sinks when I hear his deep-drawn sighs. In the dead of night, he will start and call upon Dolores in his dreams. I have, señor, a little plan of my own, which I have not yet revealed to Ramon. Anita still remains unmarried; and although not so beautiful and fascinating as Dolores, she is a handsome, frank, kindhearted girl, and as worthy as any mere mortal can be to supply the place of her sainted sister. By degrees I shall break this project to poor Ramon, and perhaps when you pass this way again you may find him a happier man."

So saying, the old lady brushed away a tear and applied herself to dishing up the breakfast of "guisado" (stew), "frijol" (beans), and "tortillas" (cakes), the courtly and handsome Ramon joining us at our homely meal, and doing the honors of the table with as much politeness and gentlemanlike ceremony as if he presided over a regal board.

To me, not the least interesting feature of this sad story, was its unintentional revelation of the infinite depths of a mother's disinterested love.

To THOSE ABOUT EMIGRATING, or who have already gone to California, with a view to settle in that delightful country, it is of the utmost consequence to know upon what terms the title to lands is held. Those who have gone, or are going, for the mere purpose of digging gold, and have no intention to remain permanently in the country, will not feel particularly interested in this chapter; while the general reader, who cares nothing about land titles, will do wisely to pass it over.

There is no question so important to the actual settlers of California, as that of their right to the lands upon which they live, or upon which they intend to live. Being a question which lies at the basis of all society, it is of course a most exciting one, and therefore should be settled with the utmost despatch. It is not a question which brooks delay, because the lands in California are not surveyed, the government of the United States is not in a position to sell a single acre; while, at the same time, a great rush of emigration is in progress, which *must* have land for cultivation. It is true that these emigrants may squat on government land, and take their chance of getting their farms whenever the land is brought into market. But the settler may not choose to hunt up land which is not claimed by individuals. He may wish a fine farm in the Napa Valley, or in that of Petaluma or Sonoma, which has already been granted to an actual occupant by the gov-

ernment of California, acting under the authority of the supreme government of Mexico. The people of California, especially those extensive
landed proprietors who were anxious for annexation to the United States,
never doubted for a moment that their estates would be at least as secure
under the protection of our government as under that of Mexico; and
numbers of American citizens did not hesitate to purchase, at fair prices,
portions of the large ranchos, considering the deeds of the rancheros, who
held valid grants from their own governments, in all respects equal to a
patent from the land office at Washington. The man who should have suggested that the United States would rob the rancheros and their grantees
of their lawfully acquired lands, would have been scouted as an enemy
and slanderer of our nation. In fact the idea never occurred to any one,
that the government at Washington would enter into a paltry controversy
with the land-owners, and endeavor to wrest from individuals what were
their rights, and what were respected as their rights, under the mean and
oppressive tyranny of Mexico. That any statesman, that any law-maker,
capable of filling a higher political station than that of town trustee,
should propose or suggest any intermeddling with the vested rights of the
Californians in their lands, was a notion never entertained, for a moment,
even by the hide-seekers. No hesitation was therefore felt by American settlers, about paying money and taking deeds for lands belonging to the rancheros; and, at this present moment, hundreds of smaller farmers have
parcelled out some of the large ranchos into farms, which still appear of
great size on the Atlantic side of the continent, but which are really none
too large for grazing purposes.

The terms of the treaty with Mexico, by which we acquired our present
title to California—for, although we conquered California, our rights by
conquest are merged in the subsequent purchase—appear to guarantee
the rights of all who held land in California at the date of the treaty; and,
even without such a provision, I suppose that nations, like private persons,
purchase lands subject to all incumbrances and prior conveyances. But
assuming that we take title as conquerors, the principle is the same, as will
appear hereafter.

The land tenures in California are based on the colonization-laws of the
republic of Mexico, which, for the most part, are transcripts of old Spanish laws, framed to encourage the settlement of remote districts in the

New World by military and other adventurers. The lands thus granted to an individual are generally of great extent; the uses to which they are put absolutely requiring that they should be so. The occupation of actual settlers is chiefly the raising of cattle and horses, and to carry on this business to any considerable extent, an extensive range of land is requisite. If the land were cut up in such small parcels as quarter-sections, or even sections, cattle-breeding and horse-raising in California would soon be on a par with the same pursuits in Illinois and Missouri.

The Spanish measurements of land are as follows:—The "sitio de ganado mayor" is a square, each side of which extends five thousand "varas Castellanas" or Spanish yards. The English designation of this quantity is expressed by the term "square league." The "sitio de ganado menor," is somewhat less than the "mayor," but both are rated in round numbers at five thousand acres respectively. Then follow the "caballeria" (lot), the "milla cuadrada" (square mile), the "suerte" (which means, literally, "a chance"), and the "huerta" or garden-spot. The two "sitios" before mentioned, are principally used for the measurement of lands, and indeed the square league is the only measurement in use for ranchos. The smaller parcels are granted only on the town lands, and for the purposes of a grazing farm would amount to nothing.

The titles were granted by the governor and commander-in-chief, and sometimes confirmed by the departmental Junta. The sessions of that body, however, were so irregular, and so seldom held, that its consent appears in but few title papers in California, nor was that consent ever deemed essential to the perfection and security of a title. The deeds specified certain conditions relating to the actual settlement of the rancho, stocking it, building upon it, and otherwise improving the property, which requirements are particularly alluded to in another chapter. Some of these grants had annexed to them, conditions too burthensome to be complied with, and of course the rancheros disregarded them. Indeed, the performance of these conditions was practically waived by the government—not a solitary case existing in the country where non-performance worked a forfeiture of the estate, although some grants provided that the land should revert to the government if all the conditions were not performed.

Another oppressive feature in some of these grants was, a proviso in restraint of the alienation or incumbrance of an estate, thus divesting it of the character of an estate in fee-simple. But this unjust and impolitic limitation was never regarded by the rancheros, who sold and mortgaged their lands at pleasure; and although these conveyances and incumbrances were perfectly notorious, and were registered by the civil authorities, and most have come to the knowledge of the government, no attempt was ever made to interfere on the part of the grantor. Indeed the insertion of clauses in restraint of alienation and incumbrance were never lawful, but void under the laws of Mexico. It has even been said that all these onerous and impracticable conditions were contrary to the policy and law of nations, and void. Those who are curious on this point can consult Vattel, chap. x., b. ii.; chap. xii., b. ii., and chap. vii., b. i., where the rights of sovereigns and private owners with respect to this kind of property are fully discussed. I am content, however, to rest the point of alienation upon the laws of Mexico herself, which never prohibited the alienation or incumbrance of estates by the legal owners, and never authorized any public officers to impose such restraints in the grants of land. In fact these latter provisos were nothing more than an arbitrary assumption of power by the local governors of California, and sometimes they had not even the governor's sanction, but were introduced by his private secretary without consulting him. Of course such unauthorized restraints could not possess the slightest validity, while the grant itself, being authorized by the law of Mexico, was entirely valid.

It is not to be supposed that these restrictions were designed merely to oppress, annoy, or control the settler. It would be most unjust to the governors and secretaries who imposed them, to assume that their motives were tyrannical. The Spanish law is ever tender of the rights of widows and minors, and while its tedious system of litigation oppresses every one else, it has a most paternal regard for those who are naturally helpless, and subject to be cheated and injured. The Spanish character everywhere partakes of this generous feeling in behalf of women and children; and if it be possible for a public functionary belonging to Spain or any of her offshoots to be honest—a proposition which I do not by any means affirm—the exception enures to the benefit of females and minors. Now these restraints on alienation were inserted in some grants for the humane object of preventing the estate from being gambled away by the reckless, or encumbered by the thriftless. But although the ranchero sold his land with the full knowledge, but without the express consent, of the government, no forfeiture was ever exacted or claimed. The land was in most instances, granted to the settler, "para du beneficia y el de su familia,"—for his own benefit and that of his family—but those words were never deemed to vest a legal title to the estate in the family, but solely in the party named in the grant; and I have no doubt that if the question had been raised in the Spanish courts, notwithstanding their leaning in favor of women and children, they would have established a precedent similar to "the rule in Shelley's case," which is found in the English law books.

The boundaries were rather loosely defined for the purposes of measurement, but were laid down with sufficient certainty to make it impossible to mistake the intent and meaning of the grantor. Some well-known landmarks were selected, such as two chains of hills, by which the two sides of the grant were bounded, the other boundaries being fixed by a given distance, measured from the next rancho, or from some other equally ascertainable starting point. The quantity of land was therefore roughly estimated or guessed at, and the words "poco ó menos" (more or less) covered the deficiency or excess.

Where lands were granted to a township, they were conveyed to the "poblacion" or population in perpetuity, for the uses of the town. The extent of these grants was commensurate with the wants of the town, and they usually consisted of tracts of four or six square leagues. Each actual resident of the town was entitled to a lot, the usual dimensions of lots being two hundred "varas" (yards) square; and the occupant was obliged to fence in or otherwise enclose his lot, and to erect a dwelling-house upon it. The lots were laid out under the direction of the civil authorities, and the town plat was subsequently approved by them. The land thus granted by the government belonged to the town, and no individual, except an actual inhabitant, could take possession of any of the land; and the rights of each settler were confined to a single lot. These town grants were made to encourage the people to live in towns for mutual security and defence, and neither the town nor the settlers could alienate the fee. Lands are granted in this way to the towns or populations of Santa Clara, San Juan, Sonoma, &c., and, whatever else may be done by our government, it is certainly to be hoped that the chartered rights of these towns, which have been the pioneers of civilization, will be respected, and ratified without delay.

Aliens were forbidden by the Mexican laws to hold property in California, unless they consented to become citizens. This exclusion, however, was never regarded, and foreigners were permitted by the local governors to hold property, establish ranchos, &c., in defiance of all such laws. Americans and other foreigners possessed large estates, and laughed at the idea of becoming naturalized Mexican citizens.

The people of California look with confidence to the government of the United States to secure to them their private property, as they held it under the laws of Mexico. The expectation is not unreasonable, and it would certainly be a sorry business on the part of our government to unsettle well-authenticated titles, many of which are fairly established by prescription as well as by grant. If the Congress of the United States should think proper to interfere with these undisputed titles, California will soon be in a state of ferment, and many of the actual settlers will be ruined men. Surely California was not acquired with any such mercenary and unjustifiable intentions; and it is to be hoped that no man will be found to advocate a law which will operate to unsettle titles and reduce the country to a state of anarchy.

If these titles shall be impeached or deraigned, we shall have, for the next half-century, an infinite amount of corrupt land-jobbing on the part of speculators, and of party-jobbing on the part of the government. Commissioners will probably be appointed for every district in that vast territory, and they will continue in lucrative and useless offices until the present land-holders and their grantees are stripped of their possessions. California will be put far back in her promising career, and a wretched and discontented race will grow up abhorring their oppressors. There is but one just and upright course to be pursued, and that is to confirm the titles granted prior to the treaty, under the authority of Mexico.

The warning voice of the eminent and profoundly erudite senator from Missouri has lately been raised in Congress on the subject of those titles. No man in the country is so familiar as he is with the history, customs, and wants of the new territories. Like a true statesman, he has large, liberal, just, and enlightened views; and the positions assumed by him cannot be shaken so long as truth, right, and justice bear sway in the national councils. The views presented by this distinguished man, on the subject of land titles are of such vast importance to California, and to all who intend to reside there, as to render it advisable to circulate them as widely as possible, and some remarks intended for this chapter are gladly withdrawn in favor of the infinitely superior arguments of the Hon. Thomas H. Benton.

LAND TITLES IN NEW MEXICO AND CALIFORNIA.

IN SENATE OF THE UNITED STATES, January, 1849.

On motion of Mr. Benton, the Senate proceeded to the consideration of the unfinished business, being the bill for ascertaining claims and titles to lands within the Territories of California and New Mexico, to grant donation rights, and to provide for the survey of the lands therein.

Mr. BENTON. As I stated to the Senate on Friday, I am opposed to the whole scheme or plan contained in the bill which is now before the Senate; and I propose to substitute for it a plan founded on an entirely different principle. The principle of the bill now before the Senate is found in the first sections of the bill, which I will read to the Senate:

"SEC. 1. That, for the purpose of ascertaining the claims and titles to lands within the territory of California and New Mexico, as required by the treaty of second of February, eighteen hundred and forty-eight, and for surveying and selling the public lands, there shall be appointed by the President, by and with the advice and consent of the Senate, a surveyor-general, a register of lands, and a receiver of public moneys, who shall act conjointly as a board of commissioners to adjudicate land claims.

"Sec. 2. They shall proceed to hold their sessions as commissioners as soon as practicable, at such points as may be directed by the President, giving public notice in some newspaper printed at each place, or if there be no newspaper, at the most public places at those points, respectively, of the time at which their sessions will commence, requiring all persons to bring forward their claims, with evidence necessary to support them. Their last session shall terminate on the thirtieth of September, one thousand eight hundred and fifty-one, when said commissioners shall forward to the Secretary of the Treasury, to be submitted to Congress, a detailed statement of all they have done; and deliver over to the surveyor-general all the archives, documents, and papers that may be in their possession." . . .

The first objection I have to this bill is, that it couples California and New Mexico in one single general land surveying district. The two countries are put together in one land district, and all the business which belongs to both, is to be transacted in one office, which office can only be in one of the two countries. Now, California and New Mexico have been always politically totally distinct, and are geographically widely separated from each other. Each consists of a mere string of settlements, one upon the Rio Grande del Norte, a river falling into the Atlantic ocean, the other, a string of settlements along the coast of the Pacific. Between them is a wilderness country of about a thousand miles in extent, the whole of it the undisputed dominion of savages, over which no man travels, except with a force sufficient to protect his life and property, moving militarily and encamping every night under the guard of sentinels, while travelling between the two countries. These two countries have never had any political connection whatsoever. Few of the inhabitants of either have ever been in the other. And to require the people of either of these strips to traverse this wilderness and go to the other for the purpose of transacting their business, is to impose on them a hardship which is intolerable—to impose on them a task which cannot be performed. There is a total disability of performing it; and when the Surveyor General's office shall be established at San Francisco, as under this bill it is to be, the people of New Mexico may give up all thought or expectation of having their business done by this Board of Commissioners. That is one objection to uniting these two countries in one land district. But there is another, which must suggest itself at once to the mind of every Senator. New Mexico is a country of indefinite boundaries: it is a country, about the boundary of which, a serious question is impending—which question, sooner or later, must receive its solution—and when it comes up, it will be large enough to occupy exclusively the authorities who may have charge of the settlement of it. The bill before us does not undertake to settle its boundaries. And it would be most injudicious and improper for it to undertake to do so. There are questions enough in the bill without mixing them up with the question of boundary between Texas and New Mexico. The bill does not undertake to fix the boundary, and it is right in making no such attempt.

But it is equally wrong in undertaking to join together New Mexico and California, when one of those countries has no boundaries by which the practical operation under this bill is to be governed. Treasury instructions must be sent out to the surveyors, defining the boundaries. Their settlement will become a subject, not of law or legislation, but of an Executive order. Sir, we all know the usual course of such things. If this bill should be passed, New Mexico, having no definite boundary, it must be acted on nevertheless; instructions must go out under it; and the rule of practice is, that the instructions are to make precise and definite whatever is indefinite and unascertained. Instructions must, then, go out, if the bill be passed, by which the surveyors will have a boundary given to them, up to which they shall work, and beyond which they shall not go. And thus we shall have devolved upon the Secretary of the Treasury, as the head of the land department, the settlement of the great question of boundary between Texas and New Mexico. The mischief that must arise from such a proceeding is too palpable to require that I should add a single word upon this point. It is manifest that it is important to keep the two countries distinct, that it is utterly out of the question to combine them, one of them being without definite boundaries, leaving it to the deputy surveyors hereafter, under Treasury orders, to say where the boundary is. I carefully abstain from saying one word about the boundary of Texas, because it is not my intention to be the means of occasioning one word to be spoken on this bill which is not pertinent to its merits.

Here, then, is a preliminary objection to the bill, that of combining two countries geographically and politically separated from each other, and of sending a question of boundary to be decided by Executive instructions to deputy surveyors. It is in reference to this part of the bill that the instructions which I have proposed require the committee to inquire into the expediency of reporting a bill for California alone, leaving out New Mexico to take her chance hereafter. And while at this point I will say that, in my opinion, there is little occasion for any Surveyor General's office in New Mexico—take the boundary of it where you please. From what I know of that country—a country which has been settled for at least two hundred and fifty years—there are no public lands in it. So far from there being any vacant land, you stand a better chance of finding titles piled upon each other three or four deep. But with respect to California, there are public lands there, and for the survey of those lands provision ought to be made. Some bill with respect to them will be required. The one which has been presented by the committee, I undertake to say— although the committee have copied an old plan which has been heretofore used—is a plan which is in violation of the treaty between the United States and Mexico; it is a plan in violation of the law of nations; it is a plan in violation of the decisions of the Supreme Court of the United States, made in similar cases. It is a plan unjust in itself, and equivalent in its operation to an entire confiscation of the whole landed property of California and New Mexico. These are large objections which I take to this plan, Mr. President, and which I will proceed to sustain by a more extended examination.

In the first place, the Surveyor General of public lands, and the Register or Receiver, or other officer constituting the board—no matter who—are made commissioners for the purpose of deciding upon land titles; and to that end all the titles of the country are to be brought before them to be examined into and adjudicated upon, and within two years to be returned to the Government of the United States here, with the opinion of the commissioners in each case, having themselves no authority to confirm anything where the amount of the grant exceeds one thousand acres. This is one general impeachment of all the land-titles of California and New Mexico. It is an assumption made by this Government that every title in those Territories is invalid; and an affirmation that not one of them should be confirmed until legislatively passed upon by the Congress of the United States; for this Board of Commissioners is to make a return of their proceedings to the Secretary of the Treasury, who is to lay them before Congress, and Congress is to pass in detail upon every claim.

Sir, this is bringing the legislative power to decide judicial questions. It is first providing a board to impeach every title in the country—to invalidate every title—to arraign every title—with no power to confirm any claim that exceeds one thousand acres; and I apprehend there never was a grant made in Mexico or California of less than a league or half a league—four thousand four hundred and twenty-eight, or two thousand two hundred and fourteen acres square. I never heard of a grant being made of less. The board can confirm nothing. And when they have thus examined into every title, the case is to be sent here to the Congress of the United States for legislative action in passing upon judicial questions concerning titles. Sir, this is a confounding of the legislative power with the judicial power; and it is subjecting claimants who have *rights* to all the humiliation of being petitioners begging favors. It is to subject the man who has a claim of *right* in his hands, to the degradation and uncertainty of petitioning for a favor. It is proposing to do a thing which cannot be done under the treaty—which cannot be done without a violation of the treaty —which cannot be done under the law of nations, without a violation of the law of nations—which cannot be done under the decisions of the Supreme Court, without a violation of those decisions—which cannot be done at all, without carrying alarm, consternation, and ruin throughout the entire provinces of California and New Mexico.

What is to be the practical operation of it? How is this thing going to work? What is the test by which the legislature is to construe them? There are three men constituting the board of commissioners, who are to be invested with power to bring before them the claims to land of every inhabitant of California and New Mexico, for the purpose of examining his title. They make their examination, and afterwards make a report, or return of the cases, to the Congress of the United States. Each claimant throughout the entire country is to come in with his title, and make it good before a board, to be composed of foreigners, whose language they cannot speak. Terror and consternation will pervade the land when these Mexicans and Californians, a conquered people, a helpless people, ignorant of our language, find that the very titles to their property are subjected, not even to the law under which they have lived, but to the pleasure of the agents of their conquerors. How is it to act, Sir? At the first summons to appear before such a board, I say—and I say it with a knowledge of what took place under similar boards in Louisiana—terror and consternation will pervade the land. What is the first feeling of these foreigners?—I call them foreigners because they are a conquered people, not yet assimilated to us; —their first feeling is, we are in the hands of our conquerors, of those who do not speak our language, who have power to do what they please.

And, Sir, what is the means which suggests itself to them as a chance of saving some part of their property from this new tribunal, and from those who possess unlimited power over them? The first feeling is, I know it well, that they must go to an American, to one of those who belong to the nation which had conquered them, and has absolute power over them, and they must give him half as compensation for going before the board and saving the other half. That is the feeling, and that is the way in which they will feel compelled to proceed. When they have given one-half—for that is the usual proportion—when they have given one-half to get an advocate to go before the commissioners, there is then no power of deciding upon cases comprehending more than a thousand acres. There are no such quantities. It is then the claimant must follow his land to the Congress of the United States, three thousand miles distant from the country where these people live. What, then, is to be done? Then they must employ that agent, or some other, to follow the claim these three thousand miles across the continent to the seat of the Federal Government, and there become an humble suitor before the Congress to get their claim heard and adjudicated. And what must they pay for this further agency? Happy will they be if they get off with the loss of the half of the remaining half. Happy, in fact, if they obtain any decision at all—if they do not, like Louisiana claimants, sue in vain to Congress ten, twenty, thirty years, for an acknowledgment of their rights. Forty years have elapsed, and many of these claims are yet unadjusted, the claimants, in the mean time, some bankrupt and dead, others clinging to a last hope, and spending the last dollar in annual attendance upon the two Houses of Congress. As it was in Louisiana, under former boards of commissioners, so will it be, and worse, because more distant, with the people of New Mexico and California, if this board is established there. Senators from States once a part of Louisiana, know full well the truth of what I say. They know the ruin brought upon many claimants in Upper and Lower Louisiana. They know that many lost their homes, which they had received from the Spanish government; that many, wearied out and disgusted, abandoned their possessions, and went off to Mexico to obtain new grants from that Power; and that, in fact, Texas was largely peopled in that way from Missouri.

I repeat it. Bad as things were under these boards in Upper and Lower Louisiana, it will be far worse with these people of New Mexico and California, so much more distant, so much more helpless, so much more ignorant of our real character, and finding themselves to be a helpless, conquered people. Terror and consternation will invade them. To purchase protection by giving up half their property will be their resource; and even that an unavailing one—for the commissioners are to have power to impeach everything, to invalidate everything, and to confirm nothing. For there is no grant of one thousand acres in California or New Mexico; they go there by leagues and half leagues, and this maximum of one thousand acres is not over a divisional fraction of any grant. No grant can be

Sketched by J. W. Revere U. S. N.   Lith. of Wm. Endicott & Co. N. York.

MONTE DIABLO - FROM THE SACRAMENTO RIVER.

divided by any number which will end with one thousand; it will be more or less.

New Mexico was conquered and settled by the Spaniards in 1594—the same century that Cortes conquered Old Mexico—and ten years before Virginia was settled. Two hundred and fifty years have elapsed since that country was granted to its conqueror, Don Juan de Onate; almost ten generations have lived and died there. Yet they are all to be called upon now to show their land titles, and to prove them also, back to the time of the conquest. All titles are to be ripped up, and rooted up, back to the original grant, two hundred and fifty years ago. What would Virginia say if she had been conquered by a foreign power, and should be served in the same manner? What would happen in that State if conquered, and called upon by the conqueror, every one to produce his title, and make it good, and wait upon Congress, as humble petitioners, until it was acknowledged?—make it good up to the time of King James the First, and Sir Walter Raleigh? Such a thing could not be done in Virginia; but the United States is strong enough to do what is worse in New Mexico, and will do it if this bill is passed, establishing a board of commissioners to impeach all titles, and send all claimants here to Congress to supplicate the legislative power to spare their lands.

California was settled in 1770—above three-quarters of a century ago—contemporary with the settlement of Kentucky; and grants have been going on ever since. What would Kentucky say, if conquered, and her conqueror should require every landholder to bring in his title, and place it before a board with power to condemn all and to confirm none, and with the privilege to the impeached owner to go three thousand miles, to some strange legislature, to supplicate for the land of his fathers? Kentucky would not submit; and yet the Californians must submit to the same, and worse, if this bill passes. It is a bill tantamount in its effects to the general confiscation of all the land titles in California and New Mexico. I say this is a violation of the treaty. I will read:

"ART. III. Mexicans now established in territories previously belonging to Mexico, and which remain for the future within the limits of the United States, as defined by the present treaty, shall be free to continue where they now reside, or to remove at any time to the Mexican republic, *retaining the property which they possess in said territories, or disposing thereof, and removing the proceeds wherever they please*, without their being subjected on this account to any contribution, tax, or charge whatever. . . . In the said Territories property of every kind now belonging to Mexicans not established, shall be inviolably respected. The present owners, the heirs of these, and all Mexicans who may hereafter acquire property by contract, shall enjoy with respect to it guarantees equally ample as if the same belonged to citizens of the United States."

"ART. IX. Mexicans who, in the Territories aforesaid, shall not preserve the character of citizens of the Mexican republic conformably with what is stipulated in the preceding article, shall be incorporated into the Union of the United States, and be admitted at the proper time (to be judged of by the Congress of the United States) to the enjoyment of all the rights of citizens of the United States, according to the principles of their constitution; and, in the meantime, shall be *maintained* and *protected* in the free enjoyment of their liberty and property, and secured in the free exercise of their religion without restriction."

Here is not only an assurance, but an absolute stipulation that their property should be inviolably respected; that the owners shall be at liberty to use it at their pleasure, selling it and removing with the proceeds as they think proper. And, in the face of this positive stipulation for the inviolable respect of property, here is a bill for the impeachment and for the destruction of their titles, for the depreciation of their property, for rendering it useless and valueless. The title is impeached the very instant it is carried before the board. That very instant the treaty is violated. So far from being respected, the title is arraigned, the value depressed at least one-half or three-quarters. Do we not all know that the value of the unconfirmed lands in Louisiana was sunk half or more? The confirmed titles are those which the United States have endorsed; the unconfirmed are those acted upon—but which the commissioners reject and bring before Congress. We all know the operations in regard to these unconfirmed claims: they are arraigned, invalidated; they cannot be sold or beneficially improved, being at the same time liable to pay taxes, and to be sold upon execution; and thus pass out of the hands of the owners for little or nothing. Now, in this treaty there is a peremptory stipulation against this invalidation of property. It is not to be impeached or violated, destroyed in any way. That is the stipulation in the treaty; and yet this bill goes to the destruction of the whole; for, sir, the property cannot be sold to any advantage while the title is thus impeached. And the owner cannot go on with any improvements; for he does not know to whom those improvements are to belong.

He can do nothing. His arm is paralyzed; his heart is sick; he looks, and looks helplessly, to a foreign country, to its mercy, and not to its justice. He may beg, but cannot demand. He may supplicate, but cannot enforce his prayer. He cannot even go into court, but must come to Congress—a legislative body, which, God knows, has more to attend to besides than they are able to do.

I have shown by the treaty that the scheme of this bill is a violation of its eighth and ninth articles. I now show you, Sir, that it is a violation of the law of nations, a violation of the decisions of the Supreme Court, as applicable to the title to lands falling under our dominion by acquisition from other countries:—

Puffendorff's Laws of Nature and Nations, lib. 8, *ch.* 6, "The conqueror acquires over those whom he subdues a despotic power with respect to their lives, but not with respect to their possessions."

Vattel.—"The conqueror lays his hands on the *possessions of the State,* on what belongs *to the public,* while private persons are permitted to retain theirs. To them the result is, they only change their masters."

United States Supreme Court.—"It is a principle of the common law, which has been recognised as well in this as in other courts, that the division of an empire works no forfeiture of previously vested rights of property, and this maxim is equally consonant with the common sense of mankind, and the maxims of eternal justice."—*5 Wheaton,* 518. *(Chief Justice Marshall).*

"In the treaty by which Louisiana was acquired, the United States stipulated that the inhabitants of the ceded territory should be protected in the free enjoyment of their property. The United States, as a great nation, regarded this stipulation as the *avowal of a principle* which would have been held *equally sacred, though it had not been inserted in the compact*."—[*4 Peters,* 512.

"The term *property,* as applied *to lands,* comprehends *every species of title,* inchoate or complete."—[*Ibid.*

"A treaty of cession from one country to another, only passes such right as the sovereign, as such, has; but does not pass what belongs to the subjects or citizens. Whether those rights are inchoate or perfect, they are all held sacred."—[9 *Peters,* 711.

"The customs and usages of the country which issued the grants are good proof in the ceded or conquered country."—[*Ibid.* 712.

"A grant or concession made by that officer who is by law authorized to make it, carries with it *prima facie* evidence that it is within his powers. No excess of them, or departure from them, will be presumed."—[9 *Peters,* 132.

"The people change their allegiance, but their relation to each other, and their rights of property, remain undisturbed."—[7 *Peters,* 87.

Puffendorff, book viii. chapter sixth, says: "The conqueror acquires over those he subdues power as to their lives, but not as to their possessions." Vattel says: "The conquered lose the possessions of the State, but not that which belongs to private individuals." Thus we see private persons are permitted to retain their property. The result is, they only change their masters. The United States Supreme Court says, it is a principle of common law, which has been recognized as well in this as in other countries, that the acquisition of a foreign country by force of arms works no forfeiture of individual rights; private property is not thereby divested. And this maxim is clearly consonant with the common sense of mankind and the principles of eternal justice. This was an opinion delivered by Chief Justice Marshall.

The treaty by which Louisiana was acquired stipulated that the inhabitants should be guaranteed in the enjoyment of their property. The United States regarded any stipulation or avowal of this principle as being scarcely needed; that titles to private property would have been held equally sacred, though it had not been inserted in the compact. The term "property" applies to every species of title inchoate or complete. A treaty of cession from one country to another only passes such right as the sovereign, as such, has, but does not pass such as belongs to subjects or citizens. Whether those rights are inchoate or perfect, they are all held sacred. The customs and usages of the country which ceded the territory are the guides to be used and followed in regard to the conquered people. A grant or concession made by the officer who is authorized to make it, carries with it *prima facie* evidence that it is within his power; no excess or departure from it will be presumed. The people change their allegiance, but their rights of property remain undisturbed.

Such are a few of the declarations of the Supreme Court of the United States, which have been brought out on trials which have been authorized by law for the purpose of ascertaining the validity of claims which have been a long time before Congress, and have at last been determined by being carried where they ought to have been at first, that is, before the judicial tribunals. Chief Justice Marshall, in delivering the opinion of the Court, declares, that a treaty makes no addition to the rights of the party; it does nothing that the law of nations does not of itself do. The treaty is only the declaration of a principle which a great nation would hold equally sacred without it; inserted, to be sure, for the purpose of satisfaction to the parties, but adding nothing to the obligation of the power receiving the sold or conquered domain. The new master is bound to protect, in all rights of property, precisely as they stood under the former power. Now, Sir, if a law shall go forth, in New Mexico and California, requiring all the people to come in with their titles, in order that they may be examined and sent to our Congress, certainly they will think that a confiscation of their titles was intended. In no conquered country of which I have ever heard, in Europe or Asia, have the people of the country been compelled to come forward and make good their titles. I have heard of no such instance; and, to give you an idea of the terror which the slightest approach to such a proceeding creates in every community, you have only to recollect the great revolt that occurred in Cairo in October, 1798—that most terrible revolt in the city of fanatics against the French who then occupied it. What was the cause of that revolt? A mere call for the land titles, in order to register them, and convert them into fee-simple estates. The great conqueror intended to benefit the land owners by giving them a fee simple title to their lands, instead of the feudal, or worse than feudal titles, by which they were held at the will of their sovereign. It was merely a call for a registration of title, for the purpose of giving them a permanent and indefeasible title, in order that they might hold the land without danger of being resumed at the will of the sovereign. Yet it made that most terrible of all revolts. I mention this for the purpose of showing the terror and consternation that are created in the hearts of a people by an interference with their titles to property.

I have now shown you, Mr. President, upon the treaty, and the law of nations, and the decisions of the Supreme Court of the United States, that such a law as this bill proposes is a violation of them all. But the bill goes further. The fourth section provides—

"SEC. 4. *And be it further enacted,* That every person, or the heirs or representatives of such person, claiming title to lands under any valid patent, grant, concession, or order of survey, issued *bona fide,* and on or previous to the seventh of July, eighteen hundred and forty-six, when military possession of the territory was taken by the United States, which were valid under the Mexican Government, or by the law of nations, shall lay before the commissioners, his, her, or their claim, set forth particularly its situation and boundaries, if to be ascertained, with the deraignment of title, where they are not the grantees or original claimants; which shall be record-ed by the secretary, who, for his services, shall be entitled to demand from the claim-ants ten cents for each hundred words contained in said papers so recorded; he shall also be entitled to twenty-five cents for each subpœna issued. . . .

Here is a deraignment of title required, which is to go back to the orig-inal concession and primary disposition of the soil. I have just said that New Mexico was settled ten years earlier than Virginia; and I put the sup-position again:—What would be the feeling, if an edict should require every person in that State to go before a board of land commissioners sit-ting a thousand miles off, to make out a chain of titles up to the time of Sir Walter Raleigh—and not only to go and make out such a chain of titles, but to pay for doing it—pay ten cents for every hundred words of their titles copied by a secretary, and twenty-five cents for every subpœna, and to be subject to punishment for not doing it? What would be the feeling of Virginia if such a law as that had given authority for this deraignment of title? (I believe I speak right if I said, arraignment). After producing this long chain of title, and paying for it, he gains nothing but the privilege of appearing as a suppliant before a strange legislative body three thousand miles off. We may be strong enough to enforce this iniquity in New Mexico and California, but we could not enforce it in Virginia or Kentucky. And against what people is such a bill to be enforced? Against ignorant In-dians, and mixed breeds, (for of such is the greater part of these people), who cannot read a word, and do not know whether a paper in their hands is a deed for land, or a bill presented against them by their baker or butcher.

I have shown that what we propose to do is in violation of the Mexican treaty, in violation of the law of nations, in violation of the decisions of the Supreme Court. I now wish to show, Mr. President, that what we pro-pose to do between man and man, between the individuals of California and New Mexico, is a violation of law which has existed long without change—for six hundred years in Spain, and of her colonies (since they had colonies)—which has been law, and approved law, since the time of Alonzo the Wise. The law of prescription, as called in the civil law—the statute of limitations, as we call it. This is the law of prescription:

Spanish Laws of Prescription.—"If one person receive from another, *in good faith,* an immoveable thing (i.e. real estate), either by purchase, or in exchange, or as gift or legacy, or in any other manner, and shall continue in possession of it during *ten* years while the owner is in the country, or *twenty* years while he was out of it; such person shall acquire the thing by prescription, notwithstanding the person from whom he received it was not the true owner; and thenceforward he shall not be held to answer for it to any man, although he should say that he could prove that he was the true owner of it."

This was the Spanish law in the thirteenth century, and has never been changed, and applies both to Spain and to Spanish America. It is wise law for the settlement, not for the disturbance of estates. It has remained without change at least six hundred years—from the time of Alonzo the Wise—in Spain—and in her colonies ever since she had colonies. People were safe under it in California and New Mexico, but if this bill passes, there is an end of their peace and security.

What I have read was the prescription where the acquisition was in good faith; there was a further provision where it was in bad faith, and all intended to quiet titles, and to give peace and security to possessors. This is it:

"If the possession acquired be *in bad faith,* title shall nevertheless be gained in the above-mentioned periods of ten and twenty years if the owner *knew* of the possession, and did not make his demand.

"Though the acquisition should be *in bad faith,* and the owner should *not know* of the adverse possession, yet a possession of *thirty* years shall gain an absolute title."—*Laws of the "Siete Partidas" of Alonzo the Wise. 3 Partidas, title* 29, *laws* 18, 19, 21.

Thus a possession, even in bad faith, was to be valid after thirty years; but we respect no time. We go back seventy years in California, and two hundred and fifty in New Mexico.

"SEC. 5. They shall examine into all *bona fide* claims arising under patents, grants, concessions, and orders of survey, where the surveys were actually made previous to the seventh of July, eighteen hundred and forty-six, when military possession of the territory was taken by the United States; whether they are founded upon conditions, and how far those conditions have been complied with; and if derived from the Spanish Government, how far they have been considered valid under the Mexican Government; and if satisfied that said claims are correct and valid, shall confirm them: *Provided,* Such confirmation shall only operate as a release of any interest which the United States may have, and shall not be considered as affecting the rights of third persons: *And provided,* That they shall not have power to confirm any claim or part thereof, where the amount claimed is undefined in quantity, or shall exceed one thousand acres; but in all such cases shall report the testimony, with their opinions, to the Secretary of the Treasury, to be laid before Congress for their determination. . . .

One error begets another. Start wrong and you must go on wrong. So of this bill. It assumes all land titles in New Mexico and California to be bad: it calls upon everybody to come in and prove up their titles. This is extraordinary power. It is inquisitorial. It is holding an inquisition upon property, and requiring the owner to appear and make good his claim. The requisition would be nugatory if there was not power to enforce his attendance, and therefore this power is given to the commissioners. Here it is:

"The commissioners are hereby authorized to administer oaths, to compel the attendance of witnesses by the subpœnas issued by the secretary, and the production of such testimony as may be wanted; to inflict punishments, either by fine, imprisonment, or both, as they may deem proper, to the same extent that courts of law are now authorized, for any refusal or neglect to obey those subpœnas or to testify; they shall have access to all papers and records of a public nature relative to any land titles within said territory, and authority to make transcripts thereof. . . .

"Every witness attending under any process from the commissioners, shall be allowed one dollar a day, and one dollar for every twenty miles travel, to be paid by the party summoning him." . . .

This power over the person is to enforce the exercise of power over property. People are to be summoned to attend the commissioners, and pay for being summoned—to bring witnesses and pay a dollar for every day's attendance and every twenty miles travel; and for not coming, or not answering, they are subject to be punished by fine or imprisonment, or both. The commissioners may inflict punishment upon them—upon the whole population of the two Territories: and thus, to sustain an inquisition into titles, contrary to the treaty, to the law of nations, to the decisions of the Supreme Court, contrary to the law of prescription, and to all justice, power is given to these commissioners over the persons of the land owners—power to inflict punishment upon them—to fine them without stint, and to imprison them as long as the board may continue.

Following up the scheme of the bill—the power to disturb and destroy everything—to decide and finish nothing—the section which I now read provides for putting the claims into four classes, and sending them to Congress for adjudication of each class. Here is the section:

"SEC. 6. *And be it further enacted,* That in making report in detail of all they have done to the Secretary of the Treasury, the commissioners shall separate the claims into four classes: class A, part one, to contain all complete titles, for less than one thousand acres, which in their opinion should be confirmed; class A, part two, those of a like character, which in their opinion should be rejected: class B, part one, those inchoate titles for less than one thousand acres, which should be confirmed; class B, part two, those of a like description, which should be rejected: class C, part one, those claims containing over one thousand acres, where, in their opinion they are sustained by proof; class C, part two, those claims of like character, which are not sustained by proof; and class D, all those cases where interferences exist between Spanish and Mexican grants." . . .

Now, will Congress ever do this work? ever unravel these classes? ever go through this complication of claims? No. Never, never, never! It has not yet finished the Louisiana claims, which were close by, and which have had Delegates, Representatives, and Senators to attend to them for forty years. Forty years have not sufficed for Congress to finish the Louisiana claims, with all these advantages: will one hundred years be enough for New Mexico and California?

The bill is fundamentally wrong—wrong even in the mode of getting at its own objects. The object is to find out the vacant land. For this purpose a knowledge of all original grants is sufficient; but this bill must know all the present possessors. If there are a thousand—and I presume there are many thousands in some instances—of settlers under one grant, each settler must now bring in his title and prove. This is absurd. We only want to know the quantity and the locality of what has been granted away by the previous government, that we may take the remainder. It is with that view, Mr. President, that the substitute which I propose requires all the grants and possessions to be laid down as they emanated from the previous government, to be laid down upon the map according to their calls or boundaries. And then, in case there be reason to believe any titles fraudulent, there is a mode of trying them judicially, of trying the cases separately and independently: to proceed against the original grant—to impeach what is impeachable, and try it judicially—and not to impeach the whole country, and condemn without trial.

———

Such are the views of one of the most enlightened, sagacious, and profound of American statesmen. His remarks are copied from the newspaper report, (The National Intelligencer), and may not be given verbatim; but they can hardly be improved even by the orator. It seems impossible that they should be disregarded.

It is not at all likely that there is a single man in the Senate of the United States, who wishes to oppress, or harass, or plunder the Californian land-holders. The honorable gentleman who introduced the bill to which Mr. Benton spoke as above, was probably not aware of its ruinous tendency; and it is not too much to expect that he will modify his views, and strike out the sweeping clauses of his bill.

But there is a disposition among the small demagogues of the country, to make a stalking horse of the public land question, and those men are overflowing with "God-given rights to the soil," and "the rights of landless men," and "the curse of land monopoly," besides other *ad captandum* phrases, which sometimes serve the purpose of hoisting small men into large offices. It is not unlikely that some few of these scant patterns of honesty, will be in favor of robbing the Californians of their land, in order that the "landless" may come in for a share. Their system of political ethics seems to recognise the "God-given right" to rob Peter to pay Paul.

It is very well that the landless should have land, and there is abundance of land for them, without robbing those who already possess it. In California, there are millions of acres of good land, which I should rejoice to see given away without money and without price, to every landless actual settler of fair character, who chose to apply for it. Let the government be as generous as it pleases with its own, and perhaps nothing would be better for the country than the free donation of *all* the public lands, both east and west of the Rocky and Snowy Mountains, to respectable settlers. But why should a private citizen be robbed of his land any more than of his money?

There are some wealthy men in California—they are few and far be-tween—and their wealth is in their lands and the products of their lands. General Vallejo, formerly general and commander in chief of California, has a large amount of land, acquired by his own daring and adventurous settlement of the north side of the Bay. For these lands he holds titles in due form, directly from the Mexican Government, and of course his titles cannot possibly be disturbed, without resorting to the most shameless and barefaced robbery, which the people of the United States will never toler-ate. He owns the ranchos of Petaluma, Soscal, and Suisun, each containing over ten square leagues of land. They are among the choicest lands on the Bay of San Francisco, and combine every variety of soil, timber, water, mining privileges, and other advantages. Over these great possessions range, under the care of mayor-domos, herdsmen and vaqueros, forty thousand head of neat cattle, five thousand mares, two thousand colts, and sheep in proportion, besides other animals. The man in the land of Uz never possessed such vast herds as this great ranchero. "My lord Esau," for whom I always felt great respect and sympathy, could not compare with him. His private caballada for his own and his family's use, contained one hundred and fifty well-broken horses, and besides them, he had eight hundred trained vaquero horses on his different ranchos, of which thirty-five were picked "caballos de su silla,"—his own private saddle-horses—splendid animals, which a sultan would be proud to bestride. During the "Bear" revolution, he lost his whole "caballada," say one thousand horses, and an immense number of cattle; but by this time he has probably replaced them, by his own superior management and industry.

Here is a brief sketch of a landed proprietor, who from the first to the last, favored the annexation of California to the United States. He has, it is true, a large amount of land, and if our government owned it they could sell it perhaps in the course of ten years, for two hundred thousand dollars. But unless they would be willing to rob a man of so much money out of his pocket, they should not think of stealing it in the shape of land. I will venture to say that this vast enterprise of General Vallejo is of a hundred times greater service to California than the parceling out of his lands into small lots would be. I believe he actually supports *more human beings* on his estates, than the same land would support if sold in small tracts. Under his superintendence—for he is a man of cultivated mind and superior judgment, as well as a man of capital—there is little doubt that in a few years these estates will show immense results. And yet, what are they compared to the almost boundless tracts of fine land in California?—a mere fraction—a drop in the bucket. The "landless" may yet, for years to come, help themselves to what they want, without the necessity of a resort to wholesale plunder.

Public lands of good quality, and the *undoubted* property of the United States government, are indeed abundant. The Spaniards never settled or granted lands north of Ross, so that from 39 deg. north latitude to 42 deg.

north latitude, extends a longitudinal strip from the coast to the Snowy Range, all perfectly new land, ready for the cultivator, and in a section of country admirably suited to the settler from the United States and the British Isles. But if the settler fancies a more southern situation, he can find plenty of valuable public land south of 39 deg., and down to the very boundary line between California and the Mexican possessions.

As a better opportunity may not occur, I will here very briefly allude to the laws by which California was governed.

In fact, no laws of any direct or specific kind existed in California. Although the Mexican laws are very elaborate, and contain many excellent provisions, and are carefully and well digested in many respects, the moral force of the government, either central or departmental, was of so little avail or consideration, that the laws were generally disregarded. Indeed, written laws of a civil nature, had been almost entirely superseded by an absolute military despotism. In a province so remote from the central government of Mexico as California, with so many peculiarities in respect to productions, face of the country, manners and customs, it could hardly be otherwise, and custom, convenience, and martial rule, took the place of law.

Thus no governor, or administrator of the customs, ever thought of being governed by the Mexican tariff laws, as passed by Congress, whenever they conflicted in the least with their own convenience; and the case was the same in Mazatlan, and the other western ports of entry of the republic lying on the Pacific. Of the money collected in those ports for duties, &c., not one cent ever found its way to the coffers of the federal government, but was expended among the employées, military and civil, of the department in which it was collected.

Private bargains were made between the consignee of a ship, appearing off the port, (always a foreigner, nearly all merchants in Mexico and California being foreigners), and the ship was admitted to discharge, or furnished with a free-trading permit, after much higgling between the authorities and the merchant. Bribery was of course resorted to whenever required—not in a private, mealy-mouthed way, but in the most open and direct manner.

The laws of the "Mesta," viz:—those which related to the government of the rural population, contain most excellent provisions. They relate entirely to the deportment of the rancheros amongst themselves, and to the rearing, tending, &c., of wild cattle and horses. They specify the marks, brands, &c., and what sorts of marks must be made, and direct the registry of each ranchero's iron at the office of the alcalde of the jurisdiction. Should the possession of an animal be contested, the law directs what is to be done; it regulates fines and penalties, punishes theft of horses and other animals, specifies the days on which "rodeas" are to be held by the rancheros of a district, alternately, and provides generally for all the minutiæ of "el campo," (the field), and for the government of the peculiar state of society existing in a grazing country.

As California must always be more or less a grazing country, these laws should be translated and put in force by the territorial or state government.

The totally absolute authority of the military governors in California, being substituted in a great measure, as I have stated, for all other authority, the community presented a singular spectacle. Still, the rights of property were held sacred, highway robbery was almost unknown, and public order was well maintained in the country. This speaks well for the character of the people, and indeed there can be no doubt, that the race is much more subservient to persons in authority than our own people are.

AT THE DATE of my departure from California, the vast deposits of gold had not been discovered. I had travelled over the richest placers* a hundred times, but it had never occurred to me to wash the golden sands over which I travelled and upon which I often slept. Had any idea of the immense treasures I was unconsciously treading beneath my feet occurred to me, I might easily have amassed the wealth of Crœsus, and instead of returning as a lieutenant in active service, it would have been an easy matter to have come in my own richly-freighted Argosy. Such is life; such its chances and changes; and, in one respect, the inward life, the life of the soul, is like unto it. A mine of untold wealth is within us, if we would but delve for it, and wash the dirt from the golden sands of our moral placers—but we pass on in the pathway of existence, not dreaming of the hidden treasures which are ready to glitter at our bidding.

It was reported, indeed, that gold had been found in the valleys of the rivers which flow into the Tulé Lakes; but the unrivalled beauties of nature excluded all ideas of avarice, and the enchantments of the distant landscape raised the eye and the thoughts above the coveted dust which lay at my feet. So may it ever be—so may we ever gaze enraptured on the

---

* This word has now become naturalized among us. It is pronounced in the singular as if written "plarthair," and in the plural as if written "plarthair-ess."

glories of that far-off shore to which our footsteps are ever tending, and where we should be most anxious to lay up treasures which endure forever.

I profess to know nothing of these gold deposits from my own observation, and perhaps Mr. Benton is right in pronouncing them a curse to California. Certain it is, that a land to which nature has been so prodigal might well dispense with them, and perhaps a hundred years hence it will be apparent that the true wealth of California did not lay in her shining sands. Whether the same eminent senator be right in predicting that those treasures will prove ephemeral no man can determine. The probability is, that large quantities of gold will be found for many years to come, and it is not unlikely that the value of that precious metal will be seriously affected by the vast additions which will be made to the currency of the world in the course of the next ten years.

What is to be the moral effect of this well-founded mania in the present anomalous condition of California, it is fearful to contemplate. She is without government, without laws, without a military force, while tens of thousands of adventurers from all parts of the earth are pouring into her golden valleys. Among these there must be many lawless and dangerous men; and it is to be feared that thousands who go out respectable, law-abiding citizens, will be transformed by the evil spirit of avarice and by associating on familiar terms with the vicious and depraved, into knaves and men of violence. It will not be surprising to hear at any moment of the most atrocious robberies and murders in the gold region, and it is to be hoped that the heterogeneous mass congregated in the valley of the Sacramento and elsewhere, will pause for a moment in their greedy pursuit of gold, and organize an association for the preservation of law and order. In the present state of affairs, it is apparent from the official documents, that it would be in vain to send troops to California. Our very men-of-war appear to be infected with insubordination as soon as they approach the magic shores of California, and ere this time a large fleet of merchantmen are rotting in the harbor of San Francisco. Where all this is to end, heaven only knows; and the most effective counteracting measure, would be to immediately quiet the land titles, and hold out inducements to settlers to turn their attention to the cultivation of the soil.

The most reliable and intelligent accounts of the gold deposits are to be found in the public documents, and the probability is, that they will continue to furnish the most authentic data respecting the auriferous regions. It is very certain that, had I been on the spot at the time the rush to the great placer took place, I could have written nothing so complete and graphic as the account furnished by the accomplished temporary governor, Col. R. B. Mason. His admirable report has been copied all over the world —published in every newspaper, and reprinted in ten thousand catch-penny pamphlets. But it still remains the most accurate and authentic history of the discovery of the gold deposits, and of the early operations of the gold collectors. It ought to be preserved in all the books which treat of California, and familiar as it is, I shall republish it in preference to any second-hand statement of my own. I shall also add the despatches of Lieut. Larkin and Commodore Jones, which will be found extremely interesting.

I begin these interesting extracts with the standard authority—the celebrated report of Col. Mason. Such valuable documents never grow stale.

HEADQUARTERS 10TH MILITARY DEPOT,
MONTEREY, California, Aug. 17, 1848.

SIR: I have the honor to inform you that, accompanied by Lieutenant W. T. Sherman, third artillery, A.A.A. General, I started on the twelfth of June last, to make a tour through the northern part of California. My principal purpose, however, was to visit the newly-discovered gold "placer" in the Valley of the Sacramento. I had proceeded about forty miles, when I was overtaken by an express, bringing me intelligence of the arrival at Monterey of the United States ship Southampton, with important letters from Commodore Shubrick and Lieutenant Colonel Barton. I returned at once to Monterey, and dispatched what business was most important, and on the seventeenth resumed my journey. We reached San Francisco on the twentieth, and found that all, or nearly all its male inhabitants had gone to the mines. The town, which a few months before was so busy and thriving, was then almost deserted.

On the evening of the twenty-fifth, the horses of the escort were crossed to Sausalito in a launch, and on the following day we resumed the journey by way of Bodega and Sonoma to Sutter's Fort, where we arrived on the morning of the second of July. Along the whole route, mills were lying idle, fields of wheat were open to cattle and horses, houses vacant, and farms going to waste. At Sutter's there was more life and business. Launches were discharging cargoes at the river, and carts were hauling goods to the fort, where already were established several stores, a hotel, &c. Captain Sutter had only two mechanics in his employ, (a wagon-maker and blacksmith), to whom he was then paying ten dollars a day. Merchants pay him a monthly rent of one hundred dollars per room; and while I was there, a two-story house in the fort was rented as a hotel for five hundred dollars a month.

At the urgent solicitation of many gentlemen, I delayed there to participate in the first public celebration of our national anniversary at that fort, but on the fifth resumed the journey and proceeded twenty-five miles up the American fork, to a point on it known as the Lower Mines, or Mormon Diggings. The hill-sides were thickly strewn with canvas tents and bush arbors; a store was erected, and several boarding shanties in operation. The day was intensely hot, yet about two hundred men were at work in the full glare of the sun, washing for gold—some with tin pans, some with close-woven Indian baskets, but the greater part had a rude machine, known as the cradle. This is on rockers, six or eight feet long, open at the foot, and at its head has a coarse grate, or sieve; the bottom is rounded, with small cleets nailed across. Four men are required to work this machine: one digs the ground in the bank close by the stream; another carries it to the cradle and empties it on the grate; a third gives a violent rocking motion to the machine; while a fourth dashes on water from the stream itself.

The sieve keeps the coarse stones from entering the cradle, the current of water washes off the earthy matter, and the gravel is gradually carried out at the foot of the machine, leaving the gold mixed with a heavy fine black sand above the first cleets. The sand and gold mixed together are then drawn off through auger holes into the pan below, are dried in the sun, and afterwards separated by blowing off the sand. A party of four men thus employed at the lower mines averaged one hundred dollars a day. The Indians and those who have nothing but pans or willow baskets, gradually wash out the earth, and separate the gravel by hand, leaving nothing but the gold mixed with sand, which is separated in the manner before described. The gold in the lower mines is in fine bright scales, of which I send several specimens.

As we ascended the north branch of the American fork, the country became more broken and mountainous; and at the saw-mill, twenty-five miles above the lower washings, or fifty miles from Sutter's, the hills rise to about a thousand feet above the level of the Sacramento plain. Here a species of pine occurs which led to the discovery of the gold. Captain Sutter, feeling the great want of lumber, contracted in September last with a Mr. Marshall to build a saw-mill at that place. It was erected in the course of the past winter and spring—a dam and race constructed—but when the water was let on the wheel, the tail-race was found to be too narrow to permit the water to escape with sufficient rapidity. Mr. Marshall, to save labor, let the water directly into the race with a strong current, so as to wash it wider and deeper. He effected his purpose, and a large bed of mud and gravel was carried to the foot of the race.

One day Mr. Marshall, as he was walking down the race to his deposit of mud, observed some glittering particles at its upper edge; he gathered a few, examined them, and became satisfied of their value. He then went to the fort, told Captain Sutter of his discovery, and they agreed to keep it secret until a certain grist-mill of Sutter's was finished. It, however, got out, and spread like magic. Remarkable success attended the labors of the first explorers, and in a few weeks hundreds of men were drawn thither. At the time of my visit, but little over three months after the first discovery, it was estimated that upwards of four thousand people were employed. At the mill there is a fine deposit, or bank of gravel, which the people respect as the property of Captain Sutter, although he pretends to no right to it, and would be perfectly satisfied with the simple promise of a pre-emption, on account of the mill, which he has built there at considerable cost. Mr. Marshall was living near the mill, and informed me that many persons were employed above and below him; that they use the same machines at the lower washings, and that their success was about the same —ranging from one to three ounces of gold per man, daily. This gold, too, is in scales a little coarser than those of the lower mines.

From the mill Mr. Marshall guided me up the mountain on the opposite, or north bank, of the south fork, where, in the bed of small streams or ravines, now dry, a great deal of coarse gold has been found. I there saw several parties at work, all of whom were doing very well; a great many specimens were shown me, some as heavy as four or five ounces in weight, and I send three pieces, labelled number five, presented by a Mr. Spence. You will perceive that some of the specimens accompanying this, hold mechanically pieces of quartz; that the surface is rough, and evidently moulded in the crevice of a rock. This gold cannot have been carried far by water, but must have remained near where it was first deposited from the rock that once bound it. I inquired of many people if they had encountered the metal in its matrix, but in every instance they said they had not; but that the gold was invariably mixed with washed gravel, or lodged in the crevices of other rocks. All bore testimony that they had found gold in greater or less quantities in the numerous small gullies or ravines that occur in that mountainous region.

On the seventh of July I left the mill, and crossed to a stream, emptying into the American fork, three or four miles below the saw-mill. I struck this stream (now known as Weber's creek) at the washings of Sunol & Co. They had about thirty Indians employed, whom they pay in merchandise. They were getting gold of a character similar to that found in the main fork, and doubtless in sufficient quantities to satisfy them. I send you a small specimen, presented by this company, of their gold. From this point, we proceeded up the stream, about eight miles, where we found a great many people and Indians; some engaged in the bed of the stream, and others in the small side valleys that put into it. These latter are exceedingly rich, and two ounces were considered an ordinary yield for a day's work. A small gutter, not more than a hundred yards long by four feet wide and two or three feet deep, was pointed out to me as the one where two men—William Daly and Parry McCoon—had, a short time before, obtained seventeen thousand dollars' worth of gold. Captain Weber informed me that he knew that these two men had employed four white men and about a hundred Indians, and that, at the end of one week's work, they paid off their party, and had left ten thousand dollars' worth of this gold. Another small ravine was shown me, from which had been taken upwards of twelve thousand dollars' worth of gold. Hundreds of similar ravines, to all appearances, are as yet untouched. I could not have credited these reports had I not seen, in the abundance of the precious metal, evidence of their truth.

Mr. Neligh, an agent of Commodore Stockton, had been at work about three weeks in the neighborhood, and showed me, in bags and bottles, over two thousand dollars' worth of gold; and Mr. Lyman, a gentleman of education, and worthy of every credit, said he had been engaged, with four others, with a machine, on the American fork, just below Sutter's mill; that they worked eight days, and that his share was at the rate of fifty dollars a day; but hearing that others were doing better at Weber's place, they had removed there, and were then on the point of resuming operations. I might tell of hundreds of similar instances; but, to illustrate how plentiful the gold was in the pockets of common laborers, I will mention a simple occurrence which took place in my presence when I was at Weber's store. This store was nothing but an arbor of bushes, under which he had exposed for sale goods and groceries suited to his customers. A man came in, picked up a box of Seidlitz powders, and asked the price. Captain Weber told him it was not for sale. The man offered an ounce of gold, but Captain Weber told him it only cost fifty cents, and he did not wish to sell it. The man then offered an ounce and a half, when Captain Weber *had* to take it. The prices of all things are high, and yet Indians, who before hardly knew what a breech-cloth was, can now afford to buy the most gaudy dresses.

The country on either side of Weber's creek is much broken up by hills, and is intersected in every direction by small streams or ravines, which contain more or less gold. Those that have been worked are barely scratched; and, although thousands of ounces have been carried away, I do not consider that a serious impression has been made upon the whole. Every day was developing new and richer deposits; and the only impression seemed to be, that the metal would be found in such abundance as seriously to depreciate in value.

On the eighth of July I returned to the lower mines, and on the following day to Sutter's, where, on the nineteenth, I was making preparations for a visit to the Feather, Yubah, and Bear rivers, when I received a letter from Commander A. R. Long, United States Navy, who had just arrived at San Francisco from Mazatlan, with a crew for the sloop-of-war Warren, with orders to take that vessel to the squadron at La Paz. Captain Long wrote to me that the Mexican Congress had adjourned without ratifying the treaty of peace; that he had letters from Commodore Jones, and that his orders were to sail with the Warren on or before the twentieth of July. In consequence of these I determined to return to Monterey, and accordingly arrived here on the seventeenth of July. Before leaving Sutter's, I satisfied myself that gold existed in the bed of the Feather river, in the Yubah and Bear, and in many of the smaller streams that lie between the latter and the American fork; also, that it had been found in the Cosumnes to the south of the American fork. In each of these streams the gold is found in small scales, whereas, in the intervening mountains, it occurs in coarser lumps.

Mr. Sinclair, whose rancho is three miles above Sutter's, on the north side of the American, employs about fifty Indians on the north fork, not far from its junction with the main stream. He had been engaged about five weeks when I saw him, and up to that time his Indians had used simply closely-woven willow baskets. His net proceeds (which I saw) were about sixteen thousand dollars' worth of gold. He showed me the proceeds of his last week's work—fourteen pounds avoirdupois of clean-washed gold.

The principal store at Sutter's fort, that of Brannan & Co., had received, in payment for goods, thirty-six thousand dollars' worth of this gold, from the first of May to the tenth of July. Other merchants had also made extensive sales. Large quantities of goods were daily sent forward to the mines, as the Indians, heretofore so poor and degraded, have suddenly become consumers of the luxuries of life. I before mentioned that the greater part of the farmers and rancheros had abandoned their fields to go to the mines. This is not the case with Captain Sutter, who was carefully gathering his wheat, estimated at forty thousand bushels. Flour is already worth, at Sutter's, thirty-six dollars a barrel, and soon will be fifty. Unless large quantities of breadstuffs reach the country, much suffering will occur; but as each man is now able to pay a large price, it is believed the merchants will bring from Chili and Oregon a plentiful supply for the coming winter.

The most moderate estimate I could obtain from men acquainted with the subject, was, that upwards of four thousand men were working in the gold district, of whom more than one-half were Indians; and that from thirty to fifty thousand dollars' worth of gold, if not more, was daily obtained. The entire gold district, with very few exceptions of grants made some years ago by the Mexican authorities, is on land belonging to the United States. It was a matter of serious reflection with me, how I could secure to the government certain rents or fees for the privilege of procuring this gold; but upon considering the large extent of country, the character of the people engaged, and the small scattered force at my command, I resolved not to interfere, but to permit all to work freely, unless broils and crimes should call for interference. I was surprised to learn that crime of any kind was very unfrequent, and that no thefts or robberies had been committed in the gold district.

All live in tents, in bush arbors, or in the open air; and men have frequently about their persons thousands of dollars worth of this gold, and it was to me a matter of surprise that so peaceful and quiet state of things should continue to exist. Conflicting claims to particular spots of ground may cause collisions, but they will be rare, as the extent of country is so great, and the gold so abundant, that for the present there is room enough for all. Still the government is entitled to rents for this land, and immediate steps should be devised to collect them, for the longer it is delayed the more difficult it will become. One plan I would suggest is, to send out from the United States surveyors with high salaries, bound to serve specified periods.

A superintendent to be appointed at Sutter's Fort, with power to grant licenses to work a spot of ground—say one hundred yards square—for one year, at a rent of from one hundred to one thousand dollars, at his discretion; the surveyors to measure the ground, and place the rentor in possession.

A better plan, however, will be, to have the district surveyed, and sold at public auction to the highest bidder, in small parcels—say from twenty to forty acres. In either case, there will be many intruders, who for years it will be almost impossible to exclude.

The discovery of these vast deposits of gold has entirely changed the character of Upper California. Its people, before engaged in cultivating their small patches of ground, and guarding their herds of cattle and horses, have all gone to the mines, or are on their way thither. Laborers of every trade have left their work-benches, and tradesmen their shops. Sailors desert their ships as fast as they arrive on the coast, and several vessels have gone to sea with hardly enough hands to spread a sail. Two or three are now at anchor in San Francisco with no crew on board. Many desertions, too, have taken place from the garrisons within the influence of these mines; twenty-six soldiers have deserted from the post of Sonoma, twenty-four from that of San Francisco, and twenty-four from Monterey. For a few days the evil appeared so threatening, that great danger existed that the garrisons would leave in a body; and I refer you to my orders of the twenty-fifth of July, to show the steps adopted to meet this contingency. I shall spare no exertions to apprehend and punish deserters, but I believe no time in the history of our country has presented such temptations to desert as now exist in California.

The danger of apprehension is small, and the prospect of high wages certain; pay and bounties are trifles, as laboring men at the mines can now earn in *one day* more than double a soldier's pay and allowances for a month, and even the pay of a lieutenant or captain cannot hire a servant. A carpenter or mechanic would not listen to an offer of less than fifteen or twenty dollars a day. Could any combination of affairs try a man's fidelity more than this? I really think some extraordinary mark of favor should be given to those soldiers who remain faithful to their flag throughout this tempting crisis. No officer can now live in California on his pay, money has so little value; the prices of necessary articles of clothing and subsistence are so exorbitant, and labor so high, that to hire a cook or servant has become an impossibility, save to those who are earning from thirty to fifty dollars a day. This state of things cannot last for ever. Yet from the geographical position of California, and the new character it has assumed as a mining country, prices of labor will always be high, and will hold out temptations to desert. I therefore have to report, if the government wish to prevent desertions here on the part of men, and to secure zeal on the part of officers, their pay must be increased very materially. Soldiers, both of the volunteers and regular service, discharged in this country, should be permitted at once to locate their land warrants in the gold district.

Many private letters have gone to the United States giving accounts of the vast quantity of gold recently discovered, and it may be a matter of surprise why I have made no report on this subject at an earlier date. The reason is, that I could not bring myself to believe the reports that I heard of the wealth of the gold district until I visited it myself. I have no hesitation now in saying that there is more gold in the country drained by the Sacramento and San Joaquim rivers, than will pay the cost of the present war with Mexico a hundred times over. No capital is required to obtain this gold, as the laboring man wants nothing but his pick and shovel and tin pan, with which to dig and wash the gravel; and many frequently pick gold out of the crevices of the rocks with their butcher-knives, in pieces from one to six ounces.

Mr. Dye, a gentleman residing in Monterey, and worthy of every credit, has just returned from Feather River. He tells me that the company to which he belonged worked seven weeks and two days, with an average of fifty Indians, (washers), and that their gross product was two hundred and seventy-three pounds of gold. His share, (one-seventh), after paying all expenses, is about thirty-seven pounds, which he brought with him and exhibited in Monterey. I see no laboring man from the mines who does not show his two, three, or four pounds of gold. A soldier of the artillery company returned here a few days ago from the mines, having been absent on furlough twenty days. He made by trading and working during that time one thousand five hundred dollars. During these twenty days he was travelling ten or eleven days, leaving but a week, in which he made a sum of money greater than he receives in pay, clothes, and rations during a while enlistment of five years. These statements appear incredible, but they are true.

Gold is also believed to exist on the eastern slope of the Sierra Nevada; and when at the mines, I was informed by an intelligent Mormon that it had been found near the Great Salt Lake by some of his fraternity. Nearly all the Mormons are leaving California to go to the Salt Lake, and this they surely would not do unless they were sure of finding gold there in the same abundance as they now do on the Sacramento.

The gold "placer" near the mission of San Fernando has long been known, but has been little wrought for want of water. This is a spur which puts off from the Sierra Nevada, (see Fremont's map), the same in which the present mines occur. There is, therefore, every reason to believe, that in the intervening spaces of five hundred miles (entirely unexplored), there must be many hidden and rich deposits. The "placer" gold is now substituted as the currency of this country; in trade it passes freely at sixteen dollars per ounce; as an article of commerce its value is not yet fixed. The only purchase I made was of the specimen, number seven, which I got of Mr. Neligh, at twelve dollars the ounce. That is about the present cash value in the country, although it has been sold for less. The great demand for goods and provisions made by the sudden development of wealth, has increased the amount of commerce at San Francisco very much, and it will continue to increase.

I would recommend that a mint be established at some eligible point of the Bay of San Francisco; and that machinery, and all the necessary apparatus and workmen, be sent out by sea. These workmen must be bound by high wages, and even bonds, to secure their faithful services, else the whole plan may be frustrated by their going to the mines as soon as they arrive in California. If this course be not adopted, gold to the amount of many millions of dollars will pass yearly to other countries, to enrich their merchants and capitalists. Before leaving the subject of mines, I will mention that on my return from the Sacramento, I touched at New Almoder, the quicksilver mine of Mr. Alexander Forbes, Consul of Her Britannic Majesty, at Tepic. This mine is in a spur of the mountains, one thousand feet above the level of the Bay of San Francisco, and is distant in a southern direction from the Puebla de San José about twelve miles. The ore (cinnabar) occurs in a large vein dipping at a strong angle to the horizon. Mexican miners are employed in working it, by driving shafts and galleries about six feet by seven, following the vein.

The fragments of rock and ore are removed on the backs of Indians, in raw-hide sacks. The ore is then hauled in an ox wagon, from the mouth of the mine down to a valley well supplied with wood and water, in which the furnaces are situated. The furnaces are of the simplest construction— exactly like a common bake-oven, in the crown of which is inserted a whaler's frying-kettle; another inverted kettle forms the lid. From a hole in the lid a small brick channel leads to an apartment, or chamber, in the bottom of which is inserted a small iron kettle. The chamber has a chimney.

In the mornings of each day the chambers are filled with the mineral (broken into small pieces) mixed with lime; fire is then applied and kept up all day. The mercury is volatilized, passes into the chamber, is condensed on the sides and bottom of the chamber, and flows into the pot prepared for it. No water is used to condense the mercury.

During a visit I made last spring, four such ovens were in operation, and yielded in the two days I was there, six hundred and fifty-six pounds of quicksilver, worth at Mazatlan one dollar and eighty cents per pound. Mr. Walkinshaw, the gentleman now in charge of this mine, tells me that the vein is improving, and that he can afford to keep his people employed even in these extraordinary times. The mine is very valuable of itself, and will become the more so as mercury is extensively used in obtaining gold. It is not at present used in California for that purpose, but will be at some future time. When I was at this mine last spring, other parties were engaged in searching for veins; but none have been discovered worth following up, although the earth in that whole range of hills is highly discolored, indicating the presence of this ore. I send several beautiful specimens, properly labelled. The amount of quicksilver in Mr. Forbes' vats on the fifteenth of July, was about two thousand five hundred pounds.

I enclose you herewith sketches of the country through which I passed, indicating the position of the mines and the topography of the country in the vicinity of those I visited.

Some of the specimens of gold accompanying this were presented for transmission to the Department, by the gentlemen named below.

1. Captain J. A. Sutter.

2. John Sinclair.

3. William Glover, R. C. Kirby, Ira Blanchard, Levi Fifield, Franklin H. Arynes, Mormon diggings.

4. Charles Weber.

5. Robert Spence.

6. Sunol & Co.

7. Robert D. Neligh.

8. C. E. Picket, American Fort Columa.

9. E. C. Kemble.

10. T. H. Green, from San Fernando, near Los Angeles.

   A. 2 oz. purchased from Mr. Neligh.

   B. Sand found in washing gold, which contained small particles.

11. Captain Frisbie, Dry Diggings, Weber's Creek.

12. Consumnes.

13. Consumnes, Hartwell's Ranch.

I have the honor to be, your most ob't serv't,

R. B. MASON,
Colonel First Dragoons, Commanding.

BRIGADIER GENERAL R. JONES,
Adjutant General U. S. A., Washington, D.C.

[NOTE.—The original letter, of which this is a copy, was sent to its address, in charge of Lieutenant L. Loeser, third artillery, bearer of despatches, who sailed in the schooner Lambayecana, from Monterey, August the thirtieth, eighteen hundred and forty-eight, bound for Payta, Peru. Lieutenant Loeser bears, in addition to the specimens mentioned in the foregoing letter, a tea-caddy containing two hundred and thirty ounces fifteen pennyweights and nine grains of gold. This was purchased at San Francisco by my order, and is sent to you as a fair sample of the gold obtained from the mines of the Sacramento. It is a mixture, coming from the various parts of the gold district.

R. B. MASON,
Colonel First Dragoons, Commanding.

HEADQUARTERS TENTH MILITARY DEPARTMENT,
Monterey (California), Sept. 10, 1848.]

Extract from a Letter from Mr. Larkin to Mr. Buchanan.

SAN FRANCISCO, Upper California, June 1, 1848.

SIR: . . . I have to report to the State Department one of the most astonishing excitements and state of affairs now existing in this country, that, perhaps, has ever been brought to the notice of the Government. On the American fork of the Sacramento and Feather River, another branch of the same, and the adjoining lands, there has been, within the present year, discovered a placer, a vast tract of land containing gold, in small particles. This gold, thus far, has been taken on the bank of the river, from the surface to eighteen inches in depth, and is supposed deeper, and to extend over the country.

On account of the inconvenience of washing, the people have, up to this time, only gathered the metal on the banks, which is done simply with a shovel, filling a shallow dish, bowl, basket, or tin pan, with a quantity of black sand, similar to the class used on paper, and washing out the sand by movement of the vessel. It is now two or three weeks since the men employed in those washings have appeared in this town with gold, to exchange for merchandise and provisions. I presume nearly twenty thousand dollars of this gold has as yet been so exchanged. Some two or three hundred men have remained up the river, or are gone to their homes, for the purpose of returning to the placer, and washing immediately with shovels, picks, and baskets; many of them, for the first few weeks, depending on borrowing from others. I have seen the written statement of the work of one man for sixteen days, which averaged twenty-five dollars per day; others have, with a shovel and pan, or a wooden bowl, washed out ten to even fifteen dollars in a day. There are now some men yet washing who have five hundred to one thousand dollars. As they have to stand two feet deep in the river, they work but a few hours in the day, and not every day in the week.

A few men have been down in boats to this port, spending twenty to thirty ounces of gold each—about three hundred dollars. I am confident that this town (San Francisco) has one-half of its tenements empty, locked up with the furniture. The owners—storekeepers, lawyers, mechanics and laborers—all gone to the Sacramento with their families. Small parties, of five to fifteen men, have sent to this town, and offered cooks ten to fifteen dollars per day for a few weeks. Mechanics and teamsters, earning the year past five to eight dollars per day, have struck and gone. Several United States volunteers have deserted. United States bark Anita, belonging to the Army, now at anchor here, has but six men. One Sandwich Island vessel in port lost all her men; engaged another crew at fifty dollars for the run of fifteen days to the Islands.

One American captain having his men shipped on this coast in such a manner that they could leave at any time, had them all on the eve of quitting, when he agreed to continue their pay and food; leaving one on board, he took a boat and carried them to the gold regions—furnishing tools and giving his men one-third. They have been gone a week. Common spades and shovels, one month ago worth one dollar, will now bring ten dollars at the gold regions. I am informed fifty dollars has been offered for one. Should this gold continue as represented, this town and others would be depopulated. Clerks' wages have risen from six hundred to one thousand dollars per annum, and board; cooks, twenty-five to thirty dollars per month. This sum will not be any inducement a month longer, unless the fever and ague appears among the washers. The *Californian,* printed here, stopped this week. The *Star* newspaper office, where the new laws of Governor Mason, for this country, are printing, has but one man left. A merchant, lately from China, has even lost his China servants. Should the excitement continue through the year, and the whale-ships visit San Francisco, I think they will lose most all their crews. How Colonel Mason can retain his men, unless he puts a force on the spot, I know not.

I have seen several pounds of this gold, and consider it very pure, worth, in New York, seventeen to eighteen dollars per ounce; fourteen to sixteen dollars, in merchandize, is paid for it here. What good or bad effect this gold mania will have on California, I cannot foretell. It may end this year; but I am informed that it will continue many years. Mechanics now in this town are only waiting to finish some rude machinery, to enable them to obtain the gold more expeditiously, and free from working in the river. Up to this time, but few Californians have gone to the mines, being afraid the Americans will soon have trouble among themselves, and cause disturbance to all around. I have seen some of the black sand, as taken from the bottom of the river, (I should think in the States it would bring twenty-five to fifty cents per pound), containing many pieces of gold; they are from the size of the head of a pin to the weight of the eighth of an ounce. I have seen some weighing one quarter of an ounce (four dollars). Although my statements are almost incredible, I believe I am within the statements believed by every one here. Ten days back, the excitement had not reached Monterey. I shall, within a few days, visit this gold mine, and will make another report to you. Inclosed you will have a specimen.

I have the honor to be, very respectfully,

THOMAS O. LARKIN.

HON. JAMES BUCHANAN,
Secretary of State, Washington.
P.S. This placer, or gold region, is situated on public land.

Mr. Larkin to Mr. Buchanan.

MONTEREY, California, June 28, 1848.

SIR: My last dispatch to the State Department was written in San Francisco, the first of this month. In that I had the honor to give some information respecting the new "placer," or gold regions, lately discovered on the branches of the Sacramento river. Since the writing of that dispatch I have visited a part of the gold region, and found it all I had heard, and much more than I anticipated. The part that I visited was upon a fork of the American river, a branch of the Sacramento, joining the main river, at Sutter's fort. The place in which I found the people digging was about twenty-five miles from the fort by land.

I have reason to believe that gold will be found on many branches of the Sacramento and the Joaquim rivers. People are already scattered over one hundred miles of land, and it is supposed that the "placer" extends from river to river. At present the workmen are employed within ten or twenty yards of the river, that they may be convenient to water. On Feather River there are several branches upon which the people are digging for gold. This is two or three days' ride from the place I visited.

At my camping place I found, on a surface of two or three miles on the banks of the river, some fifty tents, mostly owned by Americans. These had their families. There are no Californians who have taken their families as yet to the gold regions; but few or none will ever do it. Some from New Mexico may do so next year, but no Californians.

I was two nights at a tent occupied by eight Americans, viz: two sailors, one clerk, two carpenters, and three daily workmen. These men were in company; had two machines, each made from one hundred feet of boards, (worth there one hundred and fifty dollars, in Monterey, fifteen dollars —being one day's work), made similar to a child's cradle, ten feet long, without the ends.

The two evenings I saw these eight men bring to their tents the labor of the day. I suppose they made each fifty dollars per day; their own calculation was two pounds of gold a day—four ounces to a man—sixty-four dollars. I saw two brothers that worked together, and only worked by washing the dirt in a tin pan, weigh the gold they obtained in one day; the result was, seven dollars to one and eighty-two dollars to the other. There were two reasons for this difference; one man worked less hours than the other, and by chance had ground less impregnated with gold. I give this statement as an extreme case. During my visit I was an interpreter for a native of Monterey, who was purchasing a machine or canoe. I first tried to purchase boards and hire a carpenter for him. There were but a few hundred feet of boards to be had; for these the owner asked me fifty dollars per hundred (five hundred dollars per thousand), and a carpenter, washing gold dust, demanded fifty dollars per day for working. I at last purchased a log, dug out, with a riddle and sieve, made of willow-boughs, on it, for one hundred and twenty dollars, payable in gold dust, at fourteen dollars per ounce. The owner excused himself for the price, by saying that he was two days making it, and even then demanded the use of it until sunset. My Californian has told me since, that himself, partner, and two Indians, obtained with this canoe eight ounces the first, and five ounces the second day.

I am of the opinion that on the American fork, Feather river, and Copimes river, there are near two thousand people, nine-tenths of them foreigners. Perhaps there are one hundred families, who have their teams, wagons and tents. Many persons are waiting to see whether the months of July and August will be sickly, before they leave their present business to go to the "placer." The discovery of this gold was made by some Mormons, in January or February, who for a time kept it a secret; the majority of those who are working there began in May. In most every instance the men, after digging a few days, have been compelled to leave for the purpose of returning home to see their families, arrange their business and purchase provisions. I feel confident in saying there are fifty men in this "placer" who have on an average one thousand dollars each, obtained in May and June. I have not met with any person who had been fully employed in washing gold one month; most, however, appear to have averaged an ounce per day. I think there must, by this time, be over one thousand men at work upon the different branches of the Sacramento; putting their gains at one hundred thousand dollars per day, for six days in the week, appears to me not overrated.

Should this news reach the emigration of California and Oregon, now on the road, connected with the Indian wars, now impoverishing the latter country, we should have a large addition to our population; and should the richness of the gold region continue, our emigration in 1849 will be many thousand, and in 1850 still more. If our countrymen in California as clerks, mechanics, and workmen, will forsake employment at from two dollars to six dollars per day, how many more of the same class in the Atlantic States, earning much less, will leave for this country under such prospects? It is the opinion of many who have visited the gold regions the past and present months, that the ground will afford gold for many years, perhaps for a century. From my own examination of the rivers and their banks, I am of opinion that, at least for a few years, the golden products will equal the present year. However, as neither men of science, nor the laborers now at work, have made any explorations of consequence, it is a matter of impossibility to give any opinion as to the extent and richness of this part of California. Every Mexican who has seen the place says, throughout their republic there has never been any "placer like this one."

Could Mr. Polk and yourself see California as we now see it, you would think that a few thousand people, on one hundred miles square of the Sacramento valley, would yearly turn out of this river the whole price our country pays for the acquired territory. When I finished my first letter I doubted my own writing, and, to be better satisfied, showed it to one of the principal merchants of San Francisco, and to Captain Fulsom, of the Quartermaster's Department, who decided at once I was far below the reality. You certainly will suppose, from my two letters, that I am, like others, led away by the excitement of the day. I think I am not. In my last I enclosed a small sample of the gold dust, and I find my only error was in putting a value to the sand. At that time I was not aware how the gold was found; I now can describe the mode of collecting it.

A person without a machine, after digging off one or two feet of the upper ground, near the water, (in some cases they take the top earth), throws into a tin pan or wooden bowl a shovel full of loose dirt and stones; then placing the basin an inch or two under water, continues to stir up the dirt with his hand in such a manner that the running water will carry off the light earths, occasionally, with his hand, throwing out the stones. After an operation of this kind for twenty or thirty minutes, a spoonful of small black sand remains; this is, on a handkerchief or cloth, dried in the sun, the emerge is blown off, leaving the pure gold. I have the pleasure of enclosing a paper of this sand and gold, which I, from a bucket of dirt and stones, in half an hour, standing at the edge of the water, washed out myself. The value of it may be two or three dollars.

The size of the gold depends in some measure upon the river from which it is taken, the banks of one river having larger grains of gold than another. I presume more than one half of the gold put into pans or machines is washed out and goes down the stream; this is of no consequence to the washers, who care only for the present time. Some have formed companies of four or five men, and have a rough made machine put together in a day, which worked to much advantage, yet many prefer to work alone, with a wooden bowl or tin pan, worth fifteen or twenty cents in the States, but eight to sixteen dollars at the gold region. As the workmen continue, and materials can be obtained, improvements will take place in the mode of obtaining gold; at present it is obtained by standing in the water, and with much severe labor, or such as is called here severe labor.

How long this gathering of gold by the handful will continue here, or the future effect it will have on California, I cannot say. Three-fourths of the houses in the town on the bay of San Francisco are deserted. Houses are sold at the price of the ground lots. The effects are this week showing themselves in Monterey. Almost every house I had hired out is given up. Every blacksmith, carpenter, and lawyer is leaving; brick yards, saw mills, and ranchos, are left perfectly alone. A large number of the volunteers at San Francisco and Sonoma have deserted; some have been retaken and brought back; public and private vessels are losing their crews; my clerks have had one hundred per cent. advance offered them on their wages to accept employment. A complete revolution in the ordinary state of affairs is taking place; both of our newspapers are discontinued from want of workmen, and the loss of their agencies; the Alcaldes have left San Francisco, and I believe Sonoma likewise; the former place has not a Justice of the Peace left.

The second Alcalde of Monterey to-day joins the keepers of our principal hotel, who have closed their office and house, and will leave to-morrow for the golden rivers. I saw on the ground a lawyer who was last year Attorney General of the King of the Sandwich Islands, digging and washing out his ounce and a half per day; near him can be found most all his brethren of the long robe, working in the same occupation.

To conclude; my letter is long, but I could not well describe what I have seen in less words, and I now can believe that my account may be doubted; if the affair proves a bubble, a mere excitement, I know not how we can all be deceived, as we are situated. Gov. Mason and his staff have left Monterey to visit the place in question, and will, I suppose, soon forward to his department his views and opinions on this subject. Most of the land, where gold has been discovered, is public land; there are on different rivers some private grants. I have three such, purchased in 1846 and 1847, but have not learned that any private lands have produced gold, though they may hereafter do so.

I have the honor, dear sir, to be, very respectfully,

Your obedient servant,

THOMAS O. LARKIN.

Hon. JAMES BUCHANAN, *Secretary of State, Washington City.*

The following are the latest Official Dispatches received up to the present time.

From the Washington Union, January 21, 1849.

Extract from a letter from Thomas O. Larkin, Esq., late Consul, and now Navy Agent of the United States, to the Secretary of State, dated at Monterey, November 16, 1848.

The digging and washing for gold continues to increase on the Sacramento placer, so far as regards the number of persons engaged in the business, and the size and quantity of the metal daily obtained.

I have had in my hands several pieces of gold, about twenty-three carats fine, weighing from one to two pounds, and have it from good authority that pieces have been found weighing sixteen pounds. Indeed, I have heard of one specimen that weighed twenty-five pounds. There are many men in the placer, who in June last had not one hundred dollars, now in possession of from five to twenty thousand dollars, which they made by digging gold and trading with the Indians. Several, I believe, have made more.

A common calico shirt, or even a silver dollar has been taken by an Indian for gold, without regard to size; and a half to one ounce of gold—say eight to sixteen dollars—is now considered the price of a shirt, while from three to ten ounces is the price of a blanket. One hundred dollars a day, for several days in succession, was and is considered a fair remuneration for the labor of a gold-digger, though few work over a month at a time, as the fatigue is very great. From July to October, one-half of the gold-hunters have been afflicted either with the ague and fever or the intermittent fever, and twenty days absent from the placer during those months is necessary to escape the diseases. There have not, however, been many fatal cases.

The gold is now sold, from the smallest imaginary piece in size to pieces of one pound weight, at sixteen dollars per troy ounce, for all the purposes of commerce; but those who are under the necessity of raising coin to pay duties to the government, are obliged to accept from ten to eleven dollars per ounce. All the coin in California is likely to be locked up in the custom-house, as the last tariff of our Congress is in force here in regard to the receipt of money.

Could you know the value of the California placer as I know it, you would think you had been instrumental in obtaining a most splendid purchase for our country, to put no other construction on the late treaty.

QUICKSILVER MINE - NEAR SANTA CLARA.

The placer is known to be two or three hundred miles long; and, as discoveries are constantly being made, it may prove one thousand miles in length—in fact it is, not counting the intermediate miles yet unexplored. From five to ten millons of gold must be our export this and next year. How many more years this state of things will continue, I cannot say.

Extract from letter, dated October 25, 1848, from Commodore Jones to the Honorable Secretary of the Navy.

Nothing, sir, can exceed the deplorable state of things in all Upper California at this time, growing out of the maddening effects of the gold mania. I am sorry to say that even in this squadron some of the officers are a little tainted and have manifested restlessness under moderate restrictions imperiously demanded by the exigencies of the times, as you will perceive by the enclosed paper, addressed to three of the lieutenants. I am, however, happy to say that I have not been disappointed in the good effect of the means employed to prevent desertion, and to maintain order in the squadron, as but one desertion has taken place since the *rush of eight* from this ship on the evening of the 18th instant; and that the views and opinions of the few officers who were sceptical as to the *right* and efficiency of the means employed to prevent offences and to punish crime, have undergone a most favorable change, whereby I shall be enabled to keep on this coast until the whirlwind of anarchy and confusion confounded is superseded by the establishment of some legal government potent enough to enforce law and to protect life and property, which at this time is in great jeopardy everywhere outside our bulwarks.

FLAG SHIP OHIO, BAY OF MONTEREY, November 1, 1848.

SIR: By Lieutenant Lanman, who left here on the 26th ultimo, in the ship Izaak Walton, for the coast of Peru, where he expected to intercept the Panama steamers, I forwarded several communications acquainting you with my movements up to that date, which I hope you will receive early, and that they may prove satisfactory.

The enclosed extract from my last letter (No. 34) will convey the unpleasant tidings of the utter prostration of all law and order in our California possessions, brought about by the extraordinary developments of gold in this vicinity. . . .

I have the honor to be your obedient servant,

THOS. AP C. JONES.

Commander-in-chief U. S. Naval forces, P. O.

Hon. J. Y. MASON, *Secretary of the Navy.*

FLAG SHIP OHIO, BAY OF MONTEREY, November 2, 1848.

SIR: In my letter No. 24, from La Paz, I recommended the retention on this coast of all cruising ships of the Pacific squadron, and pointed out how they could be kept in repair and manned without returning round Cape Horn to the Atlantic States. When that recommendation was made I had no conception of the state of things in Upper California. For the present, and I fear for years to come, it will be impossible for the United States to maintain any naval or military establishment in California; as at the present, no hope of reward nor fear of punishment is sufficient to make binding any contract between man and man upon the soil of California.

To send troops out here would be needless, for they would immediately desert. To show what chance there is for apprehending deserters, I enclose an advertisement which has been widely circulated for a fortnight, but without bringing in a single deserter. Among the deserters from the squadron are some of the best petty officers and seamen, having but few months to serve, and *large* balances due them, amounting, in the aggregate, to *over ten thousand dollars*. . . .

There is a great deficiency of coin in the country, and especially in the mines; the traders, by taking advantage of the pressing necessity of the digger, not unfrequently compelling him to sell his ounce of good gold for a silver dollar; and it has been bought, under like circumstances, for fifty cents per ounce, of Indians. To this state of dependence laboring miners are now subjected, and must be until coin is more abundant. Disease, congestive and intermittent fever, is making great havoc among the diggers, as they are almost destitute of food and raiment, and, for the most part, without houses of any kind to protect them from the inclement season now at hand.

The commerce of this coast may be said to be entirely cut off by desertion. No sooner does a merchant ship arrive in any of the ports of California, than all hands leave her; in some instances, captain, cook, and all. At this moment there are a number of merchant ships thus abandoned at San Francisco; and such will be the fate of all that subsequently arrive.

The master of the ship "Izaak Walton," that brought stores for the squadron to this port, offered, without success, fifty dollars per month to Callao, and thence twenty dollars per month home, to *disbanded volunteers,* not seamen. We were obliged at last to supply him with four men whose terms of service were drawing to a close.* This state of things is not confined to California alone. Oregon is fast depopulating; her inhabitants pour into the gold diggings, and foreign residents and runaway sailors from the Sandwich Islands are arriving by every vessel that approaches this coast. . . .

Very respectfully, your obedient servant,

THOS. AP C. JONES,
Commander-in-Chief Pacific Squadron.

Hon. J. Y. MASON, *Secretary of the Navy.*

MONTEREY, California, October 23, 1848.

GENERAL: I arrived here on the eighteenth instant, from San Diego, and have paid the four companies of the first New York regiment in full, and they have all started for the gold mines. The three companies composing the command of Lieutenant Colonel Burton are now here, and will be mustered out to-day or to-morrow, and paid by Major Hill immediately, as the residents are extremely anxious to get rid of them; they have the place in their power. Nearly all the men of company "I," third artillery, have deserted.

We have the Ohio, Warren, Dale, Lexington and Southampton in port; but they *cannot land a man,* as they desert as soon as they set foot on shore. The only thing the ships could do, in case of an outbreak, would be to fire upon the town. The volunteers at Santa Barbara, Los Angeles, &c., behaved very well—no murmuring or difficulties of any kind with them. They complained that they were not allowed travelling allowance.

*Our ships are all short of their complements; the Ohio is one hundred and forty-five short. We can spare no more to our merchantmen.

The funds from Mazatlan have at last reached here; the amount is one hundred and thirty thousand dollars. It arrived very opportunely, as we have expended nearly all we had. The amount is a great deal more than will be required, as there are at present but two companies in California— one of first dragoons, the other of third artillery; the latter reduced to a mere skeleton by desertion, and the former in a fair way to share the same fate. I should suppose twenty thousand dollars would be sufficient to pay the present force (provided the companies are filled up) for a year. Treasury notes are good for nothing now; bills on the United States could not be negociated on any terms. Gold dust can be purchased for eight or ten dollars the ounce, and it is said to be worth eighteen dollars in the United States; consequently, all remittances are made in it.

Colonel Mason, and most of the army officers, are at Fort Sutter. Commodore Jones thinks it would be very imprudent to bring the public funds on shore, except in such sums as may be required for immediate use. He does not like to leave a ship here, on account of the difficulty of keeping the men. . . .

The gold fever rages as bad as ever, and the quantity collected has not diminished, but increased. Provisions, clothing, and all the necessaries of life, are at most exorbitant prices. Living was always expensive in this country, but now it passes all reason—board four dollars per day, washing five dollars to six dollars per dozen. Merchants' clerks are receiving from one thousand eight hundred dollars to three thousand dollars per annum salary! What the Government will do for civil officers, I do not know. Salaries will have to correspond with the times. The pay of governors, judges, &c., as allowed in the United States, will hardly compare with that paid to salesmen and shop clerks here.

I am, sir, respectfully,

Your obedient servant,

WILLIAM RICH, A. P. U. A.

Gen. N. TOWSON, *Paymaster Gen. U. U. A., Washington, D. C.*

IF I WERE TO ATTEMPT to tell all I know about the beasts, birds, and fishes of California, this volume would be swelled to more portly dimensions than I think advisable. I shall therefore confine myself to a few salient points, and leave a vast amount of details to the imagination.

And while I think of it, I will remark, that there are no buffaloes in California west of the Sierra Nevada, and the chances are that the "Buffalo Platform" is wholly unknown to the rancheros.

The buffalo being out of the question, it follows that the GRIZZLY BEAR holds beyond dispute, the foremost rank among the wild animals of California. He is the largest and by far the most powerful of all the wild beasts, and some idea of his prowess may be gathered from the earlier chapters of this book. He inhabits every part of Upper California, but if he lives in the Lower Province he keeps very dark about it, and confines himself to the mountains. He sometimes commits great havoc among the cattle, his plan of operations being to roll himself up in a ball, and then, like an eminent statesman, to "set the ball in motion, solitary and alone." He selects for this pastime an open meadow, and while engaged in this ground tumbling he cuts up all kinds of monkey-shines. He well understands the failings of the cattle, who are as curious as mother Eve, and will rush from all parts of the rancho to see the fun. In this he resembles the sportsmen of the Chesapeake, who train a little spaniel to toll the wild ducks in a similar manner. This curiosity to see what is going on is not confined to cattle, but is shared by antelopes, elk, and deer, who are easily attracted by a handkerchief flying from a ramrod. Well, the cattle will surround the bear in a wondering and gaping circle, until Cuffee—who is all the while laughing in his paw at their simplicity—seizes upon the first fat cow that comes within the grasp of his terrible claws, and, revealing himself in his true character, walks off with his prize, who thus pays the expense of the performance. Various other shifts and devices are resorted to by the bear to get hold of cattle, and he sometimes waylays them when on their way to the "rodea." An American of my acquaintance told me, that he received from the Administrador twenty cows as a fee for shooting an old bear of huge size, which had infested or invested the Mission of San Juan for many years. He had frequently been noosed, but was too cunning in the forepaw to be caught in that only fatal part, managing with great dexterity to ward off the riata from it.

The hunters say, that a pregnant she bear was never yet killed, the animal, when in that delicate situation, retiring to a secret den, where she is carefully attended by the male until an addition is made to her interesting family.

I have been present at the slaughter of three other bears besides those I have before alluded to, but they did not show fight. They tried hard to get to cover, and it is when concealed in the undergrowth that they are most dangerous to approach. A fine youth of my acquaintance was killed by a bear near Bodega. The bear, being mortally wounded, retired to cover, and was followed by the young man, against the advice and remonstrances of friends, armed only with his pistols. Ere he was aware of his danger, the bear sprang upon him, and literally tore him to pieces.

The grizzly bear will not, as a general rule, seek man to attack him, nor will he shun those who do not molest him; but if the male be surprised under peculiar circumstances, or if the female be encountered while her cubs are with her, the animal is dangerous, and will pursue a man, especially if the intruder inflict a wound. It would seem that bears are so accustomed to being avoided by other animals, that they think man should avoid them also. They have not the destructive propensities of the feline race, and there are numerous instances where they have spared men who have fallen into their power, letting them off with a few scratches, and much bodily fear. This trait is a fortunate one; for if to their terrible strength and scythe-like claws they united the cruel ferocity of the tiger, they would be formidable indeed. The only animal they dread is the little "sorillo," known in our vernacular by the monosyllable skunk, and it must be confessed, that this aversion is creditable to the taste of the bears, and will meet with universal sympathy. Indeed, so strong is Cuffee's antipathy to this small animal, that if the fragrant guest approach while the grizzly gentleman is discussing his favorite meal of a long-buried carcass—which he has stowed away himself for the sake of the "fumet"—the latter will retreat from his dainty repast with a reluctant growl, while master Sorillo quietly takes his place. And yet this huge animal, with a refined taste, does not disdain to hunt and devour small field-mice among the tulé, and the carcass of a whale, thrown upon the beach, will attract a regiment of bears.

An old hunter once took me several miles out of our way to a retired spot on the summit of a mountain, where he assured me the bears were accustomed to resort for the purpose of *dancing*. There was an old and gigantic pine, around whose base a slight hollow was regularly excavated, and the bark of the tree was completely scratched off some distance up, and the wood itself was deeply scarred. My friend assured me, that he had seen in this place a collection of bears, and had carefully approached them, keeping himself concealed, and advancing from the leeward. He solemnly asseverated, that around this tree sat the bears, and that each one of them was approached in turn by a huge old grizzly bear and led to the tree, against which they stood up and moved up and down, as if dancing. This continued until every bear had been led out by the ancient bear, and "it looked," said the hunter, "for all the world, like a lot of gals led out by a feller to dance."

Although this story seems about as tough and indigestible as Cuffee himself, still, considering the restless habits of the bear—for although in form and color he is at a distance exactly like the rocks he stands upon, his see-sawing betrays him—I am not disposed to reject the tale as wholly fabulous. But there's the story, and every one may judge for himself. I can only say, that the narrator was an honest man, and firmly believed that he had been an eye-witness to this marvellous ursine ball. The old inhabitants of California, of all degrees believe that these animals have resorts where they indulge in this fashionable amusement, and it is said that several of these ursine Tivolis exist in every district where the grizzly bear is found. I would respectfully suggest to the dancing masters to introduce, without delay, the "pas d'ours."

Many instances are known where bears have buried men who have fallen into their paws without injuring them; but this is only in cases of non-resistance.

Although I have witnessed the slaughter of five of these animals, only two attempted to make fight; the others retreated, growling, and sought a cover.

I was once with a small party at a bear-hunt, where we had baited a place with the carcass of an old mare. Picketing our horses by the "mecate," we began telling stories, and despairing of the bear, some of the party fell asleep. Suddenly, we were awakened by a deep growling, and I instantly took the end of my rope and mounted my horse. All the horses, smelling the bear, were in a state of violent excitement, and when we came to the place where the beast was tearing at the carcass, he immediately made off. Getting into the moonlight, we saw the captain of a merchantman, who had come to enjoy the sport, crying out loudly for assistance; he had mounted his horse, but had forgotten to untie the rope which fastened him to a tree. There he sat, without his hat, spurring the poor horse, which reared and plunged violently, and presenting a most ludicrous spectacle. Luckily for him, the bear was alarmed, and kept straight on, or he would have fallen a victim to his ignorance of horse-ropes. In the Black Hawk war a somewhat similar incident occurred:—A militia officer had tethered his horse to a high stump, and in the dead of night an alarm was given, and it was supposed the Indians were charging. Our officer, having mounted his horse without untying him, found it impossible to get away from the stump, and in his fright, mistaking the stump for an Indian, he exclaimed —"Mr. Indian, I surrender! I say I surrender, Mr. Indian!"

The grizzly bear has never yet been hunted by dogs; but I can easily imagine, that to those fond of hunting on a large scale, nothing could be more exciting. Indeed, Hypolyta's description of the sport is enough to stir up the blood of a huntsman:

"I was with Hercules, and Cadmus once,
  When in a wood of Crete they bayed a bear
  With hounds of Sparta; never did I hear
  Such gallant chiding; for, besides the groves,
  The skies, the fountains, every region near
  Seemed all one mutual cry: I never heard
  So musical a discord, such sweet thunder"—

But whatever dog tackles the grizzly bear must be equal to that

    —"Bred out of the Spartan kind,
  So flewed, so sanded; and whose heads are hung
  With ears that sweep away the morning dew;
  Crook-kneed and dew-lapped like Thessalian bulls,
  Slow in pursuit, but matched in mouth like bells,
  Each under each"—

The reader is already so familiar with the ELK of California, that I will say nothing more about that superb animal.

The DEER I have hardly mentioned; but for all that, they are well worth mentioning. They abound in all parts of California, and no man who understands the use of a rifle, need be without venison on the Pacific side of the Snowy Mountains.

Little that is new can be said of deer-hunting, and yet I would fain confer an ephemeral immortality on a sporting friend of mine, who has been the first to introduce a pack of grey-hounds into California.

Not far from San Francisco lives a stalwart son of the Emerald Isle—we may brag of the "universal Yankee nation," but your Irishman is the true cosmopolite—who was known to his sponsors in baptism by the simple name of Timothy Murphy, and who *is* known to the Europeans and Americans in California, by the affectionate cognomen of "Old Tim." Among the native population, however, he rejoices in the more euphonious cognomen of "DON TIMOTEO." This Herculean, ruddy-faced, good-humored Hibernian, came to California well prepared for the chase, bringing with him a splendid pack of grey-hounds, for the purpose of coursing the deer.

I have often hunted with Don Timoteo Murphy and his pack of hounds, and a more gallant sport cannot be found in the wide world. His dogs, like all grey-hounds, hunt altogether by sight, and it is a glorious sight to see them when in full cry, pursuing the fugitive deer over the hills of California. Now the fleet victim is on a lofty eminence, and his swift-footed antagonists are seen ascending in full pursuit. They have reached the summit, but the startled quarry has dashed down into the valley beyond, and for a moment the hounds are at fault. But they soon perceive him as he leaps along through brake and glen, over rocks and through the underbrush, and without stopping to breathe, they are once more upon his track. Close upon the hounds follows Don Timoteo, on his fleet and fiery Californian courser, alternately cheering on his dogs with all the phrases and exclamations in the sportsman's vocabulary, and talking Spanish with a broad Irish brogue, to the Indian boys, who officiate as henchmen and beaters, and run on foot over the broken country, with almost incredible celerity. And now the indefatigable dogs are close upon the panting buck, whose last race is nearly run. They soon come up with him, and leaping, open-mouthed upon his tender haunches, snapping and fiercely growling, they pull the victim down, and when we reach the scene of slaughter, his full and eloquent eye is glaring in death, and all is over, save the *coup de grace,* which Don Timoteo is not backward to administer.

I have attended many of these hunts with this Hibernian scion of the great family of Nimrod, and sometimes I have known the persecuted stag to take to the waters of the bay for refuge. Sometimes the Indian beaters will start a luckless little fawn, or an unfortunate doe, but the gaunt hounds pull the poor things down so speedily, that the sport is not worth much. But when the full-grown antlered stag is pursued, no finer sport can be imagined.

Unless Don Timoteo's hounds be accessible, the usual way to hunt deer is to mount a quiet horse, and with a rifle thrown across the saddle-bow, to ride in pursuit of the game. The American hunters are marvellous fellows for spying animals or Indians at immense distances through the trees. They are literally gifted with second sight, and this far-seeing faculty is similar to that possessed by sailors, who can distinguish a ship at sea long before she is visible to a landsman. For my part, I never yet stole upon a deer before the animal was warned of my approach; but the American backwoodsman can generally get within rifle range without being discovered.

The black-tailed deer is the only species known in California. It is rather larger than the deer east of the Rocky Mountains; but although the venison is very palatable and tender, it has not quite the peculiar *game* flavor of the white-tailed variety.

The large BLACK WOLF is also found in California; his habits are the same there as elsewhere, and very bad habits they are; but mankind need not fear him.

The COYOTE is a species of wolf, very much resembling the common prairie-wolf of Illinois. This animal is very destructive, and particularly so with respect to sheep, taking his mutton wherever he finds it. But he is a cowardly caitiff, and will not attack mankind. Those of our service, acquainted with this sneaking rascal, say he is really a wild dog, and it is certain that dogs readily amalgamate with the Coyote.

Then comes the LEON, or California Lion,—a generic name among the Indians and lower orders of whites, for nearly all beasts of prey—a large panther, which destroys great numbers of colts. A mare will not defend her colt when attacked by one of these panthers, but a cow generally drives off the savage beast with her horns, when he takes liberties with her calf.

The PUMA or South American panther, is also found in California, and is both a smaller animal and less destructive than the lion-panther. It resembles the wild-cat, and is substantially the same species of animal.

Of the WILD HORSE I have already had much to say, and I need not weary the reader by further remarks upon that beautiful animal, which abounds throughout California.

The ANTELOPE, shy as a young maiden, and fleet as the gale, is a very common animal in California; but in these enlightened days, when natural history is brought to every man's door, it is not necessary to describe this exquisite animal. The showman of the "Hypoferian Circus" can, doubtless, give a strictly classic account of its habits.

The HARE—the *real* hare, not to be mistaken by the London wag for a periwig—is also found, and grows to a large size. By and by, when the strides of civilization render "such small deer" an object, there will be rare coursing over the hills and dales of California, in pursuit of these swift-footed quadrupeds.

The RABBIT—a very different animal from the hare—is extremely abundant, and quite as prolific as the same family is known to be all over the globe. Every variety of this animal is found in California except the Welsh.

The SQUIRREL tribes are innumerable, and myriads of them infest the country south of the Bay of San Francisco. The holes they dig in the ground are fatal to many horses, which step into them, and break their legs. Although a small species exists north of the bay, these mischievous creatures of the larger sort never cross it, nor even the river San Joaquim.

Polecats, marmots, mice, and a hundred other small animals are to be found, in vast quantities. I do not remember having stumbled on "that same old coon," but have no doubt he is "thar."

And now a word for the feathered tribes.

The VULTURE, the EAGLE, the HAWK, the CROW, and various other carrion birds are of course abundant; but I shall not dwell upon them.

The PHEASANT is found in tolerable abundance. The CORREA, a beautiful species, with pure white plumage, is a mortal enemy to the rattlesnake, which it encircles with the prickly pear, and then pecks to death. He is called "correa," from his habit of running rapidly on the ground, and is never killed by the natives, who regard him with superstitious reverence, as the orientals do the Ostrich.

BLACK GROUSE, or heath-fowl, are also to be had for the shooting, and are by no means to be despised by the lover of game.

The Californian CRESTED PARTRIDGE is a beautiful bird, and worthy of a nook on any man's table.

PELICANS, grey and white, are very much the same as Pelicans in other regions, and have pretty much the same nine-pin attitudes.

WILD GEESE are very abundant, many varieties, including the Brant, migrating to California between September and January, and covering the whole country.

WILD DUCKS are quite as numerous as the Geese, and include the most beautiful Summer Ducks, Teal, and Grebes, besides many other varieties.

PLOVER are "too tedious to mention."

The CURLEW is as common as dirt.

BLUE CRANES, of the size of a Turkey, are most excellent eating.

WILD PIGEONS are quite as plentiful as they were in Baron Munchausen's time.

The WILD TURKEY I do not remember meeting with; but I have no doubt that excellent bird is to be found.

Speaking of the Wild Turkey reminds me of a very famous one in New York. Some say it was a Goose, but for the purposes of this story we will make it a Turkey.

A highly respectable citizen, then, who was knowing in poultry, bought a Wild Turkey for his Christmas dinner. He had made up his mind to "blow it out straight," without regard to the expense, and therefore invited divers poor cousins to his Christmas feast. At the appointed hour, the Turkey was placed on the table, and the honest citizen, full of benevolent intentions towards his indigent—not yet indignant—relations, summoned them to dinner. Drawing the carver across the steel, he began to operate on the smoking Turkey—when lo! he could make no impression. He cut, he hacked, he tugged, he perspired; but never a joint or muscle of the obdurate bird could he move. At length, "faint with excessive toil," he remarked, "Wife! this knife is very dull"—and incontinently set to work, passing the keen instrument furiously across the steel. His thumb-nail certifying that the carver was now as sharp as a razor, he renewed his labors on the reluctant fowl. But it was of no use. The bird declined being cut on any terms. At length, to the great chagrin of the family, and to the dismay of the poor cousins—who ever after believed that the pretended Turkey was a sham, ingeniously devised to mock them with a false show of hospitality—the dish was condemned to the kitchen, and the dinner was eked out with viands which the victimized guests might have got at home. The next morning, at breakfast, *that* Turkey again made its appearance on the table—whole—of course. "Wife!" says the exasperated citizen, "this is outrageous! Send off that Turkey directly and give it to the first beggar that comes to the door!" No sooner said than done. A wandering collector of broken victuals was even then knocking at the basement door, and her eyes glistened with rapture when she saw this generous meal for her famishing children thrust, without note or comment, into her wretched basket. Katy, poor thing, would for once have a good supper, and little Patrick would at last be conscious of the delights of a full stomach. Our citizen felt consoled. He had done a charitable action: a twelve shilling Turkey had gone from his door into the miserable abode of a wretched beggar. Yes; upon the whole he was rather glad everything had turned out just as it did. It was Providential; and it would do very well to remark casually to that stingy Jones, how a cooked and stuffed twelve shilling Turkey had been given away—whole—at his door, to a nameless mendicant. Our citizen slept well that night—so did his wife; every one sleeps well who feeds the hungry and clothes the naked. He awoke in the morning full of "exceeding peace," and, having an early call down-town, ate a morsel of food and sallied forth. The sun had not yet risen, but it was daylight—light enough to discern the shocking object which was stuck upon the good citizen's area-railing. Horror of horrors!—it was—yes, it was—that same old Turkey! still as hale, as hearty, as whole as ever! With an indignant growl our citizen seized the offensive bird, and, dashing it to the ground, kicked it a whole block before his choler subsided.

I have enumerated some of the quadrupeds and birds of California. It now becomes my pleasant duty to allude to the wealth of her waters.

The fresh waters are instinct with fish of various kinds.

The TROUT is a very delicate fish, and the streams are full of them.

The SALMON needs no eulogy from any man, and is also abundant.

The other varieties are not to be compared with the trout and salmon, but they are so plentiful that numerous families of Indians subsist upon them.

The SEA—the ever bountiful Pacific—yields large fish of many varieties, but I fear that the enumeration of a string of names unknown to my readers, will only add to the sins of tediousness which have been committed in this volume. But I cannot pass over the testacious kinds.

There is the OYSTER, a species of bivalve, which has been heard of on the Atlantic-side, and which is found in immense quantities on the coast of the Pacific.

The CRAB, which still perversely goes backward even there, although in the nature of things, his gait should be reversed.

The LOBSTER, which after all is nothing but a lobster, and quite as red and indigestible as his Eastern brother.

The CRAWFISH, which has become an active verb in our Western States, where a truckling politician who "backs out" is said to "crawfish."

But far transcending all, is that magnificent sea-monster known as the ABLON or PEARL OYSTER. Not only does this valuable shell-fish yield pearls, but its meat is most delicious, and weighs several pounds.

The reader will thank me for concluding this chapter with such a bonne-bouche.

DURING MY TRAVELS in the interior, I frequently met with little adventures which were pleasant enough in their way, but might not interest the general reader. I shall pass over the greater part of these incidents; but here is something which, although a very simple story, may amuse some of the old *habitués* of Washington, who will recognise the portrait of a well-known character, which is casually introduced. We will call it

THE HISTORY OF A CI-DEVANT DIPLOMATIST

One pleasant day, while riding along in the country, I came to a log-cabin, much more conveniently constructed than the houses of the Californians usually are. A pretty grove had been left standing near the house, which invested the place with a peculiar charm; for the Spaniard avoids a tree as he would a pestilence. The Americans who emigrate to California, generally allow trees to remain about on their places; a fact, the more remarkable, because the emigrants chiefly find fault with the country for its want of timber. There is indeed plenty of timber, but it is troublesome to go into the ravines and mountains to cut and collect it; and most of these gentlemen having been used to cut, slash and girdle, ad libitum, in the luxuriant forests of the West—where the great object in life is to make a "clearing"—do not fancy the bare plains of California.

Soon came the master, returning from an expedition after his cattle; and after close inspection, in spite of his bronzed face, and half-Californian, half-backwoods costume, I recognized in him an old acquaintance. We had met last in the Mediterranean, where he pursued the vocation of a special messenger of the United States Department of State.

After we had partaken of a "guisado," (ragout), the Californian national dish, composed of beef, chile, peppers, and all sorts of vegetables, he unfolded to me his story:

"Like most men of my race and country," said he, "I am naturally of a rambling disposition. After a youth of commercial disappointments, spent in rambling in foreign lands, in the course of which I learnt many languages, and acquired much experience of this wicked world, but not the solid advantages which I sought, I found myself in Washington, without a sous, looking after a clerkship, or anything else that might turn up. I here met with the celebrated Edward ——, a gentleman whose acquaintance, probably, outnumbered that of any other person in the United States. After a chequered life, he had brought up at the federal city, where he held a comfortable office.

"Ned was brought up in the Navy, and had attained the grade of lieutenant, when some relative leaving him a legacy of several thousand dollars, he resigned his office, in order to spend his money 'like a gentleman'. This was soon done, and Ned found himself, one bright morning, in a European capital, without any visible means of subsistence, except a solitary guinea, which his father—who was a physician—had received for his first fee. He was the best story-teller of his day, and a first-rate wit; and his company was sought not only by his messmates, but by the best society every where. Such a man, of course, did not despair, but making use of his wits he succeeded in getting once more to the United States with his guinea, although it had often been left in pawn for a shilling less than its value. I imagine he died in the possession of that guinea. At the time I speak of, he was hunting up the ghost of a 'claim', which he had been trying to raise for some years, bringing all his influence and abilities to bear on the surly officials.

"Ned had been a government messenger, and he advised me to obtain the same berth, promising his influence in my behalf, which was considerable. Ned had been United States Consul, and had held other loafing berths, everywhere, and was as well known at the seat of government as the capitol itself. He was a great favorite with the tradesmen, and had the free run of the capital of magnificent distances. The hotel that could secure Ned as a permanent guest was made for the season; he was chaperon in general to everybody, and knowing every one of the least consequence he *patronized* whoever he pleased, and went wherever he was treated best. He imagined that he would be rich some day or other, 'in the good time coming', when his 'claim' should be allowed, and he then intended honorably to pay off all the old scores which those who had enjoyed his custom had cheerfully charged to profit and loss. It is said that on one occasion, when Ned had been very brilliant, and had ordered some choice and expensive wine, he was told the next day, by old Mr. —— that he should be extremely happy to have him live at his hotel scot free, and consider the house his home, but when he ordered wine at ten dollars a bottle, it was carrying the joke rather too far. Ned was much offended, and with a dignified air told the astonished publican to send in his bill immediately, as he intended to leave the house. The old gentleman apologized, and urged him to stay; but Ned walked off to Fuller's, which incontinently became the fashionable house of the season.

"Well, in my capacity of government messenger, I visited nearly every habitable part of this terraqueous ball where civilization entails on man that immensely expensive and convenient evil—a government. I have done the behests of the Department of State to the courts of Europe, the South American republics, and even the Asiatic and African despotic sovereignties. Within one and the same year, I have stood in the ante-chambers of four of the sovereigns of Western Europe—all 'first-rate powers;' waited the pleasure of the Padisha, at the seraglio gate; borne a mission to his refractory vassal, Mehemet Ali; smoked a kalivan with Akbar Khan, the enemy of the English power in Cabul; visited the dominions of John Company; and returned to report progress to the 'cute' specimen of the universal Yankee nation, who, in a rusty suit of black, moves so many wires in the little old-fashioned parlor of the Department of State at Washington. I have been sent on missions secret, delicate, warlike, and peaceful—carrying mere verbal communications, in cases where it would not answer to trust to writing. Although an humble Mercury of my official superiors, I have had occasion to learn many of the dangerous secrets of diplomacy, and more than once have been placed in situations, where the discovery of my incognito would have subjected me to instant death, or worse—a lingering and secret imprisonment for life. I have, however, neither learned the lessons of deceit, nor acquired that mysterious air which is usually put on by politicians, but am a living illustration of the fact, that

> 'A light heart, and a thin pair of breeches,
> Go far through the world, my brave boys!'

"I came to this country on a mission, and liked it so well, that I resolved to settle here. Well, sir, I went first to the Pueblo de los Angeles, but having since married, I finally concluded to settle here. I own this lovely tract of two leagues; my wife is an angel, as well as a regular 'ranchera', and I am but too happy, after all my wanderings, to have brought myself at last into such snug moorings."

From this simple story the moralist may find additional evidence that happiness is independent of external circumstances, and is nowhere found in greater perfection than among those exiled to

> —"The farthest verge of the green earth."—

I will add a few scraps which may prove interesting.

The ADOBE is the chief building material of the Californians. They are made of mud, mixed with chopped straw, and then dried in the sun. Each adobe is about two feet long, and one foot wide—consequently the walls of the houses are of great thickness. They serve an excellent purpose in the climate of California, and are very cheap besides. Those who carry out frames of houses, will probably find it quite as expensive and difficult to erect and finish them as to procure the adobes and have houses built of them. These moveable houses are mere balloons, and are a constant source of expense in the way of paint and repairs. I should prefer to rely on the adobe. If laborers can be hired to put up and finish frame houses, they can also be had to erect those constructed of the adobe. The view of Monterey will give the reader an idea of the adobe house. The town of San Francisco, (my drawing of which has been lately lost or pilfered,) contained, in the beginning of 1848, only about half a dozen of these adobe houses, and the value of the picture lay in its view of the harbor, taken from the shore.

The adobe is one of the most ancient of building materials. It is beyond all doubt the same brick which Pharaoh commanded the captive children of Israel to make without straw—a thing wholly impossible. Thus, by this simple link, is Western America directly connected with the most remote antiquity, and associated with one of the most interesting passages of Holy Writ. The adobe is still found in the towns of Babylon (Irak Arabi) and in the ruins of that city itself, and of other ancient cities of Asia.

The WILD MUSTARD covers a large portion of the plains of California, south of San Francisco. It is said to have sprung from a few seeds brought years ago by an old Padre. It was not a bad idea of the worthy priest to introduce mustard where beef was so abundant.

GRASSHOPPERS are the greatest pest of the farmer in California. Some years they are very destructive, devouring all the vegetation which comes in their way; and are equal to the plague of locusts in Egypt, whose advent doubtless caused Pharaoh to think Moses "more plague than prophet."

The distance from Panama to San Francisco is three thousand five hundred and fifteen statute miles, or about twenty-one days' run of a steamer, at the rate of two hundred nautical miles a day, including all sorts of stoppages at every intermediate port on the coast, to land passengers, take in coal, &c. The distance from New Orleans to Chagres is about one thousand six hundred miles—say eight days' steaming. The transit across the Isthmus should not occupy more than two days. When the railroad, projected by Messrs. Aspinwall, Chauncey & Stephens, shall be completed, an immense tide of emigration will pour over it, both from the United States and from Europe.

The first thing the Romans did on acquiring a distant province, was to establish a *military road* running through from Rome to the capital of the conquered territory. The Roman military road was, in effect, a sort of fortification for the legions in their march. In running through a high country, the "agger" was lower than the surrounding country, making a kind of redoubt; running through a low country, it was higher than the surrounding country, thus affording a vantage ground. By means of these roads, the Romans were, in case of revolt, enabled to repair promptly to the scene of action, and to communicate securely with the heart of the empire. But *we* have *steam*, and should use it at once, to enable legions of toiling men to reach the goal of their hopes.

I once knew a Californian scapegrace to steal a horse while his owner had hold of the bridle. The owner had stepped into a shop to talk, and was holding the end of the reins in his hand, when the thief gently slipped off the bridle, hung it on a post, and rode off with the horse and saddle.

THE ROCKY MOUNTAIN ROUTE.—Every emigrant with whom I have conversed, admits that those who cross the Rocky Mountains, in emigrant wagons, with their families, undergo more hardships than they could ever have imagined possible. One of my company, who was a Rocky Mountain emigrant, once gave me an account of his terrible sufferings from hunger, during a period of twenty-two days. All that time he had nothing to eat except scraps of buckskin, and he never gave up his gun, and kept steadily on to the westward. He told me that at last, after "looking hard for a buck," he spied an Indian, and immediately gave chase. "And, sir," said he, "had I caught him, I should have slain and eaten him, as soon as if he had been a deer." These men suffer most appalling hardships, and often perish, while in sight of the promised land. The most horrid stories are told of the inhuman repasts of these poor wretches, and their deadly quarrels for the last remnant of a brother's or mother's body. But the details of such atrocities are too shocking to be dwelt upon, especially as the stories are usually derived from hearsay, and much exaggerated to suit the most depraved tastes.

HEALTH.—The high and dry character of Upper California, the absence of alluvial bottoms of great extent, the comparative scarcity of timber, and many minor causes which might be enumerated, render Upper California a most healthy country. Most new countries are troubled with ague and fever, and bilious fevers of all varieties; and I am far from saying that California is exempt from them. On the contrary, there is no doubt that large quantities of her quicksilver will be used at home in the shape of calomel, and the demand for quinine will probably be very lively. But these diseases will be contracted chiefly in the low grounds and along the valleys of the rivers, while the uplands, which compose the greater part of California, will be as healthy as any part of the world. Men who stand all day long in the mud and water digging for gold under the scorching rays of a summer sun, will be apt to sicken anywhere; and as their operations will be carried on chiefly in the fever and ague, and bilious region, the gold diggers cannot all hope to escape disease.

There are seasons when the usually healthy portions of the country become sickly. When the rains come prematurely, and afterwards a "dry spell" sets in, and then the springing vegetation rots, and the miasma arising from that cause, sometimes produces disease. But this is of rare occurrence, and it is safe to say that California is quite as healthy as any of our northern States. The doctrine of compensations is well illustrated by the fact that while the settler is obliged to draw his timber and wood a short distance, he is exempt from those diseases to which he would be subject if the whole country were thickly timbered.

A PACIFIC NAVY.—No great time can elapse before our government will perceive the policy of establishing a Pacific navy—a navy built, equipped, and maintained from the resources of California and Oregon. A respectable naval force in the Pacific will be a matter of necessity, and in a few years vessels can be built and equipped at San Francisco and manned from the vast commerce—especially the whaling trade—of the Pacific. Speaking of the whaling trade, it may well be doubted whether it will not undergo great changes when the railroad across the Isthmus shall be constructed. But I shall not stop to discuss that question. A Pacific navy is one of those obvious improvements which our government will hardly hesitate to avail of. At present, ships of war cannot be built and equipped in California, nor can the Pacific trade furnish our ships with seamen. But whenever the latter difficulty shall cease, it will be politic to send out a stationary local navy to the Pacific. It will be a great economy, and a great convenience. At present, about a year is consumed in going backwards and forwards, before and after a cruise, the officers and crew drawing their pay and rations the whole time. Thus, one year out of three is wasted, and great expense and inconvenience incurred, which may hereafter be saved by the establishment of a Pacific navy.

In a few years, when gold is more difficult to find, and a steady and wealthy population shall have settled down in California, ship-building will become a very important branch of industry. White oak of superior quality for ship-building is found in abundance north of the bay of San Francisco, and the further north you go, the larger it grows, the better its quality, and the greater the quantity. When the cheap labor of Asia shall be introduced, it is not unlikely that the New York merchant will order ships to be built at San Francisco.

EARLY IN FEBRUARY, 1847, we sailed from San Diego, in the Portsmouth, for the coast of Mexico. We hoisted the American flag at Cape St. Lucas and San José, in March following, and, with the exception of three visits to Upper California, we remained on the Mexican coast until the month of January, in the year 1848.

During this period, we visited both shores of the Gulf of California, going around from Cape St. Lucas to Guayamas and San Blas, blockading, cruising, &c. We took several valuable prizes, and annoyed the enemy in a variety of ways.

The climate, in the southern part of Upper California, is the most delightful that can be imagined. In Los Angeles and San Diego, the thermometer ranges from fifty-eight to seventy-five degrees Fahr. in the daytime, during the whole year. The nights are always cool, and the total absence of miasmatic influences, renders the atmosphere dry, transparent and balmy. The country is only tolerably watered.

In the vicinity of Los Angeles, the coast range towers above the plain, with its lofty and serrated mountain peaks, which are covered with snow during a considerable portion of the year. The peculiar clearness of the air, probably from its extreme dryness, almost wholly divests the landscape of those effects which are called "atmospheric."

Stand here! and look at those lofty mountain peaks which seem so metallic that you might suppose they were covered with burnished silver. Mark those mighty mountains, which are impending almost over your head, and seem as if they might perchance topple over and crush you. The illusion is perfect. You can scarcely believe that those mountains are very distant from you, and that mortal man has never yet attained their summits. But so it is. So clear and distinct are those ultra-marine tints, that space is annihilated; and the remote mountain is brought so near, that you seem to stand directly at its base.

In the plain itself, the richest and most brilliant wild-flowers flourish in boundless profusion, and with a rank luxuriance which far transcends all the efforts of art. All colors, all shades of colors, all hues, all tints, all combinations are there to be seen; and the endless varieties bewilder the senses. Perennial incense ascends to heaven from these fragrant plains; and the size which some of these gorgeous wild-flowers attain, would seem fabulous to an eastern florist. Among them are a poppy and a tulip, whose flaunting and gaudy hues attract the eye in all directions, and the scale descends to the humblest daisy and the meekest violet.

In the glens and recesses of the mountains are said to exist the most romantic streams, watering the finest table-lands, dashing down awful precipices, and winding through richly-wooded ravines. The timber is said to be of surpassing excellence, and the country of a very peculiar character. Here live thousands of Indians—miles de Indios—and here, before many years shall pass away, will ring the woodman's axe, and the smoke will ascend from a thousand domestic altars. It may be that the accounts of these mountains are exaggerated; but all agree that they abound in the most lovely and romantic scenery, and contain vast quantities of fertile land and valuable timber.

The GRAPE is the principal, and indeed, at present, almost the sole production of this part of our California. The vineyards of the Pueblo de los Angeles are as luxuriant and productive as any in the world. The species of grape chiefly cultivated, appears to be of the variety known to us of the Atlantic coast as the Hamburg grape. It produces two kinds of wine. One is a white wine, clear and transparent, and of a light amber tint, and in taste resembling hock. The other is a tinto, or red wine, and its taste and bouquet are something like the La Malque of Marseilles. The vineyards also produce great quantities of agua ardiente or Spanish brandy, of a very pure and colorless description, of an agreeable taste, superior quality, and the highest proof. A most delicious cordial is likewise made, called Angelica, and if the old Olympian gods could get a drop of it, they would soon vote Nectar a bore, and old Jupiter would instantly order Master Ganymede to change his goblet, and charge it with the new tipple to the brim.

Wolfskill's vineyard, in the Pueblo de los Angeles, contains forty acres of land and about five thousand vines. It produces a crop of twenty casks of wine, and an equal amount of "aguadiente."

The grape likewise grows in the San Francisco district, and so luxuriantly, that Mr. Leese made from only two acres of vines, in the year I was there, no less than twenty-six barrels of wine, and eight barrels of aguadiente.

The wild grape, which I have seen throughout all the valleys, is, when ripe, of the size of ounce balls, and of an excellent flavor. The olive, date, palm, and other tropical productions, are sparsely found in San Diego.

The grape will, hereafter, be a vast source of wealth to the people of California. The volcanic soil favors the growth of the vines, and the varieties of soil and climate will unquestionably produce varieties of wine. As yet but a single species of grape is cultivated, and that is said to have been originally indigenous. Beyond all doubt, every variety of grape will grow in that magnificent region, and when all the standard varieties shall be introduced from Europe, and grafting and scientific cultivation resorted to, who shall predict the result? Let those who, ten years hence, shall be drinking a bottle of California champagne at Delmonico's, remember that "I told them so." Perhaps the friends of temperance will mourn at the vinous prospects of California; but they should take comfort in the reflection that wine countries are not addicted to intemperance nearly so much as beer countries, and that the introduction of pure liquors will, in time, drive away the poisonous manufactured stuff, whose ravages are unjustly laid at the door of the unadulterated product of the grape.

It must be set down as a fixed fact that brandy, wine, and raisins, are to be soon added to our vast productions.

The nature of our service while on the coast of Mexico, and in the Gulf of California, was not of a kind to interest the general reader. We were chiefly engaged in blockading, and I was occasionally absent on duty in charge of prizes, which were captured without wasting much of Uncle Sam's gunpowder.

To the inmates of a ship at sea, months, and even years, seem, in the retrospect, like a very short period, as few incidents occur to mark time as it rolls on in its monotonous course. One day is entirely like another; and while the dim vista of the future stretches far away beyond the reach of imagination, we wonder at the nothingness of the past, so carelessly do we mark the ebbing sands of the present. Meanwhile, thousands of miles are passed over, with scarcely a change in our usual habits of thought or action —nothing novel appealing to our consciousness, save the variations of climate which we experience while pursuing our track in the watery waste, alternately "scorched in the tropics, and frozen at the pole."

Some men there are, however, whose systematic and regular habits of mind, render this vegetable existence not only tolerable, but even pleasant. I remember being on an Indian voyage, during which we had been more than three months at sea, when we had a celebrated mathematician for a shipmate. He had been occupied in some abstruse calculations of great length, and the quiet monotony of ship-life agreed perfectly well with the absorbing nature of his studies. On making land, every one else, having exhausted all means of amusement, was delighted, and the prospect before us was announced with great glee to our friend, as he sat absorbed in his mathematics. But the old gentleman, evidently displeased at being disturbed before his long 'ciphering' was finished, started up suddenly and pettishly exclaimed, "What a little world it is! One can hardly turn round in it." We had, since leaving port, almost circumnavigated the earth.

As few will care to be lugged about with us in our wearisome cruise, I shall merely give my impressions of the country around which we hovered so long a time.

All great peninsulas extend longitudinally from north to south, with trifling deviations to the east and west; and such, of course, is the case with regard to the peninsula of Lower California. South of San Diego, and in full view from that town and harbor, is a high and well defined table mountain. It is called the Mesa de Navaez, and the parallel of 32 deg. of north latitude passes over its summit, marking the line between Upper and Lower California. South of this line, the lofty serrania, occupying the centre of the peninsula like a back-bone, has never been explored, or even visited save by a few Indians, to whom its recesses are familiar. It is not known, however, to be inhabited by any considerable or populous rancherias of even this primitive people. Near the coast, on the west or Pacific side, there are a few fine ranchos owned by persons living in the upper district. There is, likewise, a small settlement at Ensiñada, forty or fifty miles from San Diego. Magdalena Bay is the next place in point of commercial or national importance. It has a spacious and commodious harbor, well sheltered and easy of ingress and egress. The land in the neighborhood is good and productive, but beyond a single rancho, there is no population whatever. In point of natural advantages the harbor is probably equal to any in the Pacific. It has become a place of resort, within a year past, for whalers; and a great many have visited it to take a whale called the California gray—a variety, I believe, new to whalemen. The whalers lie quietly at anchor, and the fish is caught in the bay itself.

Proceeding south, we come next to Todos los Santos. There was once a mission at this place, but there is no harbor, the few houses standing at the extremity of an indentation of the land. There is no further settlement until Cape St. Lucas, the southern extremity of the peninsula, is reached, the distance being about thirty miles farther south. The cape offers to the rolling swell of the Pacific towards the south, a lofty barrier of white and gray rocks, of volcanic origin, wrought into the most fantastic pinnacles and grotesque forms. Its extremity takes a sudden curve to the eastward, and incloses a small bay, within which there is good anchorage, well shut in from all winds except southers, which prevail in this region through the summer months.

Entering the Gulf, we come to San José, a small town, of about five hundred inhabitants, which is situated in a broad and fertile valley, with a stream of water running through it, about thirty miles from the cape, towards the northward and eastward. It has no harbor, but the road is safe, except during the souther season, and the landing on the open beach may generally be attempted.

Towards the north, (having now doubled the cape), we come first to the Ensiñada de la Palma, the first bight of the Gulf of California, and then to La Paz, which is the capital town of Lower California. It is a small place of not more than five or six hundred inhabitants, but the houses, built of adobe, with azoteas in the Mexican fashion, are good, and it is the only semblance of a town in the Province. Its spacious bay, and the island in front of it, make a fine harbor. The northern passage between the island and the main land is the broadest and best, and therefore the only one at present used by vessels of any size; but the other passage, although somewhat intricate, has plenty of water for any class of vessels. The small harbor of Pichelingue, which is a land-locked cove in the southern shore of the Bay of La Paz, offers a perfectly secure and calm place, with deep water, without rocks or other obstructions, for careenage, or refitting.

The next place of importance to the northward is Loreto, which is doubtless a magnificent harbor. Entering by a narrow passage, the bay expands into a fine amphitheatrical form, with bold shores, and without dangers, and it can be entered by night as well as by day, so well are its bold landmarks defined. There is beside a broad and deep estuary, called the "Puerto Escondido," making out from this bay, and winding for miles close under the lofty mountains near the coast, in which the navies of the world can be hidden completely from view from the gulf, or even from the outer harbor. There was anciently an important mission here, and also a royal arsenal; but both are now among the things that were.

The only remaining place of any importance on the California side is the small town of Mulegé, near the head of the gulf. It also has a tolerable harbor, and the country around it is moderately productive.

The head of the gulf, at and about the embouchure of the river Colorado, is without good harbors for affording protection from the southers, which blow hard in the summer months, and this section is infested with islands, reefs, &c., making its navigation somewhat difficult—the more so as no good survey exists of its shores.

There are some large islands, of which Tiburon Island is the most important. This island was inhabited by a numerous tribe of Indians until within a year or two, when they were surprised by an expedition from Guayamas, under the command of General Urrea, which massacred in cold blood a large portion of the population, and after destroying their villages, carried off many captives.

So exasperated were these Indians at this most inhuman, unprovoked, and uncalled-for outrage, that they retired to the main land of the adjacent Mexican Province of Sonora, and infesting the roads between its seaport, Guayamas, and the interior towns, instantly put to death every white person they encountered, without distinction of sex or age. They exhibited a remarkable degree of character for Indians; for not only did they not steal from the houses of the whites who fell into their power, but after murdering them, left all their money and effects untouched in the road. Nor did they molest the domesticated Indians of the country, who are numerous, and living on the territorial possessions of the Mexicans, are regarded and treated as their vassals.

The sea-port town of Guayamas is justly regarded as the principal commercial depot of the Gulf of California, and Province of Sonora. It is a well-built town, and contains a population of several thousands. There is considerable business done here, for it is the depot of the precious metals brought from the interior, and especially from the mines of Harispe and Chihuahua. It is said that a million and a half dollars' worth of the precious metals are sent to England from this port annually—smuggled of course. Guayamas takes also a considerable quantity of goods of English and American manufacture, as well as those of Mexico and South America. The harbor is an excellent one, perfectly easy of access, and securely land-locked. The depth of water is said to be decreasing.

In October, 1847, we bombarded this place with the frigate Congress and the sloop-of-war Portsmouth, and took military possession of it. The inhabitants retired to the small town of San José, about two leagues distant, but there was no organized resistance to our occupation; and in fact, had invasion been our legitimate business, with the crews of our ships, numbering six hundred effective men, we might have taken possession of the whole Province of Sonora, its capital, mines, and all the wealth of its inhabitants such was the apathy or discontent of the whole population of that rich and important Province.

The better part of the population is composed of Mexican-Spaniards, who own the larger part of the land, and hold to service the Indians living on it—the debased descendants of those warlike tribes which gave Ulloa and his companions some trouble, when the latter invaded their country. These Indians serve their feudal superiors in war against their local enemies. Two families of importance have for some time kept this Province in a turmoil with their feuds. The Guadaras and Iñigos are the Guelfs and Ghibellines of this part of Sonora. The end of all their wars and quarrels was to obtain possession of office, and the consequent spoils of the custom-

house, and the imposts of the country. Their lands lie in the flat and alluvial valley of the Hiaqui river, and are thickly inhabited by the Indians
of that name, who are "tall in stature, and vigorous of body," like their
ancestors of Ulloa's time, and excellent hewers of wood and drawers of
water, but not fit for fighting.

There is no other good harbor, or place of importance, on the coast of
Mexico, except Culiacan, (a small place), until we arrive at Mazatlan,
which, being in nearly the same latitude with Cape St. Lucas, brings us to
the mouth of the gulf.

The waters of the Gulf of California abound with fish of many kinds,
of which the "mero," a large sort of halibut, is the best, and grows to an
enormous size, those caught near Cape St. Lucas, weighing often three
hundred pounds. No devotee need starve in this quarter on Fridays. The
gulf also contains vast quantities of oysters, not merely your common
oysters, which are found from Maine to Florida, but the real *pearl* oyster.
The whole coast of California abounds, more or less, generally less, perhaps, in the pearl oyster. But the bay of La Paz produces pearls in considerable quantities, and of the very best quality.

Vast numbers of the same race as those wretched victims, which are
helplessly turned upon their backs at the doors of the New York eating-
houses, and exposed to the gaze of thoughtless and unpitying wayfarers,
are found in the Gulf of California. But what is the sickly, tortured trash
of those bolting machines, compared with the luscious calipash and cali-
pee fresh from the briny sea? And mind you, green-turtle-soup *is* green-
turtle-soup, in the Gulf of California, and nothing else. Whether there
ever were such a thing as genuine turtle-soup served up at a restaurant, is
a grave question to the conscience of the cook. I forbear to press it. But I
must express the opinion, that a mixture composed of the gelatinous parts
of young veal, mixed with a black sticky paste, and so seasoned as to taste
of nothing but cheap port and pepper, goes down many an unscientific
throat for the real "green-turtle"—the verdant quality being in fact outside of the bowl, and getting into it only by imputation. But at La Paz
there is no deception, and the place is probably haunted by the ghosts of
defunct aldermen.

Although the voyager, in sailing along the shores of the Gulf, when
surveying their bold and lofty cliffs, seemingly covered with vegetation,

alternating with broad and level plains and table-lands, and bounded by the verdant and towering back-bone range of the interior—the whole presenting an agreeable and varied scenery—may be led to believe the country fertile: a nearer approach will soon discover its barren character. The whole face of the country, except an occasional valley near the sea-coast, is a mass of friable whitish stone, and the surface of the earth is baked to the consistency of brick by a tropical sun, which, throughout the year, expends on it its fiercest rays. Nevertheless, in a few valleys and low table-lands, in the vicinity of the towns before enumerated, are seen the little "huertas" (gardens) of the simple inhabitants, yielding, in small quantities, all the tropical productions, of which the poor people possess the seeds or germs. All the rest of the country is taken possession of by every variety of the cactus, which attains an enormous size, and whose perennial green gives that delusive promise of fertility to which I have alluded. This plant flourishes without water, except the moisture derived from the light dews which it greedily drinks up at night. There are the melon, the Turks-head, and the tree cacti, all of great size, besides smaller sizes, of innumerable varieties, which, I regret, I am not botanist enough to describe. Their fleshy stems are well guarded with thorns, ranging from the bigness of a tenpenny nail to that of a fine cambric needle. Truly this is a botanical museum of cacti. The tree variety sometimes attains thirty feet in height, and it possesses sufficient woody consistency to make excellent firewood. These cacti are not without use to the inhabitants. Of the ligneous fibre of one species they make lines, nets, and even coarse cloth; and rough beams can be made of the spongy wood of one variety. I have often ridden through dense forests of cacti, and a beautiful sight it is to behold their flowers of the gaudiest hues, contrasting with their rich green limbs and trunks. Sometimes the blue jay and scarlet cardinal, sit chirping away on their tops, and these are apparently the only living creatures which do not fear their prickly contact.

The valley in which San José is situated is well watered, which is a great consideration in this country, where water is extremely scarce. The "huertas" on each side of the clear streams, produce dates, oranges, bananas, and other tropical fruits, besides excellent vegetables, the chief agricultural production being "panocha," or pan sugar, of which considerable quantities are exported. The nature of the soil and climate appears particularly well adapted to the culture of the cane, and there are many very fine sugar plantations.

There is a remarkable hot-spring near San José, in the bed of the river, or rather, what is its bed during the freshet season. There are several ranchos in this neighborhood, but the country is not well adapted to grazing, and the breed of animals is small and puny. The cattle are frequently affected with a kind of mange, and are seldom fat, while the horses are mere ponies.

Nothing can be stated positively with regard to the lofty serrania of the interior, but it probably has a peculiarity which may be noted in other tropical regions, viz. successive terraces or table lands at different elevations, affording various gradations of climate. It is also supposed that this serrania contains valuable mines, including gold, silver, and quicksilver—but "quien sabe?"

Some few foreigners, with whom I have conversed, who have partially explored the serrania, think that many valuable products may be had from it; but a long time will probably elapse before it will be inhabited by man. It is certain that the alpine mountain ranges produce at different elevations, pines, and oaks, besides several varieties of palms, and that the mansanilla (logwood), sandal-wood, box of large size, several species of bastard mahogany, lignum vitæ, and other hard woods have been obtained—for I have seen specimens of them myself. The sandal-wood, if it exists in quantities, would well repay the expense of an exploration, for it is already nearly exhausted in the islands of the Pacific, whence the supply for the China market has hitherto been drawn. The talipot palm grows in the gardens, and its broad leaves are used to thatch the houses of the inhabitants.

South of Cape St. Lucas, is a small cluster of islands—which may be regarded as dependencies of the peninsula—called by the Spaniards, who discovered them, the Revillagigedo islands; these are Socorro, Benedicto, and Rocapartida, which I name in the order of their respective sizes. Of these, Socorro is probably the only one of importance; and it is noted for an active volcano, which was in a state of eruption during our sojourn in the vicinity; and it is rather remarkable that shocks of an earthquake occurred during its continuance at Cape St. Lucas, leading one to the conclusion, that some sort of subterranean communication exists between the two places, as these shocks were not felt at any other part of the neighboring country. Valuable mines are already worked in the peninsula. The silver mines of San Antonio, produce to any who will work them—for they are not worked by any organized company as yet—at the rate of ten, and even as high as twenty reals on every dollar invested, and this in the rude state of mining now practised.

The use of quicksilver has not yet been adopted at these mines, but it will now be so readily procured from Upper California, that the yield can be made much greater.* No doubt the most magnificent field is open to the geologist, in the Sierras of the peninsula, and also in those of Upper California. Their mineral wealth must be immense, if we may judge from specimens already discovered by the rude and untaught efforts of the ignorant native population. Here is a virgin soil for the operations of the practical and scientific geologist; and men of capital and enterprise, will, ere long, turn their attention to it. Who can tell what vast mineral wealth such an exploration would reveal?

The climate of the peninsula is decidedly of a torrid character. I speak of the coast strip, which is the only part of which we possess any certain knowledge. The rays of the sun are very powerful every day in the year, and from the early matinal hours until nightfall, old Sol darts his fierce rays so savagely as to preclude any particular desire to be stirring out of doors. In the high mountain-ranges, the weather is probably more tolerable. The nights, however, are cool. It seldom rains, and years often pass without a shower. Indeed, showers are expected only in the summer months, and the variation of temperature throughout the year is very small. Like all tropical countries, the peninsula is visited, at long intervals, by gales of wind, principally from the south, and they sometimes increase to hurricanes, and it is then prudent to stand from under.

The inhabitants of the peninsula are few in numbers, and are exclusively of the lowest orders of the Mexican mixed race, with the exception of a white family or two of Castilian descent. They are very thriftless, and of course very poor, idle, dissolute, and ignorant. In fact, they are almost as nearly in a state of nature as many of the rude heathen islanders of the Pacific. The climate does not require them to exert themselves, either for their bodily sustenance or to raise the few articles with which they obtain, by bar-

---

* In view of a probable depreciation in the value of gold, these silver mines may become immensely valuable.

ter, the necessary wearing apparel for themselves and their families. Like other fools who compose the bulk of mankind they are excessively proud of the possession of finery and gewgaws of every kind. Their houses consist merely of cabins made of wattles of a light wood, or of reeds, and are roofed with the leaves of the talipot palm. Their furniture is composed merely of a hide stretched on four posts driven into the ground-floor, for *au rez de chaussée,* is the only story of their mansions, which are sometimes divided into two rooms by a slender and most transparent partition of reeds. A house for the lower and middling classes can be built for an expenditure of eight dollars, and makes quite a pleasant rural retreat, in its way. A few of the better class in San José and La Paz have adobe houses, but then they are the aristocracy—the haut ton—the "upper ten," and "quite the Stilton." There is no severe exertion requisite or practicable in this fiery clime, and the people are a merry, devil-may-care sort of bipeds, who take the world easily and philosophically, and perhaps are, on the whole, as happy as the victims of hot suppers and tradesman's bills, in more civilized countries. They seem always to be "descansando,"—resting—so that they enjoy a perpetual Sabbath. They are hospitable, and always glad to serve a stranger in their humble way, and it is probably no injury to their well-being that they are governed and regulated almost exclusively by their priests. On the whole, they are good-tempered, kind-hearted, and indolent; possessing a large share of that negative happiness which springs from the absence of care, anxiety, and responsibility.

The women are, many of them, very handsome, particularly when crossed with the white blood. In the many shady nooks on the banks of the river San José, one will always meet with gay and laughing groups of nut-brown wood nymphs, splashing in the crystal stream, often presenting the attitude of the goddess of the Pitti, washing out clothes, and giving rendezvous to their respective swains.

We hoisted the American flag in San José on the thirtieth of March, 1847, by order of Commodore Stockton, and soon afterwards we did the same at La Paz, taking possession of the whole peninsula in behalf of the United States. This was done without the least opposition by the inhabitants, the majority of them being well satisfied with the change. Our ship had thus the honor of hoisting the American flag as an act of military possession and occupation, at the most northern and southern points of the Californias.

LIEUTENANT COLONEL BURTON, of the New York Volunteer Regiment, with two companies, and a small battery of artillery, soon after assumed the military government of the district. In the following summer, the coast being left unguarded by a man-of-war during the souther months, one Pineda, a Mexican officer, Fray Vicento, a priest, and one Mijores, a naval officer, crossed the gulf, and going among the rancheros, with a small party, by their influence and exhortations, raised several hundred men; and, dividing this force, they attacked simultaneously La Paz and San José. The former was defended by Colonel Burton with his volunteers, and the latter by Lieutenant Heywood of the navy, and a few sailors and marines. The Mexicans were defeated with great loss. Burton and Heywood occupied adobe houses, which were pierced with loop-holes, and served very well for forts. Mijores led the attack on San José, and was killed outright for his pains, while advancing at the head of his men. He was a gallant fellow, and marched up boldly at the very front of the assailants. Not so Pineda, who undertook to dislodge Burton. This Mexican hero *backed* his men in the attack, prudently keeping in the rear, and exercising the functions of an "animador." Shrapnel shells, however, made havoc among his men, many of whom were killed. It is a sufficient eulogy on the bravery and good conduct of our officers and men to say, that they were a mere handfull, in the midst of a hostile population, cut off from communication with their countrymen, and beyond the reach of supplies or succor.

Guayamas and Mazatlan being garrisoned by our forces, and both the Californias being in our undisputed possession—except that a small body of vagabonds, under the valiant Pineda, were prowling about the interior of the peninsula—the Portsmouth sailed for the United States in the month of January, 1848.

THE AGE in which we live is the most eventful which has occurred for centuries. However trite the remark that we live in an age of wonders, it is difficult to realize the extent to which it is true. The race of man never before were conscious of the high destiny which awaits them—never before appreciated their own wondrous God-derived abilities—were never before astonished and startled at their own progressive strides—never before started back at their own enchantments, which seem to mock the fanciful creations of oriental imagination. If man believed, as of old, that he inhabited a vast plain, that the sun and moon were earth's convenient satellites, and the stars scarcely more than the ornamental spangles of her azure robe, he would dispute with omnipotence the attributes of Deity. The advance of science, almost in our own day, has revealed to us that the power and glory of the beneficent Source of life are so far incomprehensible, that the most extravagant flights of human fancy are but beggarly approaches to the most inconceivable fraction of the Almighty's attributes, the mere physical wonders of his universe, serving only to show the man who knows the most, that he knows nothing. But for these wonderful discoveries—foolishly supposed by fanatics to jeopard all religion, because conflicting with the traditional account of the cosmogony contained in the Old Testament—the whole world would ere now have embraced Infidelity, and the fool would indeed have said in his heart, "there is no God." But now, knowing that none by searching, can find out or even imagine God; appreciating, though but faintly, His mighty works, from the ground we tread upon, to the infinite systems of worlds which lie beyond the highest flights of human thought, we are kept in our proper sphere, knowing that if we accomplish a million times more than we have already done, we still shall not stand perceptibly closer to the nearest outposts of divine power. With all reverence, then, towards the Infinite and Inscrutable Creator, whose might and love pervade the universe, we may speak exultingly of what His ingenious earthly creatures have effected, more to His glory than their own.

It is almost incredible, yet strictly true, that the man is now living, within the compass of whose days the steam engine was first fashioned into a practical operative machine, not only miraculous in itself, but in suggesting, and as it were creating, vast improvements in machinery of every description to which it is applied. Men not yet past middle-life, have been contemporaneous with the introduction of steamboats, the invention of railroads and locomotives, the discovery of the magnetic telegraph and the Daguerreotype, and have witnessed the most marvellous strides of the human intellect in the departments of chemistry, geology, mechanics and astronomy. A new world, in comparison with which the earth is as a bat-ball to a foot-ball, has been added to the list of brilliant planets which revolve around our sun. Nor have the political affairs of the wondrous pigmy who sways the destinies of this little sphere, been uneventful. The French revolution, the career of Napoleon, the conquests of England in India, of France in Africa, and more recently the tendency in Europe towards the emancipation of man from the fetters of political tyranny—these and a thousand other wonderful events were witnessed by men of the present day.

But it is the career of our own country, of this western Republic—whose institutions and daily history are now regarded with universal respect and interest—which presents the most wonderful picture of the progress of the human race. Within eighty years, a few colonists, strung along the Atlantic sea-board, have achieved their independence, and become one of the most wealthy and powerful nations on the face of the earth. Occupying a vast territory, this nation has developed its resources with miraculous energy and success, and is rapidly advancing in every department of commerce, agriculture, and manufactures. Powerful in war as well as prosperous in peace, it has, by two resorts to the last argument of nations, taught the world that it may not be trifled with or treated like a child, although still in its infancy. Having shown to the world its ability to protect itself, and its prowess being universally admitted, we may hope that it has sheathed the sword forever.

But great as the nation *was,* its recent eminence does not approach its present grandeur; and mighty and opulent as it *is,* the present is but a faint ideal of its future.

A virgin empire has been added to the United States, which, at the outset, brings to the fortunate bridegroom not only far-extending lands, but also an enormous dowry in ready money.

"Westward the star of empire takes its way,"

and the seat of Empire on the Pacific, must, in the course of time, rival the seat of Empire on the Atlantic.

In acquiring California, the United States have become possessed of new elements of greatness. The abundance of the precious metals in the new territory, must rapidly elevate her commercial position, and for the present, vastly enrich the Atlantic cities. Immense fortunes will be acquired in California, and will remain there, to be invested in lands, cattle, commerce, agriculture, and even manufactures.

Of all the marvels of the present age, few have surpassed the acquisition of California by the United States, the rapid settlement of the new territory, and the sudden discovery of its mineral wealth. The results which are to flow from the immense deposits of gold, can, as yet, hardly be foreseen, but if half we hear be true, there is little doubt that the monetary affairs of the world will be very seriously affected by the depreciation of gold, the great standard and regulator of values.

One of the most magnificent regions of the world is now incorporated with the United States. The foregoing pages bear witness that in fertility of soil, mildness and salubrity of climate, and extent of resources, it is surpassed by no other country on the face of the earth. Abounding in excellent harbors, from its northern boundary to its southern extremity, it possesses every facility for accommodating a wide-spread commerce. Its contiguity to Asia will not only give immediate impulse to that commerce, but will also induce large numbers of industrious Asiatics to seek its shores in quest of employment.

Perhaps in concluding these humble labors, it will not be thought inappropriate to enumerate some of the leading products of California.

Wheat, oats, corn, rye, and all other cereal grains grow luxuriantly. In the more southern parts of the country, the fruits of the tropics flourish side by side with those of the temperate zone.

The forests yield a large supply of timber, not only for the more ordinary purposes of life, but also for ornamental uses.

The grape flourishes in unequalled luxuriance, and both in climate and geographical features, California resembles the wine countries of Europe. The sugar-cane grows so readily, that the southern part of California, will, ere many years shall elapse, furnish sufficient sugar for the consumption of the whole territory.

The pasturage afforded by the country is of the most luxuriant description, and is capable of sustaining immense numbers of domestic animals.

The vast herds of cattle and horses which roam the hills and plains of California, were until recently, and perhaps are still, the most important source of her prosperity. When a more industrious and thrifty race shall take possession of the vacant lands which now invite the settler, the business of raising cattle, horses, sheep, and other useful animals, will be immensely augmented, and every kind of agricultural pursuit will receive an impetus which will make California "the exhaustless granary of a world."

The wild animals of the country will for many years yield a large supply of peltries, while the elk, the deer, the hare, and many minor quadrupeds, will furnish large supplies of excellent food.

The numerous varieties of the feathered tribe will do their part in yielding food of the most dainty quality.

The sea will supply inexhaustible quantities of the most delicious shell-fish, and the pearl oyster will yield a double treasure.

The rivers and lakes will vie with the ocean in affording supplies of piscatory food; and in short, the resources of nature alone will, for years to come, keep famine from the doors of the most indigent.

The water-power of the country will afford every facility to the manufacturer, and the day will come when the wool, cotton, silk, hemp, and flax, of California, will be woven in her own looms.

The mines and mineral deposits will give employment to thousands of industrious men, and when the present feverish anxiety to dig gold shall subside, the attention of the people will be turned to the other metals which abound in the mountains.

United to all these natural advantages, is the unsurpassed beauty and grandeur of the scenery, which presents an endless series of glorious pictures, to cheer the heart and delight the eye.

But I count most of all upon the race of men who will mainly people and govern the country—that Anglo-Saxon race, which, transplanted to the free soil of America, has acquired new force, new impulses, new enterprise; that Anglo-Saxon race, which seems destined to possess the whole of the North American Continent which is adapted to the wants of civilized man.

In the people, after all, must rest the true foundation of greatness; and if this people fail, no other can hope to succeed. When the institutions of the Eastern States shall be extended to California; when law, order, good government, education and religion shall assume their proper position in the rising State of the Pacific, we may reasonably look for the establishment of an empire such as the sun in all his journeys has never shone upon.

I would, with great deference, venture the opinion, that the agitation now in progress in the United States in respect to the introduction of negro slavery into California, is a waste of time, temper, and treasure. Slavery can never exist in California, and if the people are entrusted with the formation of a government, they will beyond all doubt exclude slavery. The great expense and risk of transporting slaves to a country so remote, the vast numbers of Indians whose labor is so much cheaper than slave-labor can possibly be, the utter absence among the Spanish Californians of all prejudice with respect to color, the fact that the Indians are better herdsmen (vaqueros), than any African can ever become, and the ease with which any number of Kanakas from the Sandwich Islands, and the Coolies, and other laborers from Asia can be procured, render it an absurdity to suppose that negro slavery will ever be established in California. The Asiatic laborers are far more industrious than negro slaves, and possess a much higher order of intelligence; they work for very low wages,—the usual pay of a first-rate laborer in Singapore being three dollars and fifty cents per month, with which pittance the abstemious Asiatic finds and clothes himself, and saves something over besides; and, moreover, these free laborers work at their own risk of life and health, and the employer is not damnified if they run away. The introduction of slaves into California would be about as sensible as trying to carry water in sieves; for the hundreds of Indian rancherias scattered over the country, would soon become their places of refuge, and the Indians would amalgamate with them without the slightest hesitation. The nature of the country, the moderate demand for the kind of labor usually done by slaves, the fact that two or three good vaqueros under the superintendence of a competent mayor-domo can take charge of one thousand head of cattle, on a three-league rancho, to say nothing of the general indisposition of mankind to extend an institution so fraught with danger in political, civil, and social points of view, render it next to impossible that slavery should ever be allowed by the people of California.

And yet, it is said to be on account of this slavery question, that California is denied a civil government, excluded from the Union, and thus exposed to a frightful state of anarchy and confusion. If it be conceded that California is entitled to come into the Union, and that on becoming a sovereign State she will have, like the other States, exclusive jurisdiction over the subject of slavery within her borders, it seems very strange that a controversy which must be settled, and soon settled, by the people of California, should induce Congress to leave her without a government and without laws. I can understand, that if California were to remain a mere Territory of the United States, there might be some reason in prohibiting slavery; and I say this without intending to express any abstract opinion, either for or against the "Wilmot Proviso," so called—party politics being entirely foreign to my tastes. But when the local constitution must *forthwith* be made by the new State, and may at any time be amended without the possible interference of the General Government, is it not a refinement of cruelty to expose the people of California to the possible evil of a provisional government, or a government of "regulators," for the sake of a mere *pro forma* declaration of opinion in Congress, when that opinion has already been expressed in both Houses?

To those who intend to settle in California, I would respectfully offer a few words of advice. You are mostly young men, full of hope and energy. You leave behind you a land where liberty is regulated by law, and where you have witnessed the practical effects of good government. You leave behind you a happy, prosperous and enlightened people, whose free institutions are the glory of the age, and whose devotion to public order is the the best guaranty of the perpetuity of those institutions. You go to a comparatively uncivilized country, where you will be beyond the reach of those salutary restraints, which are imposed at home by custom, religion, law, the example of all good men, and the benign influences of family and friends. You go as adventurers among adventurers, and it cannot be otherwise than that you will encounter many dangerous, lawless, and unprincipled men. As you value the beloved land you leave behind; as you prize the good opinion and regard of friends and relatives; as you respect your own characters; as you hope for the glory and advancement of the magnificent region towards which your steps are directed; as you desire your own welfare, and that of your posterity—I pray you to beware of the dangers which will beset your path, and to shun with resolute determination everything which may bring upon you dishonor and the scorn of honorable men. If you meet with a lax system of public morals, be it your aim to elevate the tone of society; if you be tempted to sully an honorable name by dishonest practices, resist to the last the lures of avarice and corruption; if dissipation prevail, and you see men popular who are sunk in vice and depravity, be assured that their day will be short, and stand firmly on the Rock of Right. Virtue is the same everywhere; Truth is the same everywhere; God is the same everywhere;—and be it your aim to act, even in the midst of sin and pollution, as if the eyes of a purer society, the eyes of friends and kindred, of sisters and mothers, were ever upon you. Carry with you the great principles of political liberty, which your fathers brought to the wild Atlantic shores; carry with you a perfect devotion to those good institutions and customs, upon which are based the prosperity and happiness of the land to which you bid, perhaps, a last adieu, and remember that the good instructions you have received at home, are calculated for no particular meridian, but are world-wide in their application. Remember that a just and virtuous man is respected and trusted everywhere, and by none so much as by the depraved and dissolute. Maintain, and next to God, reverence *character*. Let it be to you a real presence—a tangible existence,—whose preservation is of infinitely greater importance than all the gold the whole world contains. The perils of the sea safely surmounted, make not a moral shipwreck; but while pursuing the shadow men call wealth, aspire to be something better than that most poverty-stricken of mortals—a mere rich man. The destiny of man is onward and upward, and let not the future generations of California have cause to say that the sins of the fathers are visited upon the children; but rather let them celebrate the good deeds of their ancestry.

Perhaps a hundred years hence, some curious book-worm, while exploring a musty library, may alight upon this then forgotten volume, and will be tempted to find out what was said and predicted of California at the eventful period of her annexation to the United States, and the discovery of her mineral wealth. The poor Indians will then have passed away; the rancheros will be remembered only as the ancient proprietors of broad lands, which will have passed into the possession of the more enterprising race who are about to succeed them; the Grizzly Bear will live only in books and in tradition; the Elk will have become extinct; the wild horse will be seen no more; author, editor, publishers, readers, all will have passed away and mingled with the dust; and perchance new philologists will have so marred our noble English language, that these poor pages will be intelligible only to the learned. CHILD OF THE FUTURE! what wilt thou then see? Will not a hundred millions of free and happy human beings inhabit the great Republic then still known as the United States of America —their habitations extending from the shores of the boisterous Atlantic to those of the placid Pacific? Will not the arts of peace flourish beyond example, and the majestic tread of man still press onward towards a yet more glorious Destiny? And California—what will she then be? Will she have fulfilled the promises of this our day, and be the highway of a mighty commerce, and replete with enterprise and opulence? Will she have become populous and enlightened, the seat of arts and learning, the generous rival of her elder sisters in all that is lovely and of good report among men? SON OF A HOPEFUL AGE! thy response may not reach "the dull, cold ear of death;" but Heaven grant it may be such as, if living, we should most wish to hear!

FIRST CALIFORNIA EDITION

1000

COPIES PRINTED
BY
GILLICK PRESS · BERKELEY, CALIFORNIA
BOOKBINDING BY COMMERCIAL BINDERY
ART WORK BY VIC ANDERSON

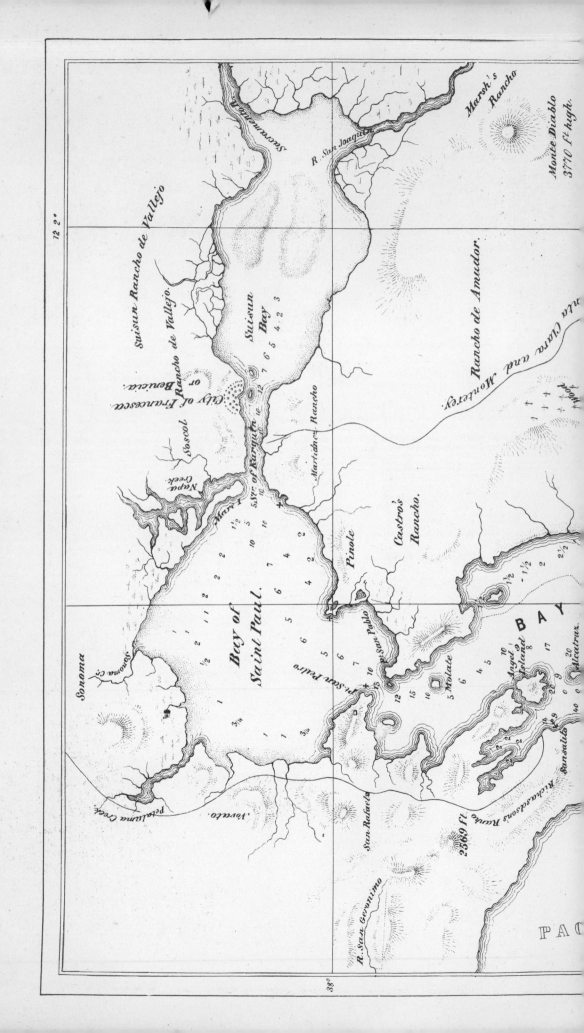